A NONSEN ECTION

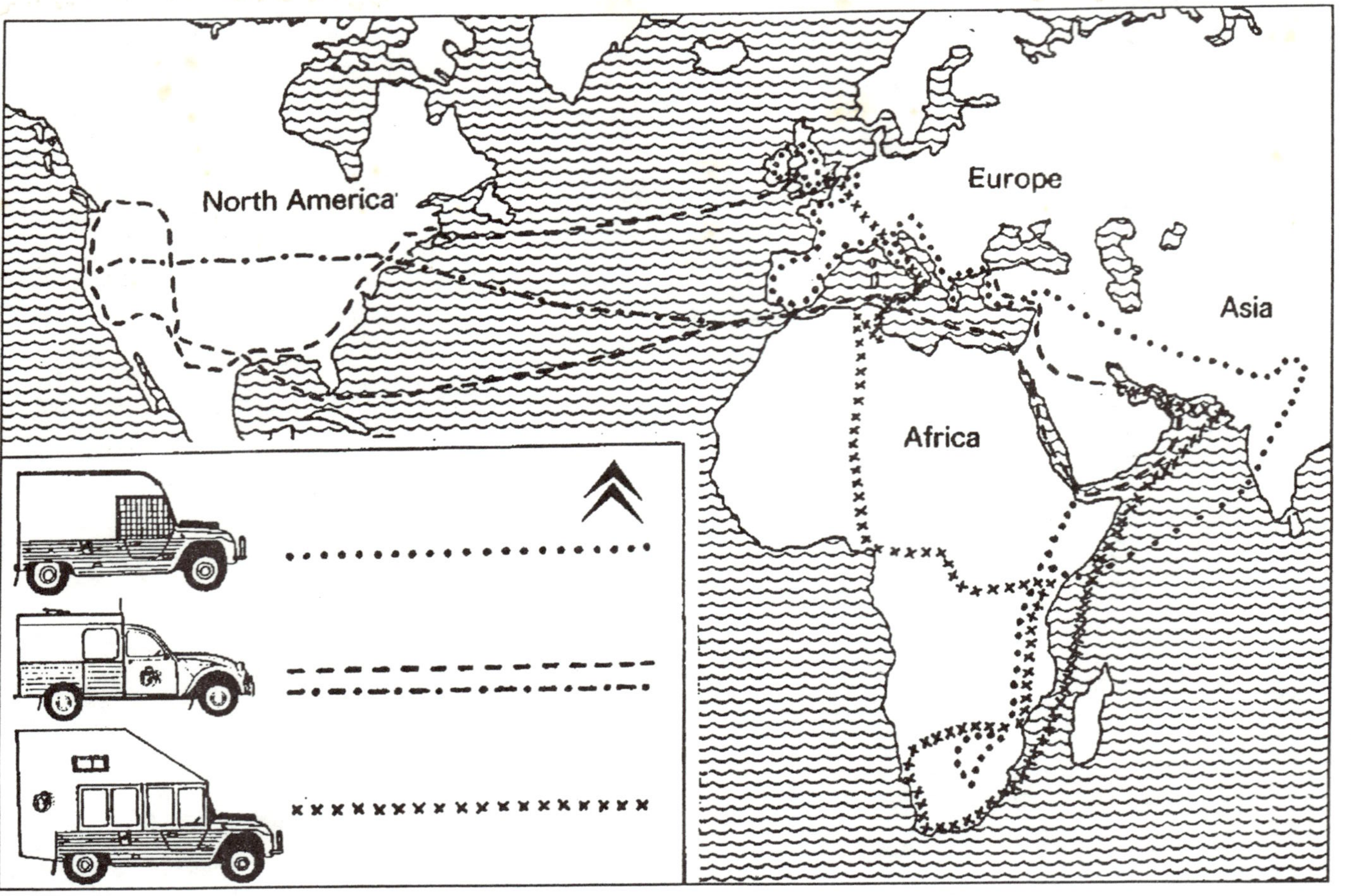
North America
Europe
Asia
Africa

A NONSENSE OF DIRECTION

OVERLAND TO EVERYWHERE IN A TOYTOWN PLASTIC CAR

by

Terence Kennedy

First published in 1992 by Globe, an imprint of
Huber & Mielke, Wingertstrasse 64, D-6902 Sandhausen, Germany

Layout : Dieter Massong
Cover : Lothar Böttrich
Map : Mike Faure

ISBN 0-9517886-0-4

CONTENTS

Für Elise.

A WORD IN YOUR EYE...

As epic journeys go, this one frequently didn't.

It has hiccupped the equivalent of seven times around the globe, through 74 countries in 17 years - and all in piddling, two-cylindered plastic cars criticised as inadequate for traversing town, let alone continents. From Afghanistan to a crackpot Sahara crossing, Liechtenstein to Las Vegas, this story has deserts, jungles and mountaintops that say otherwise.

A lot of what little we've learned en route has found its way into newspaper and magazine articles to wrap fish or line birdcages, or has provided TV-viewers with more chewing-gum for the eyes. But sandwiching 300,000 eccentric kilometres between two covers might symbolise some sort of valediction, a swan-song to wind-down our itinerant idyll, and I swore never to tempt fate with a book.

This is that book. Not so much a travel book as a book about travellers and travelling. Sometimes even anti-travel, and if you're looking for topographical splendours, words-worthy sunsets and deep psychological insights the bad news is you've come to the wrong book.

A book of bits, it's a celebration of all that's absurd and burlesque about life in a very slow lane. And it's true, or as true as you're going to get from a hack long inured to that old newspaper dictum: never let the facts spoil a good story.

So, as the sign said in our Punjab hotel: "If this is your first visit, you are welcome to it."

T.C.K.
Botswana.

1
INNOCENTS ABROAD

The Saharan sand-track became a path which became a tangled nonsense of direction and we were lost. Again.

Would blunders never cease? The car's overloaded suspension was on the brink of another sit-down strike, our ex-trailer was pushing up sand-dunes a hundred kilometres back, and now this - the latest in a series of geographical clangers to rival Columbus when he bumped into America and thought he'd found Asia. At this rate, the only way we would reach Africa's west coast was through unprecedented coastal erosion.

Elise did the only thing possible. She put on the kettle and we had a cup of foul green Algerian tea - all we could buy at the last oasis, after a leaky petrol jerrycan had turned our Lipton's reserves into 97-octane poison. Ditto the rest of our year's emergency supplies. With a final slurp of resignation we took up our compass and binoculars to trudge to the top of the nearest dune.

In this borderless sea of sand we were no longer even sure what country we were in, and looking for landmarks on the world's largest and emptiest beach is like looking for a needle in several squillion haystacks. If you're lucky, and if Tuareg metal-loving thieves haven't beaten you to it, you may spot one of the steel-pillar "balises" which the French once erected every few kilometres to mark the desert route.

This was our lucky day, though you'd never think it. Through the lenses we spotted a lone balise, shimmering upright through the haze. Astonishingly, as we watched it fell over. Then got up, fell over again, rose, and inched forward...

We bundled into the car and slewed through the sand to the last known sighting. As we drew closer, the balise changed form and gradually became a pathetic sight: a lone European cyclist struggling through the Sahara, falling over every few metres because of a minor design fault on his bicycle - it had no handlebars.

Not surprisingly, he was pleased to see us. "Merde!" he spat out a mouthful of Sahara as he rose from the desert to shake our hands. "I am bicycling to California, but my machine she is not quite right."

Indeed. No normal traveller would have touched it with several barge-poles of exceptional length tied together end to end.

The California-bound Casimir wasn't too hot on geography here in the armpit of Africa, but his abilities as an inventor would have done Heath Robinson proud. This was the uncertain start to a three-year trial run of his prototype, a two-wheel-drive bicycle. Where there should have been handlebars he had grafted a second set of pedals which were hand-driven and connected to the front wheel. Not only did the back wheel have ten gears - so did the front.

On asphalt he could overtake a bat out of hell, but in the sucking, cloying Saharan sand the contraption's reluctance to be steered by rotating hand-pedals promised regular meetings with the ground. Things were hardly helped by his astounding 40 kilos of baggage piled on the rack, dangling from the crossbar and crammed into two cut-off 20-litre plastic jerrycans suspended on either side of the front wheel.

"Mais oui," he gave a Gallic shrug as Elise prepared to annihilate some more green tea and dug out our last fresh food for this no-doubt unhappy wanderer. "What can I do? People see me riding through ze desert, they feel sorry, they give me food and drink to carry and I cannot throw it away. Alors, forget zat 'orrible tea, you will eat with me today for it is Casimir's name day!" So saying, he started to excavate in his panniers, conjuring up heavy-duty luxuries we had not dared dream of in months.

"All from kind travellers like you," he beamed as he laid out, there on our dusty blanket in the middle of a mid-Saharan nowhere, a culinary mirage of German pumpernickel, earthenware bottles of schnapps, tinned paté, a jar of roll-mops, Coca-Cola, sticky French gateaux, sauerkraut, even a deadweight family-size jar of Marmite which had confirmed forever his French despair of English cuisine.

As we ate, the young adventurer pulled a dollar from his pack and thrust it at us.

"No no!" I protested. "This you must keep - it doesn't weigh anything!"

"Mmpph - read it," he spluttered through a mouthful of knäckebröt. Turning it over, we saw a tattered message typed on a French government letterhead. Translated, it asked whosoever it may concern to allow Casimir free passage and to give him every assistance, as he was cycling across the world with just this one dollar. As Alice would have said Through the Looking-Glass: curiouser and curiouser.

Late that afternoon he wobbled off into the haze with his load lightened, pausing only to pick himself up a few times because he insisted on waving, before he disappeared from our incredulous gaze. Would we ever see his like again?

Two months and a thousand kilometres later in the Republic of Niger, we did, and he was not a pretty sight. His previously sun-seared features were wan and yellow, his clothes were in tatters and the muscle which his four-limbed pedalling had developed had wasted to string.

He grimaced stoically. "C'est la vie," he said. "I 'ave been très sick, and now I don't eat so good. The Arabs, they gave me to eat when I travel - that is their tradition. But here in black Afrique the people don't give, they take, and now I 'ave not so much anymore."

Though his health was in ruins his spirit was still strong, and after we fed him and emptied some of our medicine-chest into his mouth, we watched with concern as he pumped his four pedals uncertainly towards South Africa, at least 20,000 long kilometres away. And sure enough, a year later he defied all predictions by popping up in Cape Town, still pedalling his handlebars and asking directions for California.

Travel spawns Casimir eccentrics with all the industry of an insane asylum. The outright loonies are the saddest, heading for disaster as inevitably as a man plunging over the Niagara in a barrel.

The "Mad Vicar of Manchester" bucked the odds in the mid-1970's, pushing a sail-rigged Chinese wheelbarrow through the Sahara with the help of a Ministry of Defence army crew. The Korean we met walking across the nine-million square kilometre desert apparently didn't.

Halfway through his endless tramp, his girlfriend flew out to his oasis, his site for sore feet, to bring him new shoes and to restock the two-wheeled golfbag shopping-cart which he dragged through the desert attached to the back of his belt. Months later the travellers' grapevine reported that he had perished en route.

So, too, did two of the French family of four whose trip collapsed under the weight of its own incompetence. They had set out to cross the Sahara equipped with little more than blithe foolhardiness, in a standard and unprepared Renault R4. When a helicopter search found the survivors, the car was an unbelievable 400 kilometres from the nearest route.

Some travellers beat the odds despite loading the dice against themselves. Juan from Barcelona was such a one, having set out during his one week between jobs in Spain to "see the Sahara" with just three Seville oranges in his airline bag. An Arab trucker gave him a lift to the middle of nowhere and drove on, leaving Juan sweating, stranded, and orangeless after the first hour of thirst. He was lucky; in the only other vehicle of that day or perhaps even several days, we jammed on the brakes at the sight of the toilet-paper strip spread across the track pleading in two languages: "HELP! I am lost and have gone to look for water. Please sound your horn to call me!"

When we thought our own number was up in the sand-filled no-man's-land between Algeria and Niger after a farrago of mechanical disasters, rescue came in the unlikely, not to say fantastical, form of a German truck blaring out Oompah music at full volume and carrying three Munich ear, nose and throat specialists. In the middle of a sandstorm they gave us their business-cards with marvellous Teutonic formality. Treating the adventure as lightly as though it were a walk through the Black Forest, they were dressed in the Sixties gear of their repressed youth, satisfying a life's ambition by crossing the Sahara together. Their wives, dragged along under duress, were not amused.

Travel swashbucklers reap headlines in a world starved of swash.

From 1963 Ian Hibell has ridden, pushed or carried his bike 400,000 kilometres, including having to hack his way with a machete through Panama's infamous Darien Gap. His book "Into the Remote Places" is as gripping as a backache and guaranteed to keep armchair travellers just where they are, away from those gruelling Remote Places.

(Ian and his bike made it home intact. Less lucky was the bike of another homecoming British round-the-world cyclist; it survived seven kinds of ordure en route, only to be crushed ignominiously by the Heathrow Airport baggage conveyor).

Obsessed American globetrotter Parke G. Thomson had been to 233 countries when last we looked, and his compatriot David Kunst walked around the world in the four years from 1970. An American actually walked backwards across the U.S.A. using spectacles with rear-view mirrors, while two others would have succeeded in driving their Chevvy in reverse coast to coast in 1984, if Oklahoma police hadn't unsportingly insisted they drive in reverse reverse out of their state - i.e. forwards. At around the same time Old Etonian Sebastian Snow made "a serious attempt to perish" when he trudged from the tip of South America to the top.

Once, in 1983, we needed 14 months to struggle all the way down Africa. A Brigadier Helmsley and his wife passed us at breakneck speed in a specially-prepared Range Rover, reaching Cape Town in a record 10 days. Unlike the grand total of our sponsorship over the 17 years - two floppy hats from Land-Rover, and that only because of a clerical mistake - the Helmsleys had immense commercial backing, and presumably threw wads of money at frontier officials in lieu of the timetable-murdering bureaucracy lesser travellers must endure.

Where the Helmsleys of this world are bathed in publicity, many unsung travel heroes deserve kudos they will never get, like the crazed Frenchman we came across in Afghanistan, determined to nurse his wounded 2CV back to Paris 10,000 kilometres away - in first gear, which is all he had left after falling into a ravine. Or the Swiss heading for Australia on a Lambretta scooter, the Austrian touring Europe on a tractor, the Britons circumnavigating the U.K. on a wheeled bedstead, the innumerable optimists crossing seas in everything from a bathtub to a glorified rowboat, or even the hitchhiking Londoner robbed of everything in Pakistan. We passed him making his way back home in a loincloth.

Look in the Guinness Book of Records, and there nestling among the champions of travel beyond the call of wanderlust are two German entertainers, Manfred Müller and Paul-Ernst Luhrs.

In 20 years they set a record we might equal except in one respect, when they piloted an ancient Citroën 2CV 350,000 kilometres through 83 countries. Certainly we're within an exhaust-puff of matching their time, their tally and their distance, but if anyone's counting we're also two 2CV's down. Not dead, just rusting.

With our first semi-homemade car in its bodywork of plastic and hardboard, and with our mechanical knowledge limited to the practised inability to change a tyre, people gave us no more chance than a Hadean snowball, as we hit the road like several bags of cement...

2
DRIVING TO RHUBARBIA

Travelling the world started as our daydream and hurtled out of control towards obsession. Vagabond years and several filled passports on, we still don't know why.

Novelist Sinclair Lewis theorised that most people afflicted with the habit of travelling don't travel to see anything, but to get away from themselves, which they never do, and away from rowing with their relatives - only to find new people with whom to row. They travel to escape thinking, to have something to do, just as they might play solitaire, work crossword puzzles, or busy themselves with any other "dreadful activity." Well, yes. And no.

Globetrotting motorcyclist-author Ted Simon, asked why he did it, replied perhaps a little too glibly, "To find out why I'm doing it." Woody Guthrie neatly encapsulated the itch when he mused that "No matter where I am, I always feel I ought to be someplace else."

"Once a bum, always a bum" said John Steinbeck with typical succinctness in "Travels with Charley" (his French poodle, Charles le Chien). When he was young and the "urge to be someplace else" was on him, Steinbeck was assured by mature people that maturity would cure the itch - "but the disease proved incurable."

Literature's early road-poet, Robert Louis Stevenson, travelled not to go anywhere, but to go. "I travel for travel's sake," he said. "The great thing is to move."

The answer is all of these, yet none of them. Neither is it as easy as the shoulder-shrugging reply given by one Victorian adventurer when he said so smoothly, "Well, one has to do something, doesn't one?" When the need hit us with all the force of a sledgehammer one cold Dutch morning in the early 1970's, we were hard-pressed to find a logical motivation. We still are.

Everyone dreams of faraway places and we were no different. For years before we met, Elise (pronounced the Dutch way, Ae-lee-zuh) had nurtured the fantasy of a walk around the Mediterranean, but had found potential fellow-travellers in short supply among her stoical East-of-Holland countrymen. I had the innate restlessness, and questing for identity, so common to many young Britons uprooted from their native culture to grow up in the alien open spaces of Africa. Ours might almost have been a marriage made in heaven, if we believed in marriage. Or heaven.

Years later, an African border-official struggling to come to terms with the fact that Elise and I not only had different surnames, but even carried different-looking passports, finally got it when he announced triumphantly: "Aha, I understand, you and your woman are from two different tribes!"

Indeed. Our backgrounds could not have been more different. Elise grew up in a placid Dutch town called Oldenzaal, nestled along the border with Germany - the sort of place where, every now and then, nothing happens. In the few years since leaving school she had nursed her Walter Mitty dreams of exotic lands while removing wrinkles and guilders from solid Dutch ladies in a quiet beauty salon. Much more noisily, after qualifying and working as a journalist in southern Africa I proceeded to go deaf for a living. Night after smoke-filled night I pounded out a career as a rock drummer, later easing the decibels as I moved into jazz and cabaret to back a galaxy of falling stars, from Sixties singers Marty Wilde, Billy J. Kramer and Wayne Fontana to the much smoother but equally declined Golden Trumpet man, Eddie Calvert.

We met during a Dutch concert given by the English rock-revival band in which I was currently hitting the little time. For Elise, there to sing folk music in our supporting programme, it was hate at first sight, until she got past the ludicrous but obligatory stage persona: a drummer dressed like a one-man Carnival in Rio, playing his instrument back-to-front or while lying on the ground in a performance which could confidently have been entered for the Olympics. With the help of a couple of dictionaries we soon discovered our kindred travel spirits, an all-important shared sense of humour, and a mutual love of doing and experiencing the preposterous. As the especially apt saying has it, we definitely marched to the beat of a different drummer, and within weeks we had decided to go away together. Not just anywhere; everywhere.

Three continents would make a nice little start, we mused as we contemplated our wall-mounted Daily Telegraph World Map one snowy Sunday morning. The decision had taken all of an hour, and only that long because Elise was barely awake the first time the idea percolated into my consciousness along with the watery sunrise: overland to India, thence by ship to East Africa and down to Cape Town in time for tea.

Years on we became fairly adept at turning the travel-fantasies most people dream into reality, but in that first flush of enthusiasm it's lucky we were unburdened by the doubts and fears which more maturity brings. We had both dabbled at travel in our two young decades, but heading for India and Africa on the spur of the moment, and in a plastic car at that?

Ah yes - the notorious plastic car, which had we but known it was to become a modest trademark and a faithful friend. Back on that fateful Sunday, we knew only that we were too independent to join a tour and not intrepid enough to hitchhike.

Flying was too boring and too abrupt. In any case, I've never been a good flyer ever since the strap came off the baby-bouncer. I have a healthy respect for the laws of gravity, and things weren't helped on one memorable flight when the aircraft stopped humming muzak to itself long enough for the captain to announce: "This is your captain speaking. Welcome aboard flight 057 to, er, to -

uh -...." And as to the allure of the air hostesses, I recall an absolutely stunning blonde piling my plate with caviar, stroking my hair lightly as she bent over provocatively with the champagne and murmuring endearments. Then I woke up to find a female prison-warder ranting at me about my seatbelt.

No, having our own vehicle was the only way to go. Ever impractical, I fancied a London taxi - as nippy as a Sherman tank, with the ground clearance of a slug and with spare parts available everywhere. In London. A Land-Rover was a more obvious answer, but even our lack of a calculator left us in no doubt that it and its fuel-appetite would cause our budget to expire just past Calais.

Elise suggested a 2CV, which to an uninitiated Brit sounded only like the opening of Hamlet's most famous soliloquy. By happy, and as it turned out fateful, coincidence, a friend had one of these strange and legendary cars for sale for the token price of 10 guilders, then about £3. When we went to see it and looked under its eccentric and wobbly bonnet, I wondered why we should be buying a car without an engine. Then I realised that those few bits of leftover lawnmower squatting on the chassis WERE the engine.

As we lolloped off across the Dutch dykes in our £3 car I remained unconvinced. But three months later we were still lolloping even though I filled the tank so rarely I could hardly remember where the filler-cap was. All the maintenance it had needed was a sniff of oil in the sump and an Elastoplast on the roof, and it handled muddy canal-paths and ploughed fields as smoothly as though they were autobahns. I was converted - even when a wheel fell off and I put my foot through the floorboard in an effort to brake.

Driving a 2CV is often like keeping a pet python; you feel it calls for a little explanation. Well, many years after I underwent that almost religious conversion, at a meeting of international 2CV fans the earnest leader of the Finnish delegation endeared himself to native English-speakers. They knew what he should have said, when he explained that "In the Finland club, it is our intention to take all the fun possible out of owning a 2CV." He just about got it right, for there is an innate sense of fun in driving these idiosyncratic little vehicles, cars which stubbornly refuse to die despite being overtaken by half a century of technological march.

Lest this book be thought of as some sort of advertisement for Citroën and its quirky car, that's hardly the intention. On the contrary, despite our occasional overture, Citroën has been understandably reluctant to sponsor our oddball exploits with more than a token sticker or two, or a bit of a discount on the warehouse of spare parts we always end up carrying unused halfway across the world. I can't blame the firm, for not only has the 2CV proved itself so many times in world-beating exploits that further publicity is overkill, but each time they have seen what we have done to and with their cars, I've had the sneaking impression they've been appalled. Not without reason.

The Ugly Duckling, as the car is affectionately known, has always been an enigma. Its design dates back to the 1930's, and after the war it burst onto the motoring stage like a baby elephant arriving through a paper hoop. There was critical astonishment that the manufacturer had the gall to think motorists would buy such a ludicrous piece of mobile Meccano-set, and wags even asked whether a can-opener was supplied as standard. Within months there was a six-year waiting list.

In the famous description of which owners have long-since wearied, this "umbrella on four wheels" was designed to carry a tray of eggs across a ploughed field without breaking any, and the suspension which achieved this has gone down in automotive history. Not only is the 2CV thus an ideal car for off-road work, but its engine is virtually unburstable, its innards are simple enough for even the most ham-handed tinkerer to grasp, and because it is basic to the point of primitiveness it will go on forever despite the worst kind of punishment and neglect. It is also very cheap.

Minus a quarter of its wheels, our £3 car was not really a good bet for an 80,000 kilometre trip across the globe. Besides, under its Elastoplast-patched sunroof there was hardly enough space for the mountains of supplies we believed we would need. The answer seemed to be a plastic 2CV called a Méhari - literally from the French a speedy desert dromedaris, and how appropriate the name became for us if you don't get too literal about the "speedy." The Méhari trundled its way into the records books in 1965 as the first vehicle to have its bodywork made of plastic - not, as is often thought, fibreglass. This ABS skin was stretched over a tubular framework grafted onto a strengthened 2CV chassis, creating a mini-jeep, a sort of poor man's Land-Rover powered by the legendary 602 cc two-cylindered air-cooled engine pumping out a mighty 28 horsepower. But speedy it was not, except with a following wind on a downgrade.

Tax-free from Paris we now had our transport, but still had no travel accommodation. Early on in the planning we had decided that if the trip was to be within our means hotels were out, leaving us the option of sleeping in the vehicle or in a tent en route. Tents tend to afford scant protection against itinerant thieves, rhinos and the like, and so the car it was.

It's been said of journalists that they pontificate to the world but couldn't run a whelk stall. It would have been nice to think I bucked the trend with the whelk-stallish accommodation I cobbled onto our jeep. But... The wonder was that any of it was still standing three continents later. Hammering screws into bits of wood and sawing acres of burglar-wire with a Swiss Army knife, I jerry-built a one-and-a-half storey hardboard home of such redoubtable solidity that it held together for all of four hours on the road. That sorry tale will shortly be told, but it was to introduce us to Murphy's Law, which was to be our dependable lifelong co-traveller and an incidental star of this book. Murphy's Law, for the lucky uninitiated, decrees that anything which can possibly go wrong, will.

We packaged together a minimum of spare parts, though why we bothered beats me as I didn't even know how to change the oil, hadn't been able to find the dynamo on our £3 car, (fortunately the Méhari had an alternator even I couldn't lose, though I had no idea why), and we had reduced our helpful Epsom landlord to near apoplexy when after giving us detailed instructions for changing a tyre, he came back two hours later to find us still wrestling with recalcitrant tyre-levers. Still, we had a manual, even if it was in Dutch and I had only begun to master the language while Elise couldn't be expected to translate the technical bits. At least the pictures were good.

Our equipment, such as it was, came largely from an eccentric camping and outdoor-gear shop in London's Brixton. Just how eccentric could be judged from the sign outside, announcing in Shakespearian tones: "Now is the discount of our winter tents!" The owner suggested we take a plastic jerrycan for our water instead of metal. When I dared to question whether it would be leakproof enough, he flew into a genial tantrum.

"Leakproof?" he barked. "Leakproof? I'll show you leakproof," and he filled it with water before leaping up and down on it and declaiming its solidity as passing London gawped in amusement. How could we help but buy it?

As the months of preparation sped by we assembled a pile of maps, one or two helpful books, all our innoculations at the same time so that we were sick for days - and a mountain of tourist brochures. I don't know why we bothered with these, spectacularly unhelpful as they usually are to the non-flyer.

Those of the more Mickey Mouseish countries followed an invariable pattern. First the headline, say, "TRAVELLING BY ROAD TO RHUBARBIA." Then: "You cannot travel by road to Rhubarbia." With persistence you might unearth a host of stunningly useless facts for the motorist:

"Rhubarbian roads are often tarred and may be free of boulders. There are more than 6 benzine-stations in the country selling petrol of two grades, 34 and 36 octane. Tourists enjoy a concession, using foreign currency to pay at high prices. Visitors may bring cars only on payment of a bond which is 250% of the new secondhand value or the local price or all, depending. Such bonds must be paid in foreign money and will be refunded when you leave in Rhubarbian Custardskis, which are not usable either inside or outside the country. Foreign motorists may use their own licences if they are endorsed in advance by a Rhubarbian consulate abroad; Rhubarbia has consulates in Albania, the Azores and Upper Volta, sometimes.

"Driving is on the right, overtaking on all sides, and passing bullock-carts is forbidden, also drunk. Insurance must be purchased, but foreigners are not entitled if they have an accident and penalties are severe which Rhubarbians like to have. You will be entered in prison which is the custom and maybe released when the papers are stamped and your money has been paid to the owners of the deceased. Once again we remind you that Custardskis are not welcomed. In case of difficulties you may contact your consul. There are no consuls in Rhubarbia. Three warning-triangles must be carried, one each to be put in front and behind of the vehicle. Mud-flaps may not be worn on asphalt, and there must be a window. Police may ask to see your first-aid kit and take it. Parts for Western cars are sometimes available but always not and you should carry some keys to make your own fixing. Our garages have not the equipment but our mechanicals are very inventive and so they do not damage your car by machine; they do it by hand."

Next hurdle: the visas, those troublesome and expensive tests of a traveller's mettle. The price of just one, for Mali, would have fed us for a fortnight; let's hope, charitably, that the fee fed deserving Malians instead, though I doubt it.

Writer Laurens van der Post recalls the hero of the Victorian travelogue "Around the World on a Wheel." The cyclist set off in 1890 to circle the globe, simply by stuffing his pockets full of five-pound notes, pedalling across Europe, Russia and on back to England with nary a currency nor visa restriction. Even early this century, you could travel most of the world with just two bits of paper: a letter each from the British and the French granting you safe transit. Today there's no guarantee that would even get you into Britain or France, let alone the UN's 155 other member-states.

Some even require visas to let you out of the country - certain Arab and African states, for example, and most notably until recently the Eastern bloc countries, which harboured the perfectly valid fear that if they let their people go, they might not come back. Several countries require a sponsor's letter, and that's just for starters. To go to some parts of Africa you need a banker's letter. Cuba wants an itinerary, Russia tells you your itinerary like it or lump it, Iran and several others want letters absolving them of responsibility (for what?).

Iraq used to insist on a baptismal certificate, something not a single Christian I ever questioned possesses, though a church near that country's London Embassy did a lucrative trade in instant dunking. You could not go into Poland without validated proof of a hotel booking. And Nigeria will not entertain your application unless you can show ALL your old passports, just in case you have been to naughty South Africa. If you are thinking of going to Libya, Congo, Guinea, Angola or North Korea, travel agents' advice is simple: don't. It could take years.

Many expensively-filled passports after we first started wading through the world's swamp of visa requirements, fighting the bureaucracy which Balzac rightly called "a mighty machine worked by dwarfs," the absurdity of it all reached its peak in the Persian Gulf emirate of Bahrain. We had little trouble entering - unlike the dead body on an aircraft, whose previous occupant had been imprudent enough not to anticipate dying while transiting the country. It had thus not had the foresight to apply for a visa. After a flurry of indecision and buck-passing Immigration decided to grant the corpse a 72-hour temporary visa. When that expired and the ex-traveller was still stretched on a slab awaiting transport to a better place, Immigration came knocking on the morgue door to see whether the stiff would be applying for a visa extension.

As for moving your money around the world, things have also changed a lot. Today there's a sophisticated banking network spanning the globe, so that your funds can be transferred to Timbuktu at the touch of a computer keyboard. It's what happens when it gets to Timbuktu that's the problem, as morose and penniless supplicants stand vigil for days and even weeks trying to wrest their assets from local banks, where obstructive officials see it as their Allah-given right not to part with any more money than is absolutely necessary.

Even travellers' cheques are not foolproof, as we found in Turkey when a teller would only accept the one denomination of cheque shown in his example file and no others, albeit from the same company and with the selfsame design. Hell, what hope is there on the Third World's money-go-round when we couldn't even cash a guaranteed banker's draft from that bastion of world finance, Switzerland, in the heart of the world's money markets, New York? The lesson is simple and quickly learned: ignore the pompous officials who insist you can't take it with you when you go, stuff your funds in a bag, and hope for the best.

You may have been wondering how we would pay for the very first of what turned out to be an atlas-full of trips. Frankly, so were we. It was to be a long time before articles typed-out in cramped contortion in the back of peripatetic Citroëns would help to pay our way, so for the moment we were restricted to what little we had saved, and little it was indeed. Thank Mammon for a modest lifestyle. In any case, it has to be modest in primitive backwaters where going shopping means you might actually find something to buy if you're lucky, but just as often you don't. As time went on we mastered the knack of supplementing our savings: we put down short roots in the few remaining countries where we could not only work, but where what we earned was harder than the Monopoly money which is becoming the norm in a non-convertible, non-exchangeable, guaranteed-not-to-pay-the-bearer-on-demand currency world.

The first journey started with the balance of our life-savings after we had paid £1,000 for the car: we sallied forth with £1,400 slung in pouches around our necks. These days thanks to inflation we sally fifth, if not fifteenth, but at that time £3 a day could keep us chuntering along in a style to which we were soon to become accustomed, even with fuel gobbling fully half of it.

We were among the last of the great underspenders, largely thanks to phenomena like the Indian marketplace. In 1975 that could still provide everything we needed for three satisfactory meals a day for one week at a total outlay of one English pound. Currency black markets help, too - especially in monetary-mayhem countries like Uganda. There, not only was the black market rate for dollars or sterling an astonishing six times the official figure, but the government itself even opened black-market windows in its banks, to cream-off at least some of the cash.

By the springtime of our first lift-off every expense had been spared and we were ready to fulfil our trifling ambition: simply to set off vaguely eastwards at about 150 kilometres a day, and to keep going at more or less the same pace for 400 days until we fell into Cape Town's Table Bay.

Of course we had misgivings about the weight of the vehicle. Years later after a series of devastating Saharan mishaps we were forced to load so much gear that it was the equivalent of asking a 2CV to carry 14 people... This first experience was better, but not much, as we added to the weight of our hardboard-and-mesh house some 40 litres of water, 20 litres of spare petrol, one spare wheel, four spare tyres, a gigantic box of tools and spares, two cooking-gas canisters and a double-burner stove, pots and pans, utensils, a dozen padlocks and lots of chain, a case of emergency food rations and a cooler-box, photographic gear, an ancient Empire portable typewriter (a faithful friend which would end its days in a Dutch typewriter museum after clattering steadfastly through 74 countries), stationery, maps, guides, handbooks, a basic first-aid kit and medicine chest, a shortwave radio, a dozen books to read and then trade with other travellers, clothing for all four seasons, bedding, mosquito-net frames, and a 99-pence plastic compass. If we were lucky, on most days there might even be space for us. For a few days we also had pillows and an alarm-clock, until they joined the many items soon to find their way into roadside litterbins as we became more kilo-conscious than members of WeightWatchers. The final all-up weight: 957 kilos, in a vehicle designed to carry that much only at a pinch and heaven help us when the going got rough.

So this was it. As Peter Fleming remarked at the beginning of his seminal "Brazilian Adventure": "There are, I suppose, expeditions and expeditions. Ours was not going to qualify for either category."

We were ready to roll and if getting there was to be half the fun, getting back would be the other half. Sir Arnold Bax said one should try everything once except incest and folk-dancing and we were ready to take him at his word. On the way we might even try folk-dancing.

3
TRAVELS WITH TWO CHARLIES

Starting that very first trip was like auditioning for the Keystone Cops. Perhaps setting out from London on April the first hadn't been a good idea after all: within 48 hours a passing plant had demolished our wing-mirror, we had become hopelessly bogged in a mud-field, the entire front roof-section of the car had collapsed, several dozen kilos of our baggage had been discarded along the road, and we had caused a multiple car pile-up with the help of a pheasant. Were we destined to be the Titanic of the road on our maiden voyage?

Youth may be wasted on the young, as someone once remarked, but the naïveté and resilience of youth kept us laughing through those initial hiccups. We gathered that it wasn't going to be plain driving all the way when we trial-loaded, and unloaded, and reloaded, and unloaded the car hour after hour on that first fresh spring day. By the time we were finished and should have been halfway to Britain's south coast, the car sat several centimetres lower than intended though our spirits were high. The landlady cheered us off with a wave and a packet of digestive biscuits to see us to India, and we left to drive straight into a protruding branch. Goodnight wing-mirror, but what's a mere mirror when you're young and excited and the world awaits?

The carpenter's-nightmare bodywork creaked ominously with the weight. But for the moment, optimism ruled OK, and continued to do so as I headed right for the middle of a muddy ploughed field.

Elise gaped at me in disbelief. "Stop - are you mad?" she wailed.

"This is as good a time as any to find out what the car can take!" I retorted, wrestling with the wheel as we plunged overloaded-nose-first into the first gulping rut.

"Thump, kerr-rr-ACK," went the car just as Elise yelled that the roof was falling in and our equipment was raining. Satisfied with demonstrating that it wasn't a Massey-Ferguson after all, the car settled comfortably into the mud for a nice rest. Beside me, Elise was balanced with only her bum on the seat, in a classic "playing dead" position with her arms and legs aloft as she struggled to keep the rest of the front roof from falling in.

We laughed. That's the sort of fool thing you do before experience takes the gloss off your sense of humour. The damage was appalling as we unpacked our gear into the mud. The entire roof storage section which was to carry virtually all our excess of equipment had collapsed, and we set about reconstructing it as best you can with a few bits of hardboard, a couple of canopy-frame tubes, string and optimism. By the simple expedient of packing and unpacking the car three times in four hours we quite easily unbogged the car. But what to do about the overload? The answer was painfully obvious as we ground our way onwards: much of it was donated to litter-bins, and we often wonder at the reaction of dustmen encountering brand-new pillows in their haul. (From then on we rested our weary heads on pillowslips filled with laundry).

The following day we hit neither a pheasant nor any other cars, causing several cars to hit each other instead.

The pheasant leapt out in all its startling bulk from a roadside hedge. Now it's all very well for the manuals to say you should keep going and create an ex-pheasant rather than an accident, but try telling that to your reflexes. I braked, just in time. So did the car behind.

Those following were less lucky, hamstrung by that curiously-British habit of driving almost bumper-to-bumper at high speed. There was an almost-comic succession of crunching, tinkling, scraping, grinding noises all the way back up the hill as cars were shortened in quick succession. As the first angry delegation descended on us, it was clear this was no time to argue the legal niceties. "Quick, we're French!" I muttered to Elise, thankful for the Parisian tax-free plate on the back of the car.

As verbal slings and arrows were unleashed, we shrugged, muttered and busked through our limited repertoire of French with half-closed lips.

"Gauloises Gitanes tres bien Charles de Gaulle," I slurred.

"Ah oui," gabbled Elise. "Citroën Méhari Arc de Triomphe Place de la Concorde Renault."

"Peugeot pas de Anglais petit dejeuner" and more we mumbled and shrugged, until the aggrieved throngs dissipated to the welcome murmurs of "Bloody French!"

We sounded our "All Clear" in a relieved exhalation. Thus had passed the first mini-crisis, and surely we could cope just as innovatively with any other little googlies life cared to bowl at us? Had we but known it, our resolve was to be severely tested in the months and years to come.

As we circumnavigated Britain, we relied less on maps than on our gloriously inaccurate 99-pence windscreen compass to lead us to interesting new discoveries. Life soon settled into a comfortable routine. With an almost geriatric sense of leisure we pottered, and ate, and looked, and drove, and walked. In small towns we wandered and shopped; in tourist areas we tried to do better than the vast number of tourists who boldly go where everyone has been before, looking at everything and seeing nothing, people who go not so much to see as to tell afterwards, clicking their instant cameras and chafing at having to wait a whole sixty seconds for the print.

Elise coped happily with the unbelievable strictures of living in a mobile packing-case, adapting blithely to the necessity of having to shift masses of impedimenta every time she wanted anything from a salt-cellar to a handkerchief.

Living together for a year in our cubic metre was to be a supreme test of true love, that much was clear, as we crashed into each other with every in-house twitch. Just changing my trousers was a seven-stage lesson in contortionism. Life was lived largely outdoors despite the vagaries of an English spring, setting the pattern for the weeks and months ahead as we camped free, bathed in brooks and streams and laundered as we went, with no need of a campground or hotel except as a very occasional treat. Could there be anything more invigorating than leaving our washing out to dry in a forest above the Queen in Balmoral Castle, while I tapped away on the typewriter perched precariously on my lap?

As free-campers can testify, Britain is not always the easiest place when it comes to finding a spot for the night. Hedges, fences and a plethora of "Private - Keep Out" signs can mean driving for hours just looking for a haven, so it's little wonder we occasionally went for the far-flung spots where we knew we would not be disturbed. Absolutely the furthest-flung was the top of a mountain in the Lake District. The road from the bottom had become a track, then two ruts, then inspired guesswork, and before we knew it there was no going back as we bounced and lurched ever upwards, finding out for the first time just how tenacious a little Citroën can be. Finally at the top we puffed to a halt, and settled in for a bracing night.

"How utterly alone we are," we thought as we inflicted the searing punishment of cold water on our faces and hands the next icy morning. But we weren't. No sooner had we sat down to our soggy Weetabix than two hands came over the parapet beside our milk-jug, followed by a body festooned in ropes, hooks and picks. His pique at finding a car atop the mountain he had just so painstakingly climbed was soon tempered by a cup of tea.

On we galumphed into sparse border areas where few saloon cars venture, across territory marked interestingly on our AA map as "Extent of Overlap," and into Scotland proper, past some of the anomalies of that nation: towns and lakes with unpronounceable names, culminating in the lunacy of Loch Lochy, or past fish-and-chip shops selling Haggis and Chips, and wondering what foreign visitors must make of the cryptic signs on so many guest-house doors: "B & B, H & C in bedrooms." At 70 kilometres per hour, our top speed because of the ridiculous overload, we trundled on towards the first of what was to be many sleepless nights: in the Stranraer ferry-terminal to Northern Ireland. With several dark hours to kill before boarding, we decided to sleep in the terminal parking lot. A trucker parked his refrigerated vehicle fifty centimetres from the non-pillows in the back of our car, turned on the deafening generator and went away forever, leaving us to nurse fierce thoughts of revenge and violence as we tossed like Morpheus in the underworld.

My first return, alone, to the land of my birth the year before had been a complete Ulster education in a fortnight. Could such contradictions still exist in the Western world, I asked myself then, in a country where religious intolerance was rampant - so rampant that one distant relative, a fiery patriot of a man, had been thrown into moral turmoil by my unannounced arrival after two decades away?

For years he had gone out of his way to avoid patronising the one shop in his tiny town run by "Papists," one of the least-offensive of the descriptions he had for Catholics in the manner of so many of his bigoted, befuddled kind. Then, one fateful Friday, I arrived without warning - and the cupboards were bare. What to do? With all shops in the town closed save one - no prizes for guessing which one - could he renounce the prejudice of a lifetime and buy "something grand for the lad's tea," as his wife implored? Or would we celebrate with bread and butter?

Bread and butter it was. And the next day I kept wisely silent in an effort to preserve family harmony as "the true story" of the Irish Troubles was hammered into me, with all the finesse of a pile-driver being used to crack a nut. I was left even stronger in my belief that the Irish don't know what they want, and won't be happy until they get it.

Religious bigotry aside this was a wonderful land, as I kept emphasising to Elise our first day together ashore. She agreed with everything I said; indeed, how could she do otherwise, being totally groggy with a lack of Stranraer sleep and the delayed effects of several seasickness tablets? (She had had little benefit from the advice offered on the ship by an Aussie, who proffered Australia's national cure for seasickness: go and sit under a tree).

Our introduction to Ulster was as Irish as could be, as a friendly family took us in and offered us a bath. We accepted - but had second thoughts when we saw the tin bath being dragged into the middle of the living-room and herds of saucepans put on the stove to boil. Too late for demurral, and we accepted with good grace too the lethal green soap which is the mainstay of all well-scrubbed Irish. Antiseptically fresh, we emerged to be asked by the man of the house whether we would like to go with him to the pub, it being Friday night. At least we thought we were being asked; as it turned out "we" weren't. Only me, for whoever heard of a woman being taken to the pub on Friday? Too late, though; Elise had also beamed her acceptance, and there was an uncomfortable night ahead for our host if not for us, as we set off to collect another reveller from a nearby farm whose kitchen contained grandfather, the laundry and the family pig.

In the pub, in the middle of that Irish backwood, Elise was something of a celebrity. One farmer wrapped around his Guinness realised her accent was not entirely local, and asked where she came from.

"Holland," she replied, to be met with a blank look.

"Where's that?" the farmer asked.

Elise decided to keep things simple. "Over the sea."

The mists of incomprehension moved in. "But England's over the sea, isn't that right?" the farmer asked.

"Yes, but Holland's over the next sea."

"Oh." A long pause, then: "Ye speak English in Holland, o' course?"

"No, we have our own language, called Dutch."

"Now fancy that! Course ye use pounds and pence like we do?"

"No, we don't. We have our own money, called guilders."

He worked this through his mind for some time.

"Well now," he finally mused. "Ye don't use pounds and pence. Sure that must be awful difficult...."

Throughout the country, roadblocks, barricaded police-stations and running army patrols were an ever-present fact of life, but of Ulster's underlying troubles we saw very little, largely by choice. It was one thing for me as an unattached and quite foolhardy reporter the year before to deliberately saunter down Belfast's infamous Falls and Shankill Roads, taking pictures and talking to passers-by before being picked up and summarily ejected by the army for my own good. To do so with Elise in tow would have been unthinkable, though we did cause a stir by actually going into the almost-dormant Tourist Office in Belfast to ask for leaflets and ideas. They were so astounded at actually seeing a tourist that it was some time before we were allowed to leave, burdened with bundles of brochures which had lain for years.

The atmosphere was more relaxed across the border in the Republic - so relaxed, in fact, that wherever we stopped people ambled across to pass the time of day in that most endearing of Irish attributes, the love of a good chat. Mostly we managed, though even my ancestry availed us naught when a farmer settled in with his elbow on the roof of our van for a long monologue - of which we understood not a word, so thick was his brogue.

Ireland was the only country where people didn't actually stop work to stare at our weird vehicle as we passed. How could they, when they usually weren't engaged in any work which they could stop? Not for nothing did an eminent Irishman once reply, when asked whether his country had any word equivalent to the all-embracing, all-delaying Spanish concept of "manyana":

"No, I don't believe we have anything which conveys quite that urgency."

Through quiet towns on deserted roads we trundled, stopping often, in a country where Housman's famous lines take on a new significance: "What good is life if full of care, we have no time to stop and stare?" We did, frequently, and just as frequently enjoyed the delights of Irish hostelries. Surrounded by locals enjoying food-free dinners while trying to sup their way into the Records Book of Guinnesses before closing time, we would nurse a pint of "the gargle" and a broguery of chats, the loud insistencies of opinion on everywhich subject making it hard to hear yourself drink. But in Macroom we were so overcome by the Dublin brew that we staggered out, then managed only barely in the fog - which wasn't entirely the product of the weather - to park somewhere vaguely suitable for the night, before sinking into wonderful oblivion.

The next morning with heads like barrels and mouths fitted with carpets we woke to see our surroundings for the first time - to discover that we had parked in the middle of the town-square the night before market-day. All around us the stalls were doing a thriving trade, with hardly a polite glance at this odd red obstacle focussed in the middle.

We filled up for the last time, with fuel defined neither as regular, premium, nor several-star, but simply "Best Petrol," at a garage where a young lad approached, intrigued by our car. He got the standard guided tour, replete with references to the plastic parts. The end of the tour left him puzzled.

"The car is plastic, y'say?" he asked again.

Yes, I replied, not wanting to repeat a precise breakdown of constituent parts.

"The bodywork's plastic?"

Yes again.

"You're travelling around the world in this plastic car?"

Certainly.

"But - - " and here he hesitated. "But - has it got a REAL engine?"

Noodling back across Britain in early May made us realise what a marvellous place the U.K. could be, if only it had twelve months of early summer a year, and several thousand fewer "Keep Out" signs along those rolling English roads with their rolling English hedges which make sightseeing easy only if you're a giraffe. On we went to Europe; despite E.E.C. insistence, British public opinion still thought in terms of Britain AND Europe more than Britain IN Europe. Indeed, one True Brit went into print to express his views of the consequences now that Europe had joined Britain...

First goal: the Netherlands. Then, just to get the taste of something different we set out one day from Elise's home to nibble at Germany on bicycles. It was after all just 10 kilometres distant, but on the way back a mishap disabled my front wheel. Strong Dutch men have been moved to tears by my Great British cycling technique, so in good native style Elise took charge, bundling me onto the back of her machine as I freewheeled the other.

The wail of a siren shattered the peaceful pedalling, as a Porsche pulled up to disgorge a policeman already in the first stages of apoplexy. Had we realised that to ride two to a bicycle was almost a hanging offence in Germany, he seemed to be bellowing? When he found out I was an Englander he almost strangled on his own ire, and ordered us to walk to the border - seven kilometres away. So we walked with the cycles, and as we walked he followed in his Porsche, every centimetre of the way for one hour in case we should attempt to subvert the rules and thereby the state when his back was turned.

In the years since, we have drawn close to many fine Germans, have learned the language and can laugh at their national idiosyncrasies as they laugh at ours. But we found it hard to forgive those first-impression encounters with the unlovely side of the Teutonic character.

A belief in the innate goodness of Man is hard to sustain when you are mentally flagellated by German arrogance twice in as many days. Lost at a small forest intersection normally devoid of traffic, we stopped on the road to consult our map. A Mercedes roared up behind us (there's something about German Mercedes drivers, we soon learned, summed-up in the British cliché "the jerk in the Merc"). The driver began blowing his horn, then his top. Others would have pulled alongside - there was plenty of space to pass - to ask whether we needed assistance. Not this one, his face looking like a commercial for strychnine while he hooted and flashed.

We shrugged an apology, hand-signalled him to pass and returned to poring over the map. He hooted some more, then wobbled out of his car, slammed the door, marched to the front of our car, pulled out a notebook and gold pen and wrote down our number with all the grim determination of a gas-meter inspector in Auschwitz. Then, and only then, did he drive past, and for hours afterwards we fully expected to be confronted by a SWAT-type roadblock around every bend.

Having a German walk through our sandwiches with his windsurfer to get to the lake where we were picknicking didn't help, either, but such early impressions were soon tempered by the many fine German travellers we were to meet over the next 300,000 kilometres - some of them destined to become firm lifelong friends.

There's no doubt they're different, though - that much became clear at our first German level-crossing. As we approached, we were surprised to see none of the painters actually working with that renowned Germanic efficiency. Instead, brushes and pots in hand they waited, and chatted. Then a train approached, and the booms came down.

The men were instantly transformed. As furiously as they could they slapped new red and white warning-stripes on the lowered poles, sweat pouring from their brows as the train whizzed through. A minute later the booms went up, still dripping paint, and they relaxed to await the next train.

Through the French border we went, the laughter of the Customs officials ringing in our ears. "C'est impossible!" they had first exclaimed as they caught sight of this familiar French car in its very unfamiliar garb. Five spare tyres for a holiday in France - surely not? "Where are you going?" one asked us.

"Afrique du Sud," we replied with some pride. They laughed, and were still roaring as they waved us a bon voyage.

Still, at least the natives were friendly. As we passed through tiny hamlets, locals clustered on balconies and terraces waved with gay encouragement, and we waved back in wonderment. Whatever happened to the surly French so beloved of English bigotry?

We found out in the next town when, in mid-wave, we were overtaken by a rally car going like a Hadean bat, and then another as the crowd cheered on. We felt only slightly less sheepish than we had done on the famous Nürburgring racing circuit in Germany, when a foolish sense of romance had impelled me to drive our 602cc tortoise around the open-to-the-public track. I managed just one circuit before the dust of several Porsches and the uproarious ridicule of bystanders induced terminal humilation.

In France we had our first serious breakdown, made more serious by the fact that it occurred at lunchtime, that most inviolable and protracted of French institutions. We telephoned the local Citroën garage, and waited, and waited, from eleven in the morning through to four in the afternoon, and when the man came he looked under the dashboard, reconnected the ignition-wire which this stupid Anglais had dislodged with his foot when depressing the clutch, then left muttering. That we had waited five hours for a two-minute repair which we could have done ourselves did wonders for our morale.

It's impossible to avoid the French obsession with food, wherever you go in that land which improbably combines gastronomes and gourmets with the most foul-tasting Gauloises and Gitanes cigarettes. Not that a Briton has any room to talk, of course; there is even some merit in the comment of a French food writer who avowed that "The English have no cuisine to speak of, and if they did, they'd put mint sauce on it." Or their famous chef who said there is nothing wrong with English food - as long as you eat breakfast three times a day. Yet French milk is often undrinkable, and twice the price of the wine. And French bread must be among the worst in the world even if it adds to the scenery, as you watch Frenchmen almost gouge out the eyes of fellow-travellers in the "Metro" by wielding their long loaves. No rural scene is complete without locals bearing loaves, cyclists with thin loaves, women with droves of loaves, even, ludicrously, a policeman directing traffic with a loaf.

What we didn't expect was the treatment we got in one ultra-popular Parisian restaurant where we had gone for a meal with a friend. We queued to get in - queueing in France being a feat in itself, for the French laugh at the English propensity to form lines with feeble jokes like: "What do you have if you have two Englishmen together? The start of a queue." Once in, we expected to linger over our meal in good Gallic tradition, and we chatted, watching in some amazement as flambé dishes were set alight all around us - a habit British gourmet Clement Freud dismisses as "food you can read by."

"Madame" glided over, mindful of the throngs still clamouring for table space.

"Don't talk," she admonished us. "Eat!"

Over the Pyrenees and into Spain, our first Iberian impression was a restaurant called Purgatoria, serving, even less enticingly, Damm beer and a drink called Revoltosa. Thanks, but no thanks. We passed, stopping down the road for some minor repairs. Within minutes there was a screech of tyres as two motorcycle

Policia pulled up. New country, new laws, I worried, wondering what it was we had done to attract their displeasure.

"Inglez?"

"Si," I replied in a dazzling display of linguistic virtuosity.

He smiled. "Ghello Good morning Good afternoon Sank you Ghow you do do I like practise Eenglis Goodbye," he said in one breath, smiled again, shook my hand - and they left.

In the town of Beasain near Bilbao people were just as friendly when we had trouble finding a baker. Within minutes of learning our plight the entire population seemed to turn out to lead us to the "Panaderia." Such a pleasant fellow, that baker, as he realised here were two foreigners needing special treatment. For us he had a special loaf, which he brought out from far under the counter. Full of bonhomie he accepted our pesetas and bid us good day. At the very least the loaf was a leftover from the days of the Spanish Inquisition and could have been used to build houses. But such a nice fellow...

Fortunately Spain wasn't all like that. Far from it, as we were frequently showered with gifts of fruit, vegetables and bread - a syndrome which even increased once we reached Portugal. Our only Spanish problem was in the post office.

Trying to mail the aerogrammes we had bought the week before, we were told that postal rates had gone up in the interim. Okay, we said, sell us some stamps to stick on the aerogrammes to make up the difference.

"No es possible," the clerk regretted, managing to explain that enclosing or sticking things on aerogrammes is illegal - even stamps. We had just two choices: buy new aerogrammes and write our letters over again, or buy envelopes, enclose the aerogrammes, and pay the full airmail letter rate.

An expatriate couple regaled us with tales of twisted Spanish logic which would have filled a chapter on their own. Among the nicest was the story of their electricity bill, which should have been deducted automatically from their bank account each month. It wasn't - yet several months on, the electricity still hadn't been cut off. They took the problem to their bank manager, who came back smiling.

"No problem!" he said - an ominous phrase, as many an expat or traveller knows. "Not to worry for your bill. Our computer take it from someone else account each month by mistake, so no is necessary to do notheeng."

If Spain was poor, Portugal was poorer. The women toiled endlessly in the fields, and the men plodded along leading donkeys, or on donkeys, or even back-to-back two to a donkey. Which made one wonder why so many men sat on their asses all day... Still the shower of gifts continued. "Hello Ingles how do you do!" people would say automatically with not a sign of a Union Jack to tip them off, and they would press bread, or cakes, or fruit, or refreshment on us. God's friendliest people, without doubt - an opinion we haven't changed even in all the years and several trips to Portugal which have followed.

On that first trip, though, we weren't sure what to expect as we stood one evening near the most primitive-looking village this side of Africa, near a town called San Pueblo do Sol. Parked for the night, we had just started our meal when we sensed the presence of people. Sure enough, there on the nearby hill a group had gathered. One man, obviously the leader, would start towards us, motioning the children to stand back. Then, a few paces on, he would lose courage and retreat.

We decided to chance our luck, to stroll into the village and ask if we might stay the night where we were parked. Hand-in-hand we set out, slightly nervous, on the path to the small tumbledown four-walled mud shacks flanking the single, half-cobbled street.

The village bell began to ring, and as it did, people materialised from the doors of their houses. We rounded the last corner and there before us was gathered the entire population of the village, summoned to see us by the bell. A little unsurely we began to pantomime who we were and what we wanted to the blur of simple, eager and friendly faces. Within seconds we were a Royal Visit, and we plunged into a stuttering conversation rollicking along in English, Portuguese, Spanish and mime while they replied in their thudding consonants and slushing noises. Naturally we had permission to stay as long as we liked, and it was with genuine regret that they saw us off the next morning. In trips since we have tried to find that village again, without success. Perhaps we should not; often, all you get from looking back is a stiff neck.

Pantomime was to become a standard language as we progressed further on our travels. Disregarding the fact that by now we would have had to accumulate several hundred phrase-books, (India alone has 600 languages), it wasn't long before we realised even a phrase-book counted for naught if the locals were thrown by your mangled nuances. Take our simple need for motor-oil.

Filling-up at a petrol station, I wandered over to the attendant's kiosk, armed with carefully-rehearsed lines from our travel dictionary.

I pointed at the engine. "Oleo, por favor."

The attendant, admittedly not overburdened with brains, not too swift upstairs, looked at me blankly. I repeated the word. His expression continued to resemble the Black Hole of Calcutta. I tried varying the accent.

"OH'leo?"

Zilch.

"OLAYo?"

Nix.

"OleOH? AWleo? OhLEEo? Olé,oh?" The attendant still looked at me with his brain on hold. Just then another customer wandered over, sized up the situation and offered his help.

"Oleo," he said.

Dawning broke on the attendant's face. "Ah!" it struck. "Oleo!" And he slushed and rhubarbed on in Portuguese which clearly meant "Why didn't you say that in the first place!"

It was in Portugal that we first let down our inhibitions enough to be able to stand in a grocery-shop clucking like a chicken, or ordering squish-squish of moo, several slices of oink or a chunk of baaa. Shopping was particularly gratifying in the poverty of Portugal where you knew you were doing people a favour by buying from them. In one market-place where we bought a cabbage for a ridiculously-small amount of escudos, it would be hard to forget the look of sheer gratitude on the face of the woman selling it when she realised we were going to buy it from her. It tasted all the better for that.

Heading back up through Portugal we stopped at one of Catholicism's most revered sites, the peculiar Bom Jesus shrine, complete with the gruesome and almost lifelike dioramas of the crucifixion scenes which are more than sufficient to put you off your lunch. After the heavy symbolism and bizarre piety of it all, the shrine's souvenir shops were like something out of Kafka.

You could buy a plastic Christ on a plastic cross with a snap-on halo, a quartz clock with Jesus' arms showing the time, Last Supper drinking glasses, playing-cards showing the saints, the Virgin Mary on a teatray, a Pontius Pilate dart-board, crucifixion jigsaws, do-it-yourself glue-together Christ-kits - even one of those snow-bubble glass ornaments except that when you turned this one upside down you didn't get snow, but a hail of silver glitter which showered over Christ on his cross.

All that was missing was a seaside-souvenir pen which, when inverted, would start the Saviour slowly ascending to heaven within its barrel.

4
PASTA AND DEEP-FRIED BATHERS

Italy was closed the day we arrived. Its border was shut tighter than the proverbial maiden's knees by a Customs go-slow, and most of Europe was waiting at the gates as we joined the kilometres-long queue.

Peak-season tourists sat in the middle of the freeway, picknicking on the tarmac with their tables and chairs, coping with life in the slow lane as they suntanned or quarrelled, or stretched out on a towel in the middle of the autobahn watching portable television. Occasionally a herd of cars would be cleared and the whole confusion would be hand-pushed forward a few metres.

By the time we had inched within several hundred cars of the border, itinerant officials were wandering down the lines, demanding the odd passport. At 100 heavily-visa'd pages long, ours were odder than most, but it wasn't that which caught the attention of one sympathetic officer.

His eye had focussed on my passport's "Place of Birth." Belfast, as the old joke goes, is a nice place....to leave, and I had done just that two decades previously. But the Italian was overcome with histrionic Latin remorse at the further injustice being done to this pathetic refugee from that trouble-stricken land, who was probably at this moment fleeing the traumas of war for a precious holiday in wonderful Italia.

"Belfasta!" he declaimed, and to prove his incomparable grasp of current affairs, ratatatted us with an imaginary machine-gun. "Ah mama mia, Belfasta," he said once more with pity, and who were we to explain that he knew Belfasta better than we did if he had a TV? "Is-a all okay, my poor friend, you come to Italia, molto bene," and he waved us all the way past the waiting thousands and through the bottlenecked border. His tangible sympathy was not quite shared by those left behind to moulder, who looked like they would cheerfully outperform the worst of the I.R.A.'s atrocities on us given half a chance.

It was an auspicious start to an inauspicious stage of the trip, as we soon discovered. The English have always had a curious love-affair with Italy. Writer D. H. Lawrence swore that he loved Italy but hated the Italians. We couldn't even sum up that much emotion about this curious country.

There were highlights and lowlights, sure enough. Who could forget the traffic policeman enmeshed in the worst traffic-jam we had ever seen, who after waving his arms and gusting on his whistle for ineffectual minutes said to hell with it all, went and bought himself an ice-cream, and left the snarled vehicles to their fate while he splattered his uniform with Tutti Frutti?

Who could forget Italy's omnipresent Sunday drivers, horns blaring fortissimo as they do battle with the rest, eager to prove their machismo in confrontation with anyone who dares to intrude on their road-space? Or the drivers who refuse to allow their steering-wheel to hamper their conversational prowess as they wave and gesticulate with their passengers while the car wanders drunkenly?

Or Rome's pedestrians, some of whom actually cross themselves before crossing the street; some of whom actually make it to the other side?

Or the beach lido where tiny Guiseppe, his mountainous wife Maria and their six bambinos demanded we enjoy their hospitality, sharing some of the provisions they had brought along for 36 days in their tent: two crates of wine, lots of beer and Cokes, sacks of pasta, spaghetti, ravioli, some bread and fruit - and three flagons of olive oil?

Or Italy's chronic shortage of small change, whether epitomised in the constant handfuls of sweets or stamps you got back from shopkeepers, or in the bank which was unable to change our foreign currency unless we could round-off the difference in Lire coins because they had none.

Or Venice, where a parking attendant with a particularly bovine mentality decided our motorised Matchbox-model was a bus and should pay the same as those with 62 occupants; where tourists follow like lovesick sheep their guides who are waving red roses or somesuch aloft on umbrellas in farcical efforts to keep groups together; and where we were stunned to be charged TEN times the displayed price of a pizza because, as it was later pointed out with a smirk, the advertised price was for a takeaway and we had chosen to eat it at the restaurant's table.

Perhaps D. H. Lawrence was right, though the Italy he loved didn't have every picturesque valley filled with a belching factory as ours was, or hadn't yet been raped by the car, in an age when doing The Grand European Tour was an infinitely more exciting thing than being spoon-fed useless gee-gaws of information on an "If This Is Thursday It Must Be Italy" bus tour.

In the final summing-up we could hardly contain our indifference; we were underwhelmed by it all and longed for adventure and the lure of the REAL travelling which we knew must lie ahead. Pausing only to sink our lips into what we thought was an ice-cream cone but turned out to be disgusting whipped-cream, we fled north once more - and were no better off.

To lapse into descriptions of the delights of Central Europe would be to inflict such dullness on the reader as to cause him to flee to something lighter, like the Times Educational Supplement. As we passed our first hundred days on the road, our surroundings were chiefly notable for not being notable at all, as we killed time and distance through the clutch of instant little European countries whose maps are so easy to fold: Andorra, where our car ran out of puff some way higher than 3,000 metres; Liechtenstein, policed by 18 men and a dog; San

Marino, whose only industry is stamps; Monaco and Monte Carlo, whose casinos do so much for the Gross National Product of Kuwait and Saudi Arabia; or another nibble at the South of France, the tourist-littered "Côte d'Ordures" where the beaches of Cannes are brushed and combed every morning, and where the stench of Ambre Solaire and deep-fried bathers hits you long before you reach the coast.

The mood was hardly improved in Austria when we were attacked by cows.

Yes, I know it's a likely story and whoever heard of being attacked by God's most placid of creatures? We didn't believe it either as the four of them lumbered down on us while we picknicked among the edelweiss. We protested as they nudged us from our paraphernalia, then we shouted, finally we wielded our umbrella, all to no avail as they steamrollered on like bulls carrying their own china shop. We retreated in utter humiliation while everything was investigated and then ingested. Our Austrian tourist brochures began the long conversion into full-cream Alpine milk, along with the remnants of our picnic and, to chase it all down, our half-litre of soapy washing-up water.

Barely pausing to grin at the sight of two optimistic hitchhikers seated at a hotel terrace table, supping beer while jabbing their thumbs out at the traffic with their free hand, we headed for the famous Schaffhausen waterfalls in Switzerland. "Roll on the hardships of real travel," we had wailed during the past, warming-up weeks of bland tourism, and that's where we found one.

The moral of the story is that short-cuts rarely are, as we discovered in trying to get from the falls to Zurich the shortest way, by cutting through back roads and a tiny sliver of Germany. Little roads mean little border posts, and little border posts in Europe are where they cut the teeth of officials who aspire to bigger border posts. We had picked the littlest of all possible posts, and our budding Customs denizen thought he knew why.

"India! Afghanistan! Nepal!" His eyes lit up as he saw the visas in our passports and translated them into smuggled drug caches. Elise explained in her best German to this worst German that we were on our way to said lands, not coming from. He merely dug in deeper, rooting out all our carefully-packed goods, opening every single tin, jar and packet and in many cases destroying sealed emergency rations which were to see us through the coming year.

He thought he had triumphed. "Aha - was ist das?"

"Custard powder - Bird's," came the resigned reply.

Minutes later another "Aha!" - a packet of incense used to clear the car of cooking odours in the evenings. "From India, ja?"

"No, Woolworths, Oxford Street London."

He stopped only after stumbling across several months' worth of sanitary towels and a pillowslip-full of dirty knickers. Two-and-a-half hours from the first flickerings of his possible promotion he threw in the towel and the pillowslip with a sad "Ja, alles gut. Weiter fahren." Which translated roughly as Get the hell out of here before I burst into tears.

One would-be Swiss overlander we met years later got himself arrested trying to leave Switzerland, because of the tantrum he threw in just such a confrontation. We had acquitted ourselves calmly and well and were glad of the experience, though it hardly felt that way as we struggled to bring forth order from the chaos, and to make a sorry list of the spoiled sealed foodstuffs which would now have to be replaced.

No matter, Jugoslavia lay ahead and there, surely, Civilisation As We Know It would take a turn for the worse - or better, or at least more interesting, depending on your viewpoint. Before we hit that first encounter with Communism (a bland encounter whose passport stamp would later cause us several problems in the obsessively anti-Communist U.S.A.), we had a final brush with the free enterprise system encapsulated in one lone Englishman abroad.

Grinding our way up one of Europe's most notorious passes, the Würzen between Austria and Jugoslavia, we mentally thumbed our noses at the steaming Mercedes, B.M.W.'s and the like we saw cooling halfway up the long hot gradient, a notorious pass which has a punishing one-in-three slope in places. Up ahead of us was a curious sight: a battered English Land-Rover towing a German-registered Mercedes all the way to the top. We stopped for tea, and 40 minutes later there was the Land-Rover again, this time dragging an Opel. Later we struck up a chat with the driver.

"Always come to Austria for me fortnight's hols," he chuckled. "One week on the Würzen Pass, the rest in the Tyrol."

One week in the Würzen Pass, we queried - one of the most barren short stretches of Central Europe?

"Not for me it ain't," he grinned. "I spend that first week towing up all the cars that can't make it, charging them a few quid each time. By the end of the first week I've paid for the second."

The Iron Curtain parted with little difficulty and we were into Jugoslavia. There's a wry Russian joke about the contrast between their system and ours: under Capitalism, they say, man exploits man - under Communism it's the other way around. Certainly the Jugoslavs, with their uneasy federation of mini-republics paying slightly more than lip-service to the theories of Marx, could never be called a typical Communist state, even if the mess their economy has since become with its inflation in three digits and its dearth of goods is closer to the Eastern model than the Western.

No reflection on our own status, but I needed a couple of nuts, to replace some which had vibrated loose during our 15,000 kilometres to date. The man behind the hardware counter shrugged in resignation and pointed to the shelves behind him. There were dozens and dozens of boxes of bolts of every conceivable size - but not a single nut. That's sign number one of a good socialist economy: the ability to overproduce, on a massive scale, goods which are not needed, while underproducing just as massively those which are. Two distraught English visitors out on a never-to-be-repeated fortnight's holiday in Jugoslavia later summed it up with their despairing grumble: "How do people cope in a country where you can't even buy what you need in a supermarket to put together a complete evening meal?"

Three large Italians touring the Eastern Bloc countries for six weeks in a VW Beetle had their own solution, we learned when they invited us to join them for dinner one night. We were led to the front of the car, and the bonnet was raised to reveal their closely-packed pantry compartment. It was filled to bursting with pasta of every conceivable form, their sole sustenance for 42 days. Small wonder they appreciated the tin of baked beans we contributed to our meal together.

It was in Jugoslavia that, for the first time, we had to take care when filling-up at a petrol station, setting the pattern for several score countries to come. Choosing a brand in Jugoslavia is easy, for there is only one, of a universal quality: state-controlled poor. "Full please," I intimated at that first station, and started to pay when the job was done. Then I did a double-take at the pump reading. If it was correct, we had just taken on board enough fuel to get us to Asia - not a bad feat for a 25 litre tank.

In a babel of tongues the attendant and I embarked on frank and meaningful discussions about the 87 litres he had just pumped, settled when the car handbook was brought out to show a litre capacity which was the same even in his Cyrillic alphabet: 25. We parted not quite the best of friends, but not before a passer-by had wandered up to see us.

"You are Eenglis, excuse me?" he asked.

Yes.

"Ah - excuse me."

We waited for more. It came.

"Er, excuse me."

Yes?

"Excuse me, excuse me, you smoke?"

No.

I decided to raise the intellectual level of the chat a tad. "You are Jugoslavian?" I asked him.

"Excuse me, excuse me," he said in reply. Then he smiled, excuse me'd again, and was gone.

It was an exchange rivalled only by the one we had two days later at another filling station, when a young girl greeted us.

"Good after!" she smiled - and went away, ideally to relearn the page covering English greetings.

Not everyone was as friendly. Now and again children threw clods of sand as we passed, and if we had only known it these were probably among the least harmful of the missiles which would be hurled at us in months to come. In one village along the Albanian border shepherds waved greetings with their sticks - which had been dipped in cow-dung. The aroma was appalling as we spent the rest of the afternoon fishing in our car for excrement.

Still, sometimes we gave as good as we got, especially when we discovered a unique way of getting rid of our daily rubbish, there being few litter-bins in Jugoslavia. We simply left it openly accessible in a packet on the front of our car, and without fail it was stolen each day.

Gluttons for punishment, we didn't let up in our efforts to befriend Slavic kids. After all, surely they were no different from those in our own countries? They even read the same comics and cowboy stories, even if the Sheriff of Dodge City is known to them as Vajat Erp. Munching our lunch one day we could hardly endure the stares of the two starved-looking lads opposite us, savouring every bite in concert. Elise took out two slices of bread and spread Nutella chocolate-paste liberally. She passed them over, and we waited to see what would happen.

Very, very carefully, they scraped the chocolate-paste off the bread with their fingers and licked them clean. Then they threw away the bread.

Through the crumbling towns we meandered, towns so decrepit in some instances that they reminded us of nothing so much as Pompeii with people. By this stage, in early August, the climate cruelly resembled that spoof radio-announcer sketch from the Michael Caine film "Water": "Now here's the weather report: IT'S HOT!!!!" Forty degrees and rising and we sank gratefully into the azure blue of the Adriatic Sea - and straight onto a lethal clump of sea-urchins. My feet filled with spikes and the pain was excruciating, but it was small comfort to know my naïveté in ventilating my feet on these marine pincushions was bettered by a nearby English matron, who somehow contrived to sit down on a bed of them.

In Greece we decided to stop speaking English to each other in public. It was either that or suffer possible assaults with grievous bodily harm.

The Turks had just invaded Cyprus - an invasion for which the Greeks partly blamed Britain's unwillingness to intervene. It took just one frosty hour in the first Greek town, an hour in which postal authorities refused to give us our mail and shop assistants treated us like The Invisible Man, to realise that there was only one way we were going to get through: by taking on another nationality. The GB nationality-plate on the car was smothered under a homemade IRL for Ireland, and whenever we were in public over the coming weeks we would do what seemed to come naturally for tourists from Holland, speaking very loudly and obtrusively in Dutch. The ruse appeared to work, though we were robbed - but only because we were stupid rather than English.

Unlike other cars ours had no real windows - just acres of padlocked wire-mesh. Very effective with its nine padlocks, and offering us the best air-conditioning in the world. Theft-proof, too, provided the thieves were older than 12. At the beach in Piraeus, they weren't. Slender young arms snaked easily through the tiny holes in the mesh, and I was one wristwatch poorer, depressed not only for its immense sentimental value but because the incident revealed that our supposedly invulnerable car wasn't, while this was only Europe with worse, much worse to come.

The next day was no better as we wandered into Athens to top up our supply of visas and do some shopping. It turned out to be a day which was one of Greece's huge moveable arsenal of public holidays. We left, returning the next day which wasn't a public holiday on the calendar but which turned out to be one by popular practice. This time, we decided, we weren't leaving until we had those visas. How could we, when Elise had just dropped a contact lens in the vicinity of the car and proclaimed a national emergency?

For hours we prostrated ourselves much in the style of the Iranian-upsetting gag on the British satire show "Not The Nine O'Clock News." Their sketch showed a photo of thousands of buttocks on high as worshippers prayed in Teheran's main mosque, under the caption: "Meanwhile, in Iran, the search continues for the Ayatollah's contact-lens."

Back in Athens, we found the lens but lost the visas, the relevant consulate having both opened and closed in the time of Elise's blindness. We camped out on the pavement over the weekend, and on Monday were finally rewarded.

Finally, too, we managed to find a clinic open to give us the cholera booster shots we had sought for weeks. We knew from experience that the after-effects might leave little to be desired except death, so we fell into the car and made straight for a quiet spot in which to spend the rest of the long day's dying undisturbed.

It was not to be. As we lay suffering beside a still lake the chomping of goats distracted us from the tortoise we were watching so intently. Within moments we were fighting a rearguard action to prevent the total consumption of our exposed goods and chattels as the goats laid siege. No sooner had they gone than two friendly shepherds appeared, offering sparse conversation and a giant "carpus," the Greek name for watermelon.

Evening came, and we sat like two one-armed bandits on our back-bench tailgate de-cholera-ing. A tractor approached, bearing a farmer and his family. "Turista?" he shouted. We nodded weakly. "CARPUS!!!" he roared. Another watermelon.

Next morning, a deputation from the village. They had heard of our presence, and had brought us .... five carpusses/carpii. We had to leave then; our suspension would have stood no more.

We paused just long enough before the Turkish border for a cup of coffee in a restaurant where a waiter was administering eye-drops to a customer. And on the counter were tins of imported milk labelled in Greek. Only the name was in English: "TITS"

5
FEED THE CAT - OR EAT IT?

Dusk was gasping in over the Sea of Marmara as the car lurched along one of the world's kamikaze highways, the Trans-Asian E5 into Turkey. Sandwiched between belching hordes of mobile scrapyards masquerading as cars and trucks, we were swept onwards from the Greek border towards Istanbul in a haze of exhaust pollution and blaring horns.

Turkish Delight? Hardly, and as night spread its mantle we spied a promising-looking dirt track leading away from this bumper-to-bumper chaos, for our last night of camping in Europe. A couple of hundred metres further on, and in two coughs of a Méhari exhaust we were under the trees.

I ambled over to the nearest bush for an evening widdle. Before I could let fly, the bush did an unnerving thing. It got up and shuffled away.

Within moments the surrounding vegetation was alive and pointing guns at us. We had blundered into a super-camouflaged, plain-leaf Turkish border patrol, and it was obvious we would have to do some serious explaining.

Several whiter shades of pale, we were led at bayonet-point to the patrol-commander, luckily a man who spoke a little English. At first he was disinclined to believe we were simple tourists come to contribute to Turkey's gross national product, but after a one-hour search, a lot of probing, and with our hearts working overtime at beating a thudding retreat, we were allowed to go.

It took little perception to sense the primal hostility felt towards Greece by its age-old foe. Posters screamed out the message of hate, epitomised in the best-seller which we were to see in virtually every town and village shop: a map of Cyprus, surmounted by a portrait of elder statesman Bulent Ecevit above slogans clearly proclaiming Turkey's Allah-given right to control the island. Graphically portrayed, Turkish soldiers swarmed over Cyprus, wearing expressions which said clearly: "Kill!"

Soon we were to learn at first-hand just how deep lay that hatred for their neighbours.

Along the road to Izmir we were greeted by an effusive, and erudite, teacher of physics. Inevitably, he invited us to join him in slurping a glass of çay, (pronounced chai: tea). We chatted amiably about this and that, until I naïvely enquired about the war with Greece.

The pleasant man was immediately transmogrified. His eyes bulged and glazed, his fists clenched, his chin protruded, his knuckles turned white on the table in despotic rage and his face looked like an argument you could not possibly win. "Kill all the Greeks!" he proclaimed. "Kill them! KILL!!!" We sat stunned. Gradually, the attack abated, the werewolf metamorphosed, and we returned to discussing the cost of living, school syllabuses, cabbages and kings as though nothing had transpired.

This chilling demonstration of national hatred was just one facet of the Jekyll and Hyde make-up of the Turks - a people noted throughout history from their first mention as the biblical Hittites, for their intense barbarity and cruelty (with many instances graphically documented during the Crimean War, among others), while at the same time enjoying an unrivalled reputation for hospitality. We were to be on the receiving end of the darker side of their national character in the month which followed, but more often we were overwhelmed, even swamped, with their warm hospitality.

The first inkling of this came in a small town where, a little wary after being threatened by walking bushes, we decided to ask at the local police station if we might spend the night there.

"Marhaba!" we greeted the "Jandarma" on duty, pantomiming what it was we wished. He motioned us to wait while he consulted with higher authority, then came back to usher us inside - where some 30 police had quickly gathered in eager anticipation of our arrival. The inevitable çay was thrust into our hands while word went around the town, and before our first sugar-cube had melted in the glass almost everyone of note had gathered in that commandant's office to meet us. Along with the hordes came fruit, then food, then sweets, and more and more çay, followed by bottles of the potent national drink raki.

We sat, the police-chief, his staff and us, the teacher and other local VIPs, all sardined into that office with ordinary constables dancing attendance as the evening wore on and we wore out, keeping the conversation going in English, German, French and guesswork.

By one a.m., awash in liquid and asphyxiated by the secondhand smoke of rough Turkish cigarettes, we asked if we might sleep in the car in the courtyard. The suggestion was greeted as an immediate affront to their hospitality. The local teacher would give up his quarters and that was that, despite our protests. He led us home, and only finally let us fall onto his bed after we had quaffed yet more sticky sweets and çay. The next morning there was a knock and a delegation at the door. God help us, the day shift had arrived.

The pattern was repeated throughout Turkey with variations, bringing home to us repeatedly the fact that though we might have been tourists in Europe, in Turkey we were people from interesting foreign parts. Usually there was less actual communication than we could muster between us in that first smoke-filled police office.

The car suffered a puncture, and suddenly there were 40 people surrounding us willing to help. One insisted that the youngsters change our wheel while he take us to tea. At least we gathered that much, for none of the 40 spoke anything we could understand. Still, we followed the man to the local tea-house - in itself an honour for Elise, who must surely have been the first woman allowed into that very male preserve. We sipped and slurped, watching once more how the Turk places the sugar-cube under his tongue while pouring the tea past it from small, waisted tea-glasses.

Conversation proceeded by frustrating fits and starts, until our host had an idea: his 13-year-old son studied English at school, and could interpret for us. He was sent for, and arrived within minutes looking utterly miserable at being thrust into this adult limelight. But at least now we could progress beyond the "Turkey good, England cold" level.

A simple opening gambit was obviously needed for the nervous youngster. I ventured: "How old are you?"

He stared in abject terror.

"How - old - are - you?" I asked again.

A pause. Then finally the reply, carefully enunciated: "I - am - sitting -in - the - chair."

Elise hadn't quite heard the textbook answer.

"What did he say?" she asked.

I tried to keep a straight face.

"He is sitting in the chair."

"Ah," nodded my partner, now also having difficulty with her expression of comprehending sagacity.

Even banks doused us in hospitality - or at least eau-de-cologne, which is what happened when changing travellers' cheques in one small bank. Unbeknown to us we had arrived on its birthday, and were forced to consume tea, biscuits and confectionery, afterwards being liberally sprinkled with toilet-water whose cloying stench dogged us for days. It would have been easier to bear had we had more success in changing the cheques in the first place.

I had presented two Thomas Cook cheques of £20, and the book of examples was immediately consulted. Right enough, there under the Thomas Cook section was a picture of a cheque absolutely like ours other than its colour and its denomination.

"Cheque no good," said the teller with regret.

What? I pointed to the example in his book.

"Yes, this OK," he replied to my question. "But not same as you."

The crux seemed to be that only the £10 cheque was illustrated, therefore only the £10 cheque could be changed despite my simplified insistence that all Cooks cheques look the same. After ten minutes I knew I was beaten, put away my two £20's and changed four £10's instead. THAT was quite in order.

In the tiny hamlet of Gediz nestling in the middle of a Turkish nowhere, we found there were no hotels, no campgrounds, not even the inevitable Jendarma. We parked our car at the side of the deserted main street, cooked our meal and went to sleep, being woken only three times by soldiers checking our passports.

The next morning, as we sat on our tailgate backbench eating our bread-breakfast, we were aware as always of being watched by large collections of eyes. From the house labelled "Doktar" two small children emerged shyly, bearing a tray. On the tray were a pot of tea, two little glasses, sugar and spoons. Children in another town brought us not one but four more dreaded watermelons, and hospitality and watermelons followed us across Turkey, over the Bosporus to Istanbul, Asia and beyond.

In Bingol a policeman insisted we should dine at his home, and his woman was put to work to prepare. Leaving our shoes at the door we entered his house, squatted on the floor, and were brought an endless array of tasty dishes, each one of which was whisked away almost before we had had time to relish it. The women, naturally enough, were only briefly seen and did not eat with us, for that is not the way of things in Turkey.

It was in Turkey that we had our first sight of motor vehicles which thumb their radiators at the notion that a car is ever totally finished. Turks can repair anything, and it shows. Vehicles of 1950's vintage abound, held together by hope, optimism and wire. One car we saw was unforgettable: a Swiss-cheese bodywork, the chassis totally collapsed in the middle to drag sparks along the road, and the most remarkable wheels, with the front ones sloped inwards at around 45 degrees and the back ones genuflecting outwards. Only one part of Turkish vehicles can always be guaranteed to work, and that's the horn. Drivers are often chronically unable to see where they are going or where they have been, with their vehicles groaning under the weight of gee-gaws, knick-knacks, flashing Christmas-trees, garish acrylic fluff, mirrors, curtains, acres of mud-flaps, chrome add-ons, even Spartacus-type spiked wheel-hubs to unleg any pedestrian who strays too close.

Theft, we had been warned, was a serious problem from Turkey onwards. So had evolved a complex system of locking and unlocking every time we entered or left our car, a routine which on a good day involved no fewer than nine padlocks. Usually we got it right. When we didn't, the result could be mortifying, as it was when we pulled into a garage for petrol.

As the inevitable throng materialised to surround us, we realised with sinking hearts that we had locked ourselves in, irretrievably. There was nothing for it but to trust to human nature - a dicey business in Turkey - and pass the keys out to the attendant, asking him to let us out. The show was an immense success.

Turkey it was which first made us realise just how much we like kids - preferably pickled in a jar on a shelf. Here's a quote from an English Automobile Association leaflet: "Motoring in Turkey is often fraught with unexpected difficulties. In the more remote areas there is, for example, danger of children throwing stones at passing vehicles; two possible solutions to this problem are either to wave at the children, or to stop."

Well, we tried both, to no avail. The stones were thrown, frequently, and had we but known it disaster would strike within weeks. For the moment, ducking the missiles - and occasionally the children - was a harrowing ritual.

The stones were bad enough, but the children themselves came to represent a constant daytime nightmare for us just as they did for all the other travellers we were to meet. There were kids who hurled stones, or dung, or clay. There were those who pulled bits off the car, or who scratched the windows, or bent the wing-mirrors. There were even Mafia-type gangs demanding protection-money to ensure nothing happened to your car. Frequently, with our eccentric car exercising a magnetic pull on mischief-makers, we would have children hanging on the spare tyres on the outside, or making maximum use of that supple Citroën suspension, or kicking the car as they hurtled past on bicycles, ripping off our nationality plate, stealing the rubber bonnet-catches or mangling the windscreen-wipers.

The pattern of mindless adolescent vandalism was repeated across the country, and climaxed during one bad stretch when we travelled with two German VW-buses for safety. They must have regretted their offer, for our car attracted kids like sugar to an ant, as it chugged along gleaming red in the harsh light. On the other hand, we often drew the troublemakers who would otherwise have assaulted the VW's. Yüksekova was a case in point.

There, in the heart of Kurdistan, a region which has been the nemesis of many a traveller, we stopped to shop, and were surrounded. We tried walking, gathering an entourage of children as we went. By the time we had reached the end of the street, our original party of six had swelled to a hundred, and the taunting began as they threw clods of earth and then stones.

We retreated in laager formation, as the taunting turned to touching and female backside-fondling. With two of our number actually walking backwards we finally reached the "safety" of the car. It was a false haven, for no sooner were we inside than the hordes began climbing over the vehicles, particularly the Méhari which began to rock alarmingly. Citroën boasted that these cars couldn't roll, but what a hell of a time to be proved wrong, I reflected as I slammed the car into gear and took my foot off the clutch.

The car didn't budge - how could it, with our two cylinders hardly a match for a score of kids pushing in the opposite direction? Though I was deeply afraid of the consequences if we injured a child, rising panic forced me to throw the car into reverse, then into first, then reverse again - and eventually we rocked our way out of town under a barrage of stones.

Thanks to such lovable Turkish kids we were forced to undertake some major renovations. After one notable incident when a group bearing blades decided to improve Michelin's tread-pattern on our spare tyres, there was nothing for it but to remount them inside the car, thus reducing our cramped living-quarters to something more like living-eighths. And we bought yet another padlock.

Convinced that the worst was past, we trundled on alone for a few days, and one quiet afternoon found us parked in the lee of some barren rock-mountains doing our daily chores - writing, cleaning, repairing the car and our mosquito bites. Elise was constructing our modest lunch when a group of women approached. Unlike the usual black-clad Turkish females, these wore gay, colourful dresses and jangling bangles, and we were intrigued at this sight of our first real Asian gypsies.

They came close, jabbering. Too close, as they began touching and feeling everything, opening Elise's saucepans, fingering her earring, trying to cadge souvenirs from us. We stayed calm and unyielding, and at the approach of a taxi they retreated a short distance. With hindsight we had done something no traveller in unknown parts should do: we had manoeuvred ourselves into a corner, for we were alone and I had immobilised the car by stripping a part for repair.

The gypsies came back, their numbers swelled to nine. This time we locked ourselves in, and hoped. Through the wire-mesh which served as windows they jabbed their fingers, trying to hook anything hookable. Bitter experience had taught us never to leave anything accessible, so their attempts were frustrated, which made them even angrier at these foreigners who obviously had so much but were willing to give nothing. They shouted, then spat through the mesh, then threw stones. It would end in worse than tears, of that we were sure as we sat, trapped - when to our rescue came a passing "Dolmus," or taxi-bus.

The women took flight, and I leapt out of the car to fiddle frantically at making it driveable. The taxi-driver and his friend approached to see if we were all right; we were, just. Then they began to size us up - particularly Elise. The driver took me aside, explaining amiably how Turkish tradition required that one good deed be repaid by another. He and his friend wished to borrow my wife "only ten minutes in back of taxi, not long," he assured me, on the principle, no doubt, that no greater love hath any man than that he lay down his wife for a friend. I stalled while Elise threw together our belongings while fending off wandering Turkish hands. She scrabbled for the only real weapon we carried, our tiny tear-gas aerosol, while I groped surreptitiously for the biggest frying-pan we possessed.

We were lucky. Sensing finally that they were on a loser, they backed off, as trembling limbs and several months' supply of adrenalin gave the lie to our image as intrepid, fearless travellers. Never again would we park where we would invite trouble, we vowed, particularly when the car was disabled.

One of the most frequent questions asked of any overlander is what sort of weapon he carries. The simple answer must usually be "none." International legislation leaves the traveller almost defenceless, forbidding as it does the carrying of any recognisable weapon over borders - so that had we been caught with our minuscule tear-gas spray smuggled in the guise of a contact-lens cleaner, we could well end up as an Amnesty International case history. Other travellers have their own solutions, from shirt-pocket flare-pistols which make a loud bang, to oven-cleaner sprays or ammonia-filled water-pistols or even, comically, the German we met whose specially-wired vehicle played a loud recording of a growling dog. But in the end there is no weapon better than common sense combined with a little luck, a lesson we were to learn repeatedly over the coming years as we suffered attack and robbery, though fortunately never with the serious physical violence which overtakes so many travellers.

One Swiss was knifed in a bazaar for taking a photograph. Unfortunately the photograph was of someone's wife, which is rarely a good idea in Turkey. We envied several Germans their unique solution to the problem of being unable to photograph people: a special lens which has a dummy smoked glass on the front, and a hole in the side with a mirror set at 45 degrees in the manner of a sideways periscope. Ideal for serious people-snappers, all it takes is an accomplice placed in front of the camera for a fake portrait, while the real picture is taken at right-angles.

The contradictory nature of the Turkish character was summed-up for us in two more incidents.

In Cappadocia, home of the famous fairy-tale-like rock formations into which have been hewn houses and chapels, we saw the less-acceptable face of the Turk. Two desolate English hitchhikers had paid for a taxi-ride to this isolated region from the nearest town. Once there, they had been dumped and stranded when they refused to be blackmailed into paying double the fee to get back. Overloaded though we were, we could hardly leave them to walk some 50 kilometres through barren and perhaps hostile rock-desert.

We're still puzzling over the second incident years later. As we sat eating at a roadside stop, a truck pulled up bearing the initials of the Turkish Ministry of Works. The driver ambled over, carrying a small furry bundle which turned out to be a kitten. He thrust it out at us.

"Yemek," he said. "Yemek!"

I mimed that we couldn't carry a kitten on our travels.

"Yok, yok," ("No, no,") he exclaimed. "Yemek!"

So I looked it up in the phrase-book: "To eat."

Strewth, surely he didn't intend us to eat that lovable, mewling creature? We will never know, having parted in a haze of mutual incomprehension. Cynics in the travelling fraternity swear that Turks relish cooked kitten. We prefer to believe he wanted us to feed it, but oh how we've wondered...

We left Turkey amid drownings of official tea. The Iranian side of the frontier was less convivial - particularly for the British Land-Rover group which preceded us. Impatience and their First-World inability to accept a Third-World approach fertilised what started as simple irritation, when a customs official showed his determination to carry out a thorough scrutiny. Within a very few minutes there was every prospect of a dam-burst.

"I search everything!" Customs declared, and tempers flared in the dusty courtyard which housed the border offices. He began to burrow in the car, flinging into the dirt everything removable.

The Land-Rover driver's blood-pressure soared with his efforts not to shake the customs man warmly by the throat.

Then, finally: "STOP!" he exploded, and there was a loaded silence.

"Okay, sunshine, are you intending to throw everying onto the ground?" he asked the officer in suddenly-controlled tones.

Certainly, came the reply.

At that, the driver picked up his scattered possessions, tossed them back into the car, got behind the steering-wheel and started the engine.

"If that's the case, you'll do it properly," he said simply - then put the car into low-range four-wheel-drive and drove straight for the dozen steps leading up into the customs hall. His audience stood agape as the vehicle bucked and bounced, clawing its way up the stairs, into the midst of an astounded throng of bus-passengers unpacking their luggage to be searched. He stopped, switched off the engine, lit a cigarette, and waited. By the time we left several hours later, our opinion of a Land-Rover's stair-climbing abilities was immensely enhanced, but the search itself was only just moving into top gear.

Our first glimpses of Iran showed it to be little different from the East of Turkey: landscapes of infinite brown, sparsely populated. Amid vast desert panoramas and immense bare mountains, the only detail for hundreds of kilometres might be one forlorn tree, dry, dusty and barren. The sheer scale of it all reinforced for us the first glimmerings we had encountered in Turkey, that our naïvely-planned "schedule" of covering an average 150 kilometres a day was hopelessly inappropriate. In a country the size of Britain, France, the Low Countries and Germany put together, we realised that driving would mean getting from town to town with little or nothing inbetween, whether the distance was a hundred kilometres or several times that.

Iran, unlike Turkey, then had the surface trappings of modernity as the Shah aspired to drag his country kicking and struggling into the twentieth century. New towns were springing up everywhere, fuelled by the oil wealth. Each had its statue to the Shah, with squares and green lawns to contrast the overall brown of the landscape. People with no inkling of the world beyond their village had electricity and running water, modern shops and the ultimate ostentation, neon signs. In the bigger towns there was a palpable striving towards Westernisation in everything from dress and films to cars. Teheran, soon to become notorious as the violent blood-letting valve for all of Persia's pent-up frustration, was a case in point.

In Teheran you were struck by the European-ness of the city. You were struck by its deafening noise. But most of all, if you were just slightly unlucky, you would be struck by the motor car.

Its accident-rate was an astounding eleven times greater than the European average as traffic vied for position in a motorised rugby-game without the ball. Every day was Pamplona in Teheran; few cars were undented, and what traffic system there was seemed more like a free-for-all and Allah take the hindmost, as drivers jostled for advantage. You passed or were passed on whichever side offered the least chance of disaster, while red lights were a suggestion, not an order, and meant only the challenge to make it through unscathed. No point in stopping for amber; if you did the car behind wouldn't and your car would be shortened, and all this took place at such breathtaking speed that if you dared to stand on the brakes you would be strawberry jam. Never a squeamish driver, I quivered in Teheran, where you aimed at your destination rather than drove to it, praying in a sudden onset of religion, knuckles blanched white in a hopefully death-defying grip on the wheel.

Our first introduction to that schizophrenic city ran true to oddball form, as we scoured the map to reach the conclusion we knew only too well already: we were lost.

"Hello, speak Ingliz?" came the voice from a passing panelbeaters' delight.

So did he, albeit haltingly as he offered to lead us to the campground. "First, we go to my business," he said.

His company ran most of Teheran's buses, and we had arrived just in time for a special treat - or so he maintained. The "treat" was his alone, and a twisted one at that. Once a week he got an almost carnal kick out of paying his employees their wages, one by one and maddeningly slowly, virtually making them grovel for it. We watched with some unease, then suggested we would, finally, like to go to the campground.

"Sure, no problem," he agreed. "I show you - but first I rest. I have headache now. You stay here, I come back in few hours." We started to protest, carefully, but before getting much further than actually preferring to go on if it was all the same to him, we found ourselves locked inside his office, with our car and all our possessions outside.

It was a harrowing few hours, wondering if we were about to become a newspaper headline:

"KIDNAPPED!" - in 62-point bold type across The Sun.

"Minor Incident in Iran: Ambassador To Submit Note" - The Times.

"U.S. Evacuates All Personnel" - Washington Post.

"Sexy Elise Lookalike Takes Your Eyes Hostage on Page Three!" - Daily-Mirror.

"Brit Globetrotters Said Hijacked - Persian Harem?" - The National Enquirer.

"Tourists abctuded" (sic) - The Guardian.

"All lies!" - Iran's Kayhan newspaper.

"Test Your Ability To Be A Good Hostage With This 20-Question Quiz" - Cosmopolitan.

"Bomb the Bastards!" - Soldier of Fortune.

"Two Spend Year Inspecting Iranian Bus Fleet" - Coachbuilders Monthly.

A key grated in the lock, and in came our captor with coffee, biscuits and not the slightest twinge of an apology. As though locking travellers in his office was the most normal of actions in that most abnormal of cities, he chatted, told us how wonderful his bus company had become thanks to his efforts and his alone and what a favour he was doing when he paid his drivers in person - then he took us to the campground, pumped our hands, and left.

The next day continued as our visit to Teheran had begun: peculiarly. For our second anniversary we did something really special - we broke open a box from our carefully-hoarded Variety-Pak of breakfast cereals. Luxury is a very relative term when you're on the road with little of nothing. That evening we went unsuccessfully in search of an advertised "Pink Panther" film, dodging the inevitable approach by street-touts all the way: "Hashish, good hashish, no?" No - a non-use of this commodity which, we were quickly realising, put us among the perhaps ten per cent of travellers on the Asia trail who were actually there to see what there was, rather than visions which could be induced.

With some relief we left Teheran for a resort on the Caspian Sea, there to struggle for the first time with serious bowel problems which wrung our insides into outsides as they put our stomachs at odds with our appetites. Delhi Belly, Gyppo Gut, Mussolini's Revenge, The Trots - whatever you called it in every country it came with the territory, and as we covered rather a lot of territory we would soon count with gratitude the days when we didn't have it, eating like a horse to stockpile for the next attack. Indeed, in some countries that's exactly what we did: ate like a horse, when oats and barley were among the few available foods.

Nothing you could do would grant you immunity, though one American couple we met at the Caspian had it all worked out. They had planned it so well: mounted atop their VW bus was a huge, coffin-like box. For their year-long trip they had brought 365 paper plates each, 365 paper cups, half a supermarket of canned food, lots of dehydrated delights, in short everything they would need for a 12-month trip so that they wouldn't have to buy a single, suspect, local product en route. They got sick from the water.

At the Caspian a small convoy took shape which was to become the nucleus of a caravan through much of Asia further on - indeed, even on into Africa.

John and Pat were a couple of middle-aged Cockneys who had met on a London bus; he was driving it, and she was punching the tickets. One day, just as we had, they decided to opt out of Civilisation As We Know It, buy a van and drive to exotic places. Travellers tend to congregate, but they collected more congregators than most - thanks partly to Pat's endearingly-English insistence on frying-up huge panfulls of chips wherever they went, an undreamed-of luxury for most of the half-starved Europeans on the road. John had his own endearing attributes, not the least of which was a droll English sense of humour and a willingness to help anyone with their mechanical problems. The more openly adventurous of the two, his desire to see places strange and wonderful was tempered by Pat's distate for foreign toilets, so that they could only travel as far at a stretch as a bus laden with a Porta-Potty and several dozen kilos of chemicals would go.

Geert and Olga were Dutch, and had pointed their ancient Citroën van at Asia on a late honeymoon. Much-liked though they were, the rhythmic nightly creaking of their honeymoon-suite van-springs soon began to play on everyone's nerves, making sleep impossible. John solved the problem, presenting them with four carefully-measured logs to jam under each corner of the car before retiring.

Absolutely the strangest of the new arrivals was Horst.

Horst was an East German teacher who had successfully crossed to the West and was now making-up for all the freedom he had missed in his youth. We knew he was odd, but didn't realise just how out to lunch he really was until some time later.

Right at that moment, all we were aware of was a tiny, dirty Citroën 2CV belching towards our camping spot in a cloud of soot, its suspension totally sunken on one side so that it heeled like a yacht in high wind. Horst had travelled nearly 70,000 kilometres on his own with all his baggage on the seat behind him - hence the lop-sided suspension and the fact that his two nearside tyres were bald while the offside ones were like new.

The first morning we were camped together he saw John and I tackling the engine of the Méhari.

"Vot are you doing?" he asked.

Servicing it, we replied.

"Wunderbar - can you make it for me too?" he asked. "I never had one!"

We thought he was joking until we opened the bonnet of his car. It's true that 2CV's don't have much of an engine, but Horst's appeared to have none at all. Or could it really be lurking somewhere under that mountain of muck in the engine compartment? John's mechanical instincts were affronted by what he saw: an air-filter with no space left for air, spark-plugs buried in sludge, and a battery whose terminals looked like an Alaskan snow-scene. Further questioning revealed an astonishing tribute to the durability of the legendary 2CV, for Horst's car had had just one service in 70,000 kilometres: the first, free one at 1,000.

"Ja, one time a friend put new plugs and points," he added. "But nothing else except sometimes I give extra oil."

Nothing for it, thought John, but to roll up sleeves and plunge in. We did, for one solid, dirty day, servicing the car thoroughly using our extra parts and his expertise. The result was astounding.

The car refused to go. Not a cough, not a splutter, not a hiccup. Yet for 70,000 kilometres it had chundered on in a state of total benign neglect. The shock of a service was too great for it to bear.

We dismantled, we cranked, we pushed, we even towed the thing up and down for kilometres on end trying to coax some reaction. Finally, miserably, it retched into life. John's oft-stated mechanical philosophy probably stems from that incident. "If it's working," he's fond of saying today, "leave it alone."

There was more peculiar about Horst than just his car. One evening he arrived back at camp bearing a triumphant acquisition: a complete "abha," or chador, which he quickly donned. It cloaked him in black from veiled head to foot, leaving only his hands visible. Very amusing, we chuckled - until he announced his intention of seeing the East in this disguise. Still we thought he was joking, until we met him one day emerging from a mosque, where he had been "at prayer" with the local women. Naturally the ruse was fraught with immense danger, but as days went on we saw less and less of Horst as he slipped away in his black shroud, bent on entering parts the others couldn't reach - an imitation-female latter-day Lawrence of Arabia or the legendary Arabist Richard Burton, but without so much as a word of Farsi to get him out of trouble.

Gradually, too, we saw him become more involved with the drugs so easily available, drugs which caused him to become stranger still. Eventually he drifted away from us one day and was not seen again. Much later, in a camping-courtyard toilet hundreds of kilometres away, we puzzled over this freshly-scrawled graffiti: "Horst was here because of . . shit!"

Horst it was who succumbed to that bane of the traveller's life in Iran, the carpet-sellers. Where most of us spent many of our waking hours actively fending-off the omnipresent rug-merchants, Horst was in his element, and actually wanted a carpet. Nothing unusual in that, perhaps, and several travellers did return with examples of the Persian carpet-weavers' art. But Horst actually parted with 2,000 German marks, the equivalent of many hundreds of pounds, for a carpet which he had not seen from a merchant who promised to send it on to Berlin. Eventually...

Carpets caused us to have fists shaken after us in a tiny Iranian village, when we swerved the car to avoid driving over rugs laid across the road. It was precisely what we shouldn't have done, we only learned later. Some types sell better when worn, so are laid in the road precisely so that people, carts and cars will move over them - a principle we were later to find applying to grain in Africa.

It's harder to dodge the carpet-sellers. Even the most innocent of approaches would end in carpets, whether it was the student ostensibly wanting to practise his English by showing you round his town - and carpets - or the visitor admiring your strange car who invites you home for tea. And carpets.

A favourite ploy was to forge a common bond with the potential victim.

"Where are you from?" the tourist would be asked.

"London," might come the reply.

"Ah! I have a brother studying at university in London," the conversation then reveals - and the bond is forged, with carpets as its aim.

John became a dab hand at de-carpeting our forays into town, by the simple expedient of beckoning the tout's ear close, then bellowing a deafening expletive into it. He it was, too, who took the "university ploy" to its ultimate, ludicrous climax.

"Where are you from?" asked the inevitable seller-in-disguise.

John's broad Cockney accent made a three-course meal of Europe's tiniest, virtually unknown principality.

"Liechtenstein," he grinned.

"What a coincidence," said our tout, sweeping inexorably towards disaster on the crest of his patter.

"I have a brother studying at university in Ligh - , Lish -, er, Leek....."

6
ONE ROOM: TEN AFGHANIS

Afghanistan opens up a whole new world of ignorance to the traveller. Countless colonisers, from the imperial British to the recent Russians, failed to unravel its puzzle - why should the humble traveller have any more success?

It takes only the most superficial of encounters to make you realise what a Rubik's Cube of a country it is. It's a land where there's a thriving black market changing money at LESS than the bank-rate - because the hopelessly inefficient banking system might change your cash within a day, or then again it might not. Everything in the bazaars is sold scrupulously by weight, notwithstanding the fact that no merchant we ever saw had any standard weights, so that our daily dish of Kandahar yoghourt weighed two spark plugs and a rusty bolt.

In a country without even a railway, and with a house-of-cards infrastructure even before the ravages wrought by invaders, it's hardly surprising tourism has never been high on Afghanistan's list of priorities. Today it's virtually non-existent, but even in the mid-seventies there was never more than a trickle of hardy masochists.

Crossing the dusty tract of no-man's-land from the Iranian border towards the "Afghan Cusotm Post" (sic), there's hardly an inkling that you are about to enter one of the world's most closed of societies, the true beginning perhaps of The Mysterious East, and an acrimonious battlefield throughout history. Ahead, behind that innocuous sign, lies a Bermuda Triangle of a country which for centuries has been the spot marked on the map with a cross waiting for an accident to happen. From the savagery inflicted by Genghis Khan to the ill-advised Russian incursion, Afghans have endured stoically and fought back viciously, almost enjoying what Jonathan Swift called - in their case perhaps appropriately - "War, that mad game the world so loves to play."

Tawdry reality brought us back to basics in the "Cusotm Post," as we confronted a harrassed official flustering behind a mound of muddled paper on a creaking desk, his foetid office filled with people, some of whom had waited since the previous day. The forms were thrust out, to be filled in triplicate - no carbon paper, naturally - and after an hour and a half he took our forms, lost half of them, found them again, lost his rubber-stamp and his temper, looked at his watch (four o'clock), announced he had had enough for the day, was closing the cusotms post and that everyone had to come back again the next day.

That next day we waited for four hours outside the insurance "Ofis" for the insurance man to come back from praying. Compulsory car insurance in Afghanistan is about as useful as a liferaft in a desert, but who were we to deny them yet another precious trickle of "real" money? Had a German couple coming the opposite way been more ready to part with some capital, they might have avoided the slight inconvenience we saw occurring as we finished our own formalities. They stuck to their principles by not crossing any official palms with silver - or green to be more exact, with the almighty dollar more a passport than the passport itself. The outcome was inevitable: their van was positioned over an inspection-pit hacked roughly out of the ground, as officials drilled holes in it "in search of smuggling."

Entering the first town, Herat, was like a slap in the face after the westernisation of Iran. To step out of your car-shaped time-machine was to be transported straight back in history to an era when transport had a leg at each corner. Donkeys, camels and horses traipsed the dusty streets, streets filled with scrofulous hole-in-the-wall shops selling everything by the light of paraffin lamps.

Once you could buy slaves, opals, diamonds, gold; now it was ice-cream and fizzy drinks, Japanese watches and gaudy trinkets along with fly-encrusted meat, spiderweb-festooned preserves, sacks of rice marked "Gift from the United Nations - Not for Sale," refilled non-refillable lighters, magnificent curved Afghan daggers, ancient Martini-Henry rifles, carpets, well-thumbed photographs of (unveiled) Western women, little mounds of hardly-cured hashish, hookah pipes, always Coca-Cola, cheap and nasty imported ghetto-blasters (tent-blasters?) and cassettes of the most banal of the West's pop-music. Proprietors sat cross-legged and barefoot outside their shops, slowly uncurling like stamp-hinges in the morning sun.

Traffic was infinitesimal, yet each street had its own uniformed traffic-policeman, waving his arms ineffectually and whistling at a streetful of nothing. All around was a sea of white, bobbing turbans floating above a babble of conversation as the men sat on the pavement, slurping tea and discoursing loudly. You passed, and all conversation ceased as though someone had hit the sound button. Eyes swivelled, and the women in our group were mentally undressed, slowly, from head to toe. Small wonder, with what few local women you saw wandering like perambulating bin-liners, shrouded in a veil with only a minute number of holes offering them a dim window on this man's world. Equally cautious were our ladies, too, in a vain effort to sidestep the wandering hands magnetically attracted to their interesting bits. The female travellers' standby remedy was a rolled-up newspaper, swung purposefully and accurately at the crutch of any male who strayed into the female's space-bubble, much to the hilarity of the watching tea-drinkers.

And the buses! Mobile scrapyards as they puffed and gasped and wheezed and belched hooting through the empty streets. The insides were crammed with sweating humanity, clinging, squashing, crushing into every nook and cranny. Intrepid travellers hung on to the outside, and those who would breathe air with the dust and pungent body-odour, opted to ride on the roof-rack, clutching uncomplainingly with each lurch the vintage vehicle made while their turbans unravelled in the wind.

In the town, we pulled up at "The Herat Hotel for Esteemed Travellers." One room: 10 Afghanis, which was the currency and not the state of the room's population. Usually. So for less than the price of a Western loaf we could have all not-so-mod cons. A pipe which at certain unspecified times of the day would spout choleric water from the wall: The Shower. A hole in the ground with a plastic jug of water next to it: The Toilet. A wall-to-wall carpet of cockroaches. A health-bed: if you valued your health you left it to the bugs and slept on the floor. And nearby, a dingy, musty room filled with crumbling tables and staff where, for 15 Afghanis, you could have what the menu described as "Rice and Everything."

"Please provide me with your passports for safekeeping," smiles the manager, and, smiling back, you decline, knowing full well that passports delivered into such safekeeping are quite liable never to be seen again.

Leaving the town, you drive endlessly on a road laid alternately by the Americans and the Russians during their tit-for-tat efforts at buying Afghan friendship - mile after endless hundreds of miles of concrete slabs laid end to end, the monotony relieved every so often by the sight of a wanderer, walking. From where, to where, you will never know though you stop to give water - only that he may have wandered days, and will trudge for more before he reaches the next outpost.

Occasionally you pass a shepherd, whose life is so little that the mere sight of your approaching cloud of dust causes him to run to the road just to catch sight of what it is that his way comes. You stop, regularly, to top-up Afghanistan's foreign reserves, at roadblocks where you must park, walk a hundred metres to a hut on top of a hill, pay a toll, sign a book, then wait on the cushion provided while the official tries not to give you a receipt.

On through the forbidding, empty desert our convoy rumbled from Kandahar, and then disaster struck in the infamous North-West Frontier Territory.

Kids, you'll recall, can be adorable in this part of the world. They love to give you things, like stones thrown at high velocity as you pass. Every traveller soon develops an instinct. You can smile and wave. Or, if it looks dangerous you stop, dish out some platitudes, sweets or picture-postcards to pacify. (Writer Redmond O'Hanlon recently backpacked 400 3-D pictures of Queen Elizabeth into the Borneo jungle as peace offerings, and gave away every single one). You can, in really dangerous instances, pick up the metal tube which you have salvaged from people travelling in the opposite direction, and point this instant rifle at the kids, who should then disappear before you can say bang.

All these ideas have one thing in common. They rarely work. In this case we had no time to try any of them, with everything happening so quickly. Yet it is printed on the mind like a movie in slow-motion: the child stepping out from the side of the road almost into our path, bending down, choosing a large rock, and from a range of 10 metres lifting his arm and hurling the missile straight at us.

The windscreen exploded as I reeled with a blow to the forehead, blinded. Drivers' instinct took over as I pumped the correct pedals while Elise wrenched the steering-wheel, and within seconds the car had stopped. I tumbled out of the seat, blood streaming down my face, yelling significant doubts about the child's parentage. Our companions stopped too, and while two of our convoy colleagues ran off in hot pursuit, our Cockney companions did what any good English people will do in the face of a crisis: they made tea.

Four first-aid boxes were produced and emptied onto the gash on my forehead, and by the time the damage had been patched the hot-pursuit team was back, crestfallen. They had narrowed the distance on the culprit until the outskirts of a small village; then, from a house, a large, bearded, turbanned and, more importantly, armed Afghan emerged to bar their way.

It could have been worse, we reasoned, estimating that I had missed a trip to Kabul's United Nations Eye Hospital by millimetres. The windscreen had been less blessed, and after smashing out its remnants and swathing ourselves in as many clothes as we could muster to combat the biting cold we set off, wrapped like parcels and filled to overflowing with tea and sympathy. When delayed shock and the cold set in, we appreciated the camaraderie of travelling-friends, who took it in turns with Elise to drive our car the draughty road to the capital.

My concern with the windscreen saga was quickly dispelled, washed away in a sudden tidal-wave of the amoebic dysentery which was to plague us both for weeks - and later, for years - afterwards. On what seemed like my death-bed, like a drowning man visions of past meals flashed before me. I dreamed of Black Forest cake, Choc-99 ice-creams and waffles, but managed only flat Coke and carrot-juice on the better days. Had we but known it, the pattern was being set for the weeks and months to come, with a 50/50 ratio of health to halfway-hale-and-heartiness for both of us which was not to change until we sailed away from Asia and its virulent bacteria.

As for the windscreen, perhaps it was fortunate that our colleagues had been unable to find a replacement, and that we had to jerry-rig a piece of scratched perspex instead to get us to the first glass-shop in Pakistan. Fellow-travellers in a VW bus might have wished they had been equally unsuccessful in finding a new part for their vehicle. By the time they hit Afghanistan they were sorely in need of a roof-rack. As chance would have it, one dusty town contained a dealer with the familiar VW sign above his yard. "Sure, no problem! I fix you good roof-rack!" he beamed, agreeing to charge them only two-and-a-half times the realistic price. They paid, then went shopping while the rack was fitted. It was a good, solid job - the rack was welded, in a mess of blistered paintwork, to the roof of the car.

Temporarily recovered from our gastric wars, we set off towards the Russian border and the fabled Hindu Kush - "Kush" means death, probably because of all the dangerous mountain passes. We were heading for Bamiyan with its 54-metre Buddah, de-faced (literally) by Genghis Khan. Thence, crashing and bouncing onwards over the rocks and ruts in low gear, on to Band-i-Amir, high in the mountains to a settlement where even the ubiquitous Coke machine was hardly to be found.

To say it was cold is to say the Sahara can be warm. Our cheap car thermometer wouldn't register lower than the -10°C limit its needle passed that night, and we almost froze trying to doze fitfully in our car. In the depths of that long night Elise groped sleepily for one of our better inventions, the funnel attached so cleverly to a tube going out through a hole in the floor. As she answered her early-morning call of nature, she wondered only groggily why her socks seemed suddenly wet... The tube had frozen closed - and equally frozen was the water for our early-morning reviving cup of tea. Not that having water would have helped, for our gas-stove no longer worked in such Arctic temperatures.

The day which followed made it all worthwhile, once we had shaken off the Afghans who kept appearing offering us a "Horse-no?" No, we definitely didn't not want a horse-no, preferring instead to wander for five hours by feet-yes through some of the most awe-inspiring, and little-seen, mountain-lake scenery in the world: a series of startling blue lakes set against a barren brown backdrop of desert rock.

Thence back to Kabul to linger and malinger alternately, at times caught up in waves of dysentery so severe it seemed touch-and-go whether we would expire before our visas did. It was between gusts that I had the brainwave of ordering a cake for Elise's birthday.

How do you explain a Western birthday-cake to a flat-bread and biscuit baker who doesn't speak a word of English? Somehow, with pen, paper and waving hands I managed, and the result was a masterpiece. The baker thought so, too - he tried to charge triple the agreed price when I went to collect it, but I wasn't having any of that so we settled for double... A sponge cake of dubious quality and no doubt rampant with more bacteria, it was covered with centimetre-thick icing. And scrawled on the top in my very own handwriting - Afghans don't use Western script, and he had only my sketch to go by - it proclaimed "Elise, with love."

The actual presentation might have been more propitious.

Both of us were racked by disease on the birthday morning, and it took more willpower than I thought I had, to ease me out of our mobile sickbed and down the road to the baker to collect the cake. Like an alcoholic reforming by getting through just one day at a time, I managed by stages, and returned bearing the gift and greetings. Then disaster struck, as I bumped our emergency pan - the one filled with the unspeakable by-products of the night's sufferings. It splattered over us both, blanketing us with muck and tears. But what the hell, when you're young and in love...it's still an unmitigated disaster. The cake wasn't eaten for days.

Our frequent duels with the Kabul post office were also symptomatic of what was to come, as we grappled with the simple but complicated process of posting a letter.

The scenario was to be oft-repeated in the following months, and goes something like this: You enter the post-office, bearing letters. The official weighs them, demands the fee, then puts the money away and the letters to one side. Sceptical as any good traveller should be, you ask for the stamps. He tears them out and puts them with the letters, turning away once more to signify the transaction is closed. It isn't. You insist on the stamps being put on the letters. He does so, with poor grace - but you notice he has stuck down only a small corner of each stamp. Knowing that by time-honoured tradition he will pull off the stamps when you have left and sell them again (hence the corollary, that Asian stamps are often poorly-coated with gum), you demand that they be fully stuck. Now both angry, you because your precious communication with The Outside World looks set to be sunk for a few stolen cents, and he because you have tumbled to his fiddle, you end up wielding serious abuse at each other as you next demand that the stamps be franked beyond any shadow of a resale doubt, and then that the letters are actually put into the mailbox or bag instead of disposed-of in a fit of post-row postal pique. You leave knowing that your chances of being heard-from at home this time are less than good.

Yet, you realise even after just a few weeks, it's impossible not to like the Afghans. Brigands they may be to a man, and totally indolent - they have mastered the knack which many a Westerner would covet, of being able to do nothing whatever of any significance without the merest flutter of guilt. But they have suffered, and continue to suffer, stoically. They are proud, fierce, and guardians of one of the most remarkable and as-yet-unspoiled-by-tourism landscapes in the world. We were among the last generation of overland travellers permitted a rare glimpse into that byzantine world, in a brief cracking-open of the doors which the Russians later closed. Despite the ravages of the war which killed one million and displaced three times that number, with Herat reported 40 per cent destroyed and other parts just as badly ravaged, the door may eventually creak open once more on what one jaded traveller rather unfairly called this armpit of Asia; if it does, it will take all our willpower to resist our sensible rule never to retrace our steps.

Our final encounter with an Afghan ran true to the form we had come to expect as we headed for the Pakistan border. "STob" said the sign, and we stobbed. Resplendent in several days' growth and a tattered uniform, an Afghan official ordered us out of the car and began to rummage. What is this, what is that, he demanded to know? How do you explain the function of a Tampax or, ludicrously, the battery-powered toothbrush of one of our companions, to an illiterate hill-tribesman? He was on safer ground when he came to the pouch I was wearing, containing our small supply of dollar bills.

"Hah, dollars good!" he exclaimed, fingering them lovingly.

"Yes, good," I replied with somewhat less enthusiasm.

"Dollars very good," he persisted - and battle was joined, with the winner to be he with the most time and tenacity as we debated the goodness of dollars. I won; whatever else we may not have had on the road, the listlessness and laissez-faire of Asia had taken us and time was rarely a factor - that and the knowledge that following travellers will be treated largely according to the precedents you set.

Next stop the border, having carefully followed the intriguing directions offered by a helpful Indian diplomat: "You are taking the black-top road for one furlong until you are coming to a bifurcation..." We slept that cold night in the lee of the infamous Khyber Pass, waking for our breakfast of black tea and "naan," the local flat-bread, to watch truck drivers stacking shards of wood under their engines and setting fire to them. Not perhaps the safest way of warming your engine, and we treated their smoking vehicles as though they had rampant b.o., but it worked.

By this stage of the game little that bureaucracy can throw at you is surprising. Spending several hours at the border has already become a norm, offering opportunities to meet other travellers. One Australian hitchhiker arrived in the dingy immigration office sporting a ballpoint protruding from his pocket. He asked for an immigration form.

"Perhaps," said the official with all the subtlety of a hurled brick. "The price of this form is one pen." Ultimately, the hiker paid.

For us it was easier, possibly thanks to the perceived magic of the name Kennedy. Tedious it may be to profess amusement for the thousandth time at a joke about being from the American presidential family, but who's proud when it lubricates formalities? So we smile, and laugh at this most original and refulgent of witticisms once more, and drink tea, and sign dusty ledgers while pompous officialdom scribes incompetently. "Have you any tomatoes?" he demands, and for once you are totally flummoxed. To be asked whether you are carrying drugs, or dirty pictures of unveiled ladies, or undeclared foreign currency, is one thing, but tomatoes? A banned Afghan import, it transpires, and you lose your precious cache from the Kabul bazaar, later to see it relished by Immigration round the back of the "Ofis."

Finally, then, on up the Khyber - a visual treat denied to later travellers when war and a half-hearted attempt to stamp out the smuggling trade closed the famous pass to foreigners from the early 1980's. Our route followed the road past the original, centuries-old and still-used camel caravan trail and the sign which warns that "It is against the law to photograph women in local costume in

Pakistan." Past, too, another series of signs on the dangerous hairpin bends, the first saying "Slow," the second "Slower," the third "Dead slow," the fourth "Even slower..."

It's little wonder that countless would-be invaders throughout history have met their match in the magnificent Khyber Pass. Grinding your way up it you begin to realise why, as it towers impenetrably beside you while the track claws its way up the edge of dark, bleak mountains. Cliffs flank the sides, each as often as not surmounted by a fort from which defenders could reign almost unassailably.

And then you are in Pakistan proper - a cacophonous melange of deafening traffic driving on the "other" side of the road. Everywhere the flavour of the Raj persists, in the malls and the English signs, even in the railway station called Charing Cross. Taxis buzz past groaning under the weight of a dozen occupants in a space designed for four, fighting for road-space amid the bullock-carts, horse-carriages, scooters, buses, trucks, and pedestrians. The rules of the road are simple: Big is Best, so that trucks will - and do - force smaller vehicles like ours into the ditch. You drive on the right or the left depending on where you want to go, honking incessantly. One American we met wore out his horn getting through Pakistan, and we soon realised that it took two of us to pilot our vehicle: one to perform the mechanical functions of steering and changing gear, the other to operate the horn at five-second intervals in the often-forlorn hope that it would clear a Citroën-sized path ahead.

While we opted to camp in the courtyard of a Lahore church, our friends decided on a hotel. It turned out to be an interesting experience.

As they checked-in, the manager approached, smiling ingratiatingly and insisting on shaking the European lady's hand - pulling on her rings in the hope one might fall free, a frequent Asian trick. He led them to their room, they asked where to find the bathrooms, then he departed.

She decided to use the toilet, but soon after installing herself in the cubicle, began to feel just a little uneasy, as though she were being watched.

She was. Above her, suspended from the toilet ceiling partition was the manager, beaming down at this show of shows. "Hello my dahleeng," he said when discovered. "I love you..."

Our toilets were safer, back in our churchyard. Indeed, they were the only safe haven in the whole yard, where we could write-up our diaries without collecting people like demented human flypaper. Even so, I was tracked down by one tenacious Pakistani.

"Excuse me sahib," he beamed through his betel-juice-stained red lips. "I am understanding from your car that you are British?"

I agreed.

"Acha, what a wonderful coincidence!" he gushed. "I too am wanting to be British. Please advise me."

(That day I was to make the mistake of answering requests for our British address with the real one, instead of the line which usually suffices: 12 High Street England. Months after we returned there continued a barrage of perfervid Pakistani correspondence, written almost to a formula. The first paragraph invoked God to shower us with countless blessings, the second was a reiteration of the opinion that we were among the finest, nay THE very finest, people in all creation, and the third asked for U.K. sponsorship, the rest being filled with questions as to whether Bradford was far from London, or whether it would be better for him to enter via Dublin or whether, adding a new twist to an old phrase, I could recommend him to a good tailor).

We wallowed in the oriental aura of the bazaars, ambling past stalls where salesmen would implore you in that gloriously archaic English so beloved of the Indian sub-continent: "Purchase here, sahib. Purchase, purchase, purchase!" Occasionally we did, but more often we just strolled, watching the children of no more than twelve hard at work in tailor-shops.

In the spectacle-shops there was a thriving trade in spectacles with plain glass, pandering to the vanity and the snobbery of Pakistanis. The fact that we counted an average of only one in twenty pairs of glasses actually sporting real lenses is reminiscent of what apparently happened to the Parker Pen Company. Their agent cabled for a consignment of several thousand Parker pen-tops. When the company cabled back that they normally supplied only the whole pen, he explained that sporting a Parker in your shirt pocket was THE status symbol, but that most Pakistanis were illiterate. Hence the request - which was subsequently filled.

There seemed nothing you couldn't buy in this bazaar and much that you wouldn't want to. One poorly-patronised stall offered just three types of item: stuffed owls, genuine imitation wind-up gramophones, and collections of 78-rpm records by the man who did the music for World War Two, Glen Miller. Perhaps the most unnerving stall of all was The Dentist, where we watched the "doctor" providing a popular show, filling and extracting teeth using tools more suited to a car workshop. No fancy drills, no anaesthetics - just say "ah" and the mouth is filled with Victorian forceps and a load of bazaar dust kicked up by passing bullock-carts.

Around the bazaars would be tethered the inevitable goats so that, when the stress of work became too great for the stall-owners, they could squeeze themselves a fresh glass of goat-milk. And the prices! With civil servants earning the best wage in the country, equivalent to about ten English pounds a month, it's hardly surprising that a magnificent, full-size wicker chair cost just four rupees, which at that time was around 40 English pence. Or that we could buy a week's-worth of food for less than a pound.

Not for the first time, and certainly not for the last, we were conned in Lahore. Sensible people have to be silly about something, and it is a traveller's right to set himself up to be taken, repeatedly.

The two Pakistanis sidled past with their inevitable "Change money mister?" and the offer of a very good rate. We talked, and negotiated, and I conducted myself splendidly in beating them down to just £20 and a small, spare radio for several hundred rupees. "Don't do it, something's not right," muttered my sceptical partner, but I was flushed with success as the money, and our radio, changed hands. No sleight of hand, as so often happens when part of the proferred wad mysteriously disappears in the exchange. No, the niceties were scrupulously observed after I had inspected the offered banknotes which any fool could see were genuine. Both amounts were passed across simultaneously, obviating the other possibility, that they would run off clutching both my pounds and their rupees. A good deal all round, I congratulated myself as they made off, quickly. Rather too quickly...? Still, we had what was beyond doubt several hundred Pakistani rupees, and at a favourable rate, so celebrations were in order as we penetrated the bazaar to shop.

We couldn't buy a thing. How could we have known there was good - i.e. new - Pakistani money, and bad, or old? At midnight a month before, all the country's existing paper money ceased to be legal tender, and no amount of shameless pleading, even all the way up to the State Bank, could turn my Monopoly money into the real thing. A bitter blow to a tight budget, and needless to say I learned no lessons from it. (Surprisingly, the story has a happy ending. Almost a year later, in a Victoria Falls bank in Rhodesia, we were spotted as Scruffy Overlanders by a manager who was also a keen numismatist. He bought our paper at its face value, and may he have much joy of it).

Back on the road again, we were soon at the border-crossing with India. No need to pick one, because at that time, with India and Pakistan again pantomiming at each other across no-man's-land there was only one frontier-post open, at Wagah, and that only for foreigners.

From a distance as we parked we could hear a strident south-London accent declaiming loudly from the Immigration Office.

"I know me rights!" it bellowed. "You have to let me through! I demand to be let through! You have no right to stop me!"

I wonder. The owner of the voice turned out to be a skeletal European clad only in a loincloth. In the East in search of a drug-induced Nirvana, he had sold everything in search of the ultimate fix, even down to his clothes, his blood and his passport. "You have to let me through!" he continued to demand, much to the embarrassment of Pakistani officialdom unused to dealing with Britons in the raw. Where he was headed, or how, or whether he was finally allowed in we never found out. When we cleared the border four hours later he was still there, pounding the table with his naked, emaciated arm.

7
A DIFFICULTY FOR EVERY SOLUTION

Travelling in India is like picking up a razorblade. At the time you don't feel all that much, but soon, watching the blood welling you think "Oh, that went deep." Quite how deep we were not to know until years afterwards. For the moment it was enough to wallow hopelessly. We impressed like Plasticine, saw everything and understood nothing.

If all the world's a stage, India is appallingly badly cast. How could it be otherwise in a nation with its own space and nuclear programmes alongside the globe's most grinding poverty? Or where a population renowned for its passivity can be so roused by the stopping of a TV soap-opera that they will storm the studios? There's only one way for the punch-drunk visitor to take India, and that's morsel by morsel with a pinch of garam masala. Like a streetside curry, it doesn't do to analyse too deeply.

Much of what you see in India is to credulity what lockjaw is to conversation. The mind cannot remain unboggled by the roadsign we saw halfway down the country: "Bombay," it announced: "396 miles, 415 yards and 2 feet." Other classic notices are long cherished by my notebook, like these gems gleaned from Indian hotels:

"You are invited to visit our restaurant where you can eat the Indian foods in a European ambulance. If you wish for breakfast in your room, lift the telephone, ask for Room Service, and this will be enough for you to bring your food up."

"We will be happy to dispose of all your family. Our hotel is situated in the shadiest part of the town."

"Ladies are requested not to have children in the bar."

"If your wife needs something to do, she should apply to our suggestive head porter."

"In case of fire, please do your utmost to alarm hall porter."

In a decrepit elevator in downtown Delhi: "To move the cabin, push button of wishing floor. If the cabin should enter more persons, each one should press number of wishing floor. Driving is then going alphabetically in natural order. Button retaining pressed position shows received command for visiting station."

Or my favourite of them all: "To call the Room Service, please to open door and call Room Service."

There was a sign in the window of the Bombay Same Day Cleaners: "48 hour service! We do not tear your clothes with machinery. We do it by hand."

A freighting company in the same city advertised that customers should "Hand your baggage to us. We will send it in all directions."

Elise found this one in the ladies room of a Delhi restaurant: "For sanitation purposes please sanit in the pots provided and not on the floor."

And from a disaster report in an Indian newspaper: "The fire killed 300 people, many of them men, women and children."

Ah, India! What do you reply to the taxi-driver who has endured countless delays trying to negotiate wandering herds of sacred cattle in the main city streets, when he asks you earnestly, "Tell me sahib, what do you do about this problem in London?"

And how do you react to the man standing beneath Bombay's famous Gateway, selling leaflets? "THE END OF THE WORLD," they are entitled - and under the title, in small letters: "Tenth Edition."

The British Empire, it is said, was founded by people who didn't like the climate at home. In the even less equable climate of India, I wonder how many of those early colonists were defeated by an environment closely akin to being locked in the stocks, for they threw anything at you there, too. By the time we left we were as good as defeated, having found only dark at the end of the tunnel after two months and 4,000 kilometres of stumbling around in search of enlightenment. Many a traveller has met his nemesis in India. I would like to say we were different. I would like to, but...

Immense vistas of frustration, tormenting us to an almost homicidal degree, were still to open up before us as we crossed the border for our first encounter with India's bureaucracy. Britain left many enduring legacies in India, but the one she has most to answer for is the civil service, which is like Whitehall run amuck. For two hours we felt as though we were swimming through clotted cream in an avalanche of paperwork, none of which appeared to have any sense at all.

The final official, a man with the IQ of a telegraph pole, took down a dusty ledger, spent ten minutes trying to find our visas in our passports, and then began writing precisely what they said: "This visa entitles the bearer to enter India for a three-month period from initial date of entry...." and so on, paragraph for paragraph. And each entry in his ledger was the same back into the mists of time, transcription after transcription of the same visa in which only the names changed. We were unlucky. His attention was distracted for a moment, and when he picked up the threads of his labours he was unable to find the place in our visa where he had stopped copying, having to enlist the help of two more officials to search-out what came after the word "initial."

So we were in, heaven help us, in a country as vast as Europe minus Russia, containing 550 million people and all of them on the road ahead, or so it seemed as we picked our way gingerly through the throngs, passing carefully-metricated signs: "Speed limit 32 km\hour," they said - precise conversions from 20 miles.

There were the Indian road gangs hard at work, several score people doing the work of one Caterpillar machine in the West. Masses of people achieved little, slowly. Women carried baskets of pebbles on their heads, men cooked mixtures of tar in little pots. Each spade had not one but two people to work it - one on the handle, pushing, the other pulling a rope attached to the blade. Several men were down on their haunches with tiny hammers chip-chip-chipping at little slabs of stone. The results were laid into the spot being repaired, then another worker would approach, splash a spoonful of tar over the strewn pebbles, and the road repair continued, endlessly, using technology as timeless as the people.

In Amritsar we wandered and wondered at the Sikhs' holiest shrine, the fabulous Golden Temple, later to be the scene of the bloody carnage which would close it indefinitely to tourism. We had had too good a run of five whole days of good health, so inevitably the bug struck again and we were sicker than a sick sikh, in an agony I made worse by unthinkingly swatting a mosquito which had landed atop my naughty bits. Not dreadfully amusing at the time.

Fresh mountain air would do us good, we reasoned, and headed north for Kashmir, one of the world's anomalies.

Srinagar, the capital known to the locals as "Heaven on Earth," was once the playground of the British in the days of the Raj. The local Maharajah decreed that no Briton might own land there, so they took to the water, building magnificent houseboats which still fill the lake. The surfeit of boats and dearth of tourists makes it almost impossible not to be battered into submission by hordes of touts offering laketop accommodation: "Houseboat-houseboat-houseboat-mister!!!" They descend on travellers like a collapsing tent, making escape almost impossible. No-one in Srinagar, it seemed then, was not renting houseboats. When two German travellers stopped their van to pick up a light casualty and take him to a doctor, he still found time amid his agonies to groan from the back seat: "Houseboat, mister?"

We shared "The Field Marshall Montgomery With Fully Sprung Seats" with these friends, shopping from passing canoes called shikaras which offered an amazing variety of goods, one even carrying ancient packets of Tampax. After we moved ashore again, I offended local sensibilities by shitting on a shrine.

With the car parked beside a splendid hilltop, I had set off for one of those most pleasant of travellers' interludes, toilet-roll under my arm. On the crest of the hill, pondering the view while nature took its course, I was snapped from my reverie by the angry approach of a shouting Kashmiri. He ranted on at me for defiling a holy place, while I hopped and skipped into some form of respectability. Though I apologised profusely he blathered on, steamrollering my plea of an ignorance of local geography. In mid-blather, he stopped.

"What is that?" he asked, pointing to the toilet-roll.

We take toilet tissue for granted, but it's not easy explaining Western hygiene politely to a total stranger more at home with a small jug of water. He was bemused - then asked if he might have some and I obliged. Now it was my turn to be curious. Why did he want it?

"I will use it to make bandages," he explained, and we parted the best of friends, sacrilege or no.

Personal hygiene is a whole new can of worms in India, as we were rapidly discovering - and not just in the innumerable billboards exhorting Indians to use toothpaste, in a country where toothbrushes cost a Maharajah's ransom. Undaunted, many simply smeared the paste onto their teeth with their fingers. Things were murkier when it came to more alimentary matters.

Indians, as every traveller knows, are wont to squat when the urge arises, wherever and whenever and to hell with surrounding humanity. One town council thought it had a modernising idea in building fine new urinals for men. Later we watched as men did indeed make good use of them - squatting beside the buildings to urinate against the wall. Less amusingly, our eventual trip to Africa aboard an Indian passenger ship would be made distinctly uncomfortable as uneducated Indians used drinking-fountains to hawk and spit out their phlegm, or filled the showers with excrement. After that, even watching women eating their lunch with hands unwashed after collecting cow-dung patties would have seemed normal, though it didn't at the time. And we would hardly have blinked as we did when an itinerant entrepreneur bearing a reed-mat came up offering to perform a relaxing massage (in the middle of the town square, with a gawping cast of thousands) or, more intriguingly, "Clean your ears mister?"

Our expedition moved on, slowly for fear of reducing India's population. But our care and the constantly bleating horn were in vain when the car hit an elderly man.

That's not entirely accurate, for it's just as likely he conspired to hit us in the hope of reaping substantial compensation from the rich Europeans - a ploy which was, and probably still is, widespread in this land of relentless poverty where parents will even maim their children, in the hope of giving them a chance of survival as crippled beggars entitled to alms.

The road was a normal one for India: wall-to-wall people, many of them squatting on it in that simian crouch Asians can maintain for hours; ox-carts lumbering along with their drivers asleep; holy cows which may not be budged; sheep and goats; monkeys darting across; taxi-tricycles (average total earnings for their drivers three rupees - or about 30 British pence on a good day); flotillas of cyclists all ringing their bells in a cacophony of utter futility; even the odd freight-carrying elephant lumbering into our way. Anything mobile is dragooned into service, roadworthy or not, as we realised in passing an ex-bus which was lolloping crab-fashion down the road. Once a proud example of the Tata factory's coachbuilding abilities, now it was a hulk, having been in one or a dozen accidents. The whole front was smashed in, the chassis buckled, the wheels warped, no glass in the windows, doors and bits of bodywork hanging lopsidedly from the front, the driver perched atop a seat in the now non-existent driver's cab as the vehicle spluttered and groaned semi-sideways.

It was full of people - passengers sitting blandly in this memory of a bus as though it were quite normal, which it probably was in India. A travellers' tale tells of an Indian double-decker bus overloaded with the usual double complement of passengers, when the weight of humanity caused the entire rear platform to collapse, spewing passengers onto the road. The driver stopped, the story goes, checked how many passengers had been so summarily ejected, refunded their fares, and drove on.

This, then, was the traffic nightmare of India, an organised chaos which had already seen a policeman order a truck to back into us, temporarily denting our front grille but thank Citroën for a plastic car with its panels which pop back into shape. That accident was par for the course, and so was the later one in Agra when a truck-driver decided simply to push us out of the way as he came around a tight bend, or the many times we were forced off the tarmac by thundering trucks because there's one rule of the road in India and that's to give way to anything big.

Which lands us back with the reason we started to measure our Asian trip not in kilometres per litre, but in kilometres per windscreen.

Approaching Lucknow, both of us were driving intently, crawling through the hordes in second gear, Elise on lookout duty and operating the horn while I tried not to run down too many people. The law of averages says that if you have a dozen near-misses a day your luck must run out, and it did as an old man detached himself from the throng, stepped left, then changed his mind, decided to cross the road without looking, stepped right and crash - exit another windscreen.

I should be ashamed to admit my first thought was for the windscreen. India does that to you. We stopped, and a crowd coagulated as the man looked up at us, then began to writhe and moan. At a quick glance (which was all that had happened to him when all was said and done) he didn't appear to be suffering anything worse than bruises - but as we were told afterwards, he was being advised to stay down in the hope of getting hospital money from the wealthy foreigners.

The crowd pressed in, as did the atmosphere. Two American friends on a motorbike arrived just in time, sized up the situation and told us to get the hell out and leave them to sort it out. It was wise advice, as we left to the first thrown insults and stones. The Americans made sure the man was intact, offered an eagerly-accepted handful of rupees and all that remained to be repaired was the windscreen. By now somewhat fatalistic (India does that to you, too), I vowed I would not put in any more Asian glass, waiting instead until we reached Africa. On we groped, peering through layers of cracks, splinters and shards of glass held together by insulating tape and optimism.

Americans Don and Becky were to travel together with us for several weeks. Interrupting their studies in law school for a Grand Tour of Europe and Asia, they had opted to use a giant B.M.W. motorcycle with an engine capacity one-and-a-half times greater than that of our one-ton plastic tortoise. It was hopelessly excessive for the purpose, and though it had five gears they never managed to get above third, or second for long peopled stretches of India. Its size was a distinct handicap, too, when the diminutive Becky was left alone to manoeuvre it, or collapsed under it, or fell off it, and the locals enjoyed the show immensely.

Come to that, the locals enjoyed any show immensely. Rural Indians have all the time in the world and lives so little, that the arrival of a traveller is finer entertainment than even the most dire of Bombay's dire movies. Wherever you went, even in the most remote area apparently devoid of people, Indians could materialise miraculously within minutes, to stand and stare in convincing imitations of windowdressers' dummies.

Over and over we tried to turn this into contact and conversation, even steeling ourselves to the dreaded phrase put to every traveller dozens of times a day: "What is your country?" Or "What is the purpose of your visit?" You didn't have to be a misanthrope to find all this wearing, for it meant you rarely had the privacy just to stop and look. But, stubbornly persistent, you might once again trot out your answer, knowing well that it would provoke no reaction and the questioner would linger, satisfied, mute, curiosity sated. Only rarely did we succeed in bridging the gap which left us regarding one another like outer-space aliens. Eventually we resigned ourselves to the constant gawp with much less good grace than the effervescent Don was able to muster.

He revelled in the cabaret. If a tyre was to be changed a hundred would press in while he exaggerated every movement. If he brushed his teeth, the madding crowds would look on in awe. And when his dental floss was wielded a sword-swallowing fakir could have elicited no more appreciation. If the press became too much he would persuade the throngs back, then draw a line in the sand with a stick, demonstrating that the line was a barrier not to be crossed while the show - our daily routines - tried to progress as though nothing was abnormal. And the crowds would crane on, some almost falling flat on their faces in their efforts not to cross the seeming force-field of that line in the sand.

At times it became all too much. When a cycling Indian hove into view and grew roots right in front of us to watch us forever as though he was rehearsing for a part in Madame Tussaud's, obscuring the very mountain scenery we had stopped to admire, our patience was not equal to his. "Don't just do something, stand there," we said with all the irony we could muster, but the sarcasm was as lost as we were in that most familiar of Indian travellers' dilemmas, how to cope with being a mobile freak-show.

Kilometres on we had become more blasé about the whole business, daring to deal with Indians in a manner which would have brought instant retribution anywhere else. Where else, for example, would you dare to tell an enquiring policeman to go away?

It was barely New Year's Day 1975, and we had fallen asleep after Elise had concocted an astonishing celebratory meal in the back of our cramped car, six glorious courses cobbled together from the few foods available locally and some tins saved for just such an event. We even rounded it off with our special "find" from a local shop, a tin of Cadbury's Drinking Chocolate showing the familiar label, aromatic wisp rising from the prepared cup and all. Only it wasn't Cadbury's, as we found when we tried to drink it and retched with disappointment; it was a rip-off called Bradbury's which ought to have flown the skull and crossbones and may they rot in hell with their undrinkable powder.

So, nonetheless, we dozed into 1975 until there was a knock on the side of the car. With sleep-filled eyes we peered out to see a policeman on his bicycle, come to see this strange car parked along his stretch of road. "What do you want?" we demanded.

"I am coming to investigate," he replied.

"Go away, we're sleeping," I grunted.

"Yes sir, sorry sir," he said - and went. Then he thought better of it, and decided he would have to make a full report. Out came the notebook as he asked for "informations." I grunted terse answers, and then he began to write down the informations displayed on the back of our car. For twenty minutes as we tossed inside our sleeping-bag we could hear him spelling it all out: "Over-land.....Lon-don....Eur-ope..." he muttered as Elise fell asleep between each word and by the time he reached Africa I had gone too. I woke up as he began on our nationality stickers, spelling out each letter of the GB and NL, but by the time he had started in on the Citroën badge, the numberplate, the logo of the Dutch garage which had performed our first service, and the sticker which said "I think your car looks funny too," all sleep had gone and there was nothing for it but tea.

There was less forbearance in our encounter with the Agra taxi-driver.

The afternoon of our arrival at the spectacular Taj Mahal had been written off, after the ever-present throngs of hasslers ruined any hope of savouring the atmosphere of the palace itself. We got up in the dark the next morning, fortified ourselves with tea and set off to see this most special of buildings at sunrise.

The streets were almost bare, save for one persistent taxi-driver.

"Sir, sir, you want taxi?" he chattered as he waggled his head at us.

"No thank you."

"I give you good taxi, little rupees."

"No."

"Is being best taxi, cheap-cheap."

"No, go away!"

"Sir, very good taxi, take you anywhere."

"Go away, dammit. We want to be alone."

"But is number one taxi, very cheap."

I could take no more. My cup of tolerance had indeed runneth'd over as I grabbed his shirt, placed my mouth next to his ear and bellowed:

"FUCK OFF!!!!!"

There was a stunned silence. Then, carefully:

"It means you don't want taxi....?"

The Taj Mahal was beautiful, naturally, though we got lost leaving. "Is this the way to Arrah?" I asked a pedestrian.

"Oh yes sahib."

I didn't believe him, so I asked another, then four more, and all agreed this was the way to Arrah. It wasn't. An hour later I tried again.

"Is this the way to Arrah?"

"This is Patna."

Asking directions in India is like unravelling spaghetti, where people will tell you what they believe will please you most. Why should they make you unhappy by revealing you are miles from Arrah and getting further away every minute? So they head-waggle their agreement whatever you say; we tested the theory several times.

"Is this the way to Delhi?" we would ask. Yes, naturally.

"Is that the way to Delhi?", indicating a totally different direction. Yes, yes without doubt.

"Is this the road to Timbuktu?" Certainly, sahib, and the poor sap could hardly have understood why two foreigners doubled-up with laughter in the middle of that Indian nowhere. Is it any wonder we ended-up regarding India and Indians like a demented self-sealing fuel-tank - something you could shoot holes into, but some resilient inner lining will always close over them and nothing comes out?

Indian reasoning reached its climax in Delhi's main post office when we went to look for our mail. "Kennedy, with a K," I said after an hour spent queueing, and he brought out the shoebox marked K. Nothing. I tried the T's, then the E's, and we were desperately down to middle names before inspiration struck.

"Let me see the M's!" I demanded, and Elise looked at me in bewilderment. Voila! There were all our letters, along with thousands which would never be collected, some of them years old as they mouldered in this enormous box of M's: Mr., Mr., Mr., Mrs., Miss, Mrs., Mr., Mr. and on back into the mists of postal time. (The lunatic logic of this was repeated years later in the library of an Arab newspaper for which I was writing, when missing photos could be found under P for picture).

Nepal was altogether much easier. Seven sets of wrong directions and two hours completing Indian exit formalities followed by ten minutes on the Nepalese side and we were in, Himalaya bound. Pokhara was like something out of an Asian Hans Christian Andersen, a tiny town of cardboard-cutout buildings nestling in the lee of giant mountains beside a cluster of lakes - all peopled by a friendly if often indifferent folk who are achingly poor yet scrupulously honest, as we found when villagers ran after us to return the camera we had stupidly left lying.

In Pokhara we packed a tin of corned beef, vitamins, army-ration chocolate, six hard-boiled eggs, boiled potatoes, a canteen of water, glucose sweets and our weatherproof "Space-blanket" and headed for the hills. Trekking is easier said than done when you've spent eight months living in the back of a car, with your only regular exercise confined to an early-morning up-down up-down up-down then open the other eyelid. At 4,000 metres and 5°C we began the Himalaya Slowstep: step, gasp, gasp, gasp, step, as we set off on the long walk upwards into the heart of the world's most mysterious mountain range, Everest reaching eight kilometres into the sky somewhere far ahead. The women paused to smile shyly under their killing loads of bundled firewood suspended on their backs by a strap around the forehead, the children clapped hands and greeted us with an enthusiastic "Namaste," and all was sweetness and light until the blisters set in.

For a few cents we ate, and slept, on the rough floors of "hotels" along the mountain track. And in one of these I made two mistakes. First I asked where to find the toilet, and was led in a welter of giggles out into the street where the world's highest and most rarefied toilet lay waiting. Then I asked for water to brush my teeth, and was deeply ashamed when it arrived hours later after a daughter of the house had been sent miles down a mountain to fetch it.

In the foothills of imposing Annapurna, where we believed the hand of man had never set foot, we stumbled across a British horticulturist who corrected our hopeless sense of direction, and then we were there, on the roof of the world and high with it all.

Further on in Kathmandu we were still high on life though most other European travellers of the time were high on far more noxious substances. Kathmandu was for years the pot of pot at the end of the drug rainbow, and there was a distinct "them and us" gulf between travellers and dope-heads. Indeed, one of the few times we became angry in that most tolerant of cities was at seeing indigent Europeans, reduced to poverty by pot and looking like walking slums, begging amid all the squalor of Asia. Should we have been disgusted, too, by the German package-tourists jetting-in to overrun the place as though they owned it? At least one made us laugh, when he finally got a reluctant Nepalese girl to turn around for a photograph by unexpectedly bellowing the first few bars of "Deutschland Über Alles" at the back of her head.

It was a memorable Christmas Eve, celebrated so far from the Christian world in that convivial mountain kingdom. With German travel companions Klaus and Kristel we set off for a restaurant and ate our way twice through the menu. Thence to a pie-shop for some of Nepal's famous and no-doubt dysenteric concoctions. On the way home our mock-disgust at such gluttony was tinged with sickness of another kind: homesickness for the first time, brought on by the thought of a real European Christmas so many thousands of miles away. As if to order, a strange thing happened.

As we meandered through those tiny streets, wafting through the night came the discordant sounds of a carol, "Oh Come All Ye Faithful." Then, in the distance, a flicker of candles bobbed towards us, followed by singing European faces. Suddenly Christmas was real as we joined this band of lonely foreigners carolling through the streets of Kathmandu to the delight and astonishment of the Nepalese.

A Christmas party among the friends who had shared the long hard road, then a sad parting the following day as we left our companions to strike out southwards. And God help us we were back in India again, spending two hours changing a travellers' cheque, because every transaction has to be okayed and signed by six people in three departments and then the manager who would rather not be bothered by the whole transaction at all, until you make it clear you will stay there with your foot in his door until gangrene sets in.

Something snapped in India - a syndrome to which many travellers can attest. Even the most gentle of people become killers, and when the umpteenth child threw the umpteenth stone at us my paranoia broke loose and I hurtled from the car with murder in my heart. I made a flying leap at fleeing youth, and naturally I nabbed the slowest one who had nothing to do with the whole affair. His face took on the terror-stricken look of a massacre about to happen and his bowels emptied and there I stood, perplexed, ashamed, defeated.

We found out how that child must have felt days later as we headed for a somnolent Indian village, following a Government jeep at some distance. Nothing was heard but the sound of endless Indian time decomposing in peace, when suddenly there was a flurry of activity up ahead and the agony of an engine about to burst. Men appeared as if from nowhere, hurling rocks at the jeep with hate in their faces.

As we stared in disbelief the jeep appeared to disintegrate, shattered glass flying everywhere as it screamed madly backwards towards us, its occupants streaming blood. I never panic except in a crisis, and made a complete botch out of jamming on the brakes, throwing our car into reverse and careening in terror out of the village. The stone-throwing, stick-wielding crowd surged on and we knew with sinking hearts and our wills not yet made out that they would soon overtake us...

Which is precisely what they did. They thundered straight past, intent only on the jeep, which disappeared in a trail of debris over the hill. The crowd returned and beckoned us to carry on through their quiet village as though nothing had happened. Only the Government was the enemy in a bitter dispute over taxes, we learned later, and this frightening explosion by a people renowned for their passivity darkened the murky waters of our incomprehension even more. It did at least partly help to explain the violence which surrounded the partition of India and Pakistan in 1947, when up to a million people died in bloody confrontation.

In the holy city of Varanasi\Benares the stoicism of the Hindu was displayed in a different context. Creeping along in a traffic-jam of rikshas near the banks of the River Ganges, we noticed that the occupant of one of these man-drawn taxis looked decidedly uncomfortable. "How does he manage to sit for long like that, perched so stiffly on the bench?" I asked Elise as the riksha drew alongside.

"Easily," she replied. "He's dead."

And so he was, being wheeled down to the river to be placed atop a funeral pyre, less-than-diligently cremated, and then thrown into the Ganges where, not more than a few metres away, people bathed, people drank from the river, and vultures picked at the floating feast.

We were watching all this in fascinated horror, snapping forbidden pictures, when an educated voice asked: "Is that a Canon camera you're using?"

We turned to see a man dressed in a flowing saffron robe, sporting a beard and a conspiratorial grin. "I prefer a Nikon myself, particularly with a good zoom," said this "Sadu," or Indian holy-man. For seven years he had travelled in search of wisdom, eating the food which good Hindus are obliged to offer him, sleeping in their huts. He had given up all in search of enlightenment, and the road had been hard for he was 52 and didn't look a day over 70. We talked, knowing full well towards the end where the talk was leading, and though he didn't actually ask for money he simply reminded us of his "condition," telling us that even holy men had to eat. We gave.

Which is not something you normally do in Asia, we knew from experience. Particularly in this holy city the visitor is besieged by beggars and cripples of all shapes and afflictions. Some limp only as they come into sight, some forget which leg is supposed to be lame as they press their case. Others display the most revolting disfigurements and woe betide the traveller whose heart is broken and who parts with money, for he will soon be swamped under an avalanche of beggars as word gets out. Hardened to it all, we occasionally even tried Winston Churchill's famous riposte - naturally to no effect whatsoever:

Beggar: "Please sir, I haven't eaten for days."

Churchill: "Well force yourself, my good man, force yourself!"

We needed normality, such as it is in India, and headed for a Western-style restaurant serving plates of bacteria-laden food, as our medical history would prove. Normality was a long time coming, though, as a waiter shuffled out of the kitchen bearing a cooked chicken. He stumbled, dropped the chicken, trod on it, picked it up, dusted it off on his filthy uniform, looked around to check if the relevant customer had seen, sidled back into the kitchen, then came out bearing the same chicken to serve it with a flourish.

Perhaps an ethnic Indian restaurant would be better? The "Best Easting

House" sign (sic, as we were at the end of it) belied the fact that no-one in this pungent hole-in-the-wall spoke English. But the owner wiped his nose with his dishcloth as he babbled, lifting the lids of the dozen pots bubbling on the fire for us to select. Each smelled more malodorous than the next, clotted with raw sewage swimming in a cesspool. We made a random choice while other patrons laid bets on our chances of survival: the beggar with the small change cadged to fuel him through another day, the clerk picking his betel-juice-stained red teeth with a fork, the introspective sadu or holy man claiming his religion-decreed right to a free meal, a chattering group in from a village whose debris of devastation on the table looked as though they had passed the food up through it to their mouths.

As the dishes of offal in slime arrived at our rickety table, the jabber of conversation slackened in expectation, then stopped as we raised the first spoonful to our lips.

My mouth burst into invisible flames. Elise was taken suddenly short of Kleenex, a reservoir of water and a fire-extinguisher. This was no ordinary hot curry; this was hell, the holocaust and "Fahrenheit 451" rolled into one. Mouths opened in food-filled grins around us as we cried helplessly through every bite, determined to finish though our taste-buds be crippled for life. Tears coursed down our flaming cheeks as we shovelled in spoonful after spoonful, frantically to condense the agony, tasting nothing, though briefly guessing with our tongues what each bite might be as a blind man prods at the world with his equally nerveless stick. Beside us the sadu watched wistfully as we super-spooned, his hopes of snaffling the leftovers dashed. The others involved themselves gleefully with the drama, pushing forward their remedies, from half-eaten chunks of "naan" bread and partly-demolished chapatis to draughts of effluent-coloured water and lip-curdling sugar-cane juice, when all we really needed was asbestos innards.

"Acha, curry good yes?" said the clerk as we staggered from our seats an eternity later, heads swirling, gullets gutted, palates napalmed but our dishes proudly empty.

We wanted to agree, but no words came out. Nodding dumbly through the tears as we threw down some cash, we fled for fresh air, rampaging diarrhoea, and days of numb nothing where our taste-buds should be.

On then to Bombay, which boasts what is said to be the finest hotel in the sub-continent, the glittering Taj Mahal Hotel, and that's where we stayed during those final halcyon days. Well, not exactly. In its carpark to be precise, camping under the benign and remunerated gaze of the watchman. We were discovered there by a personable Indian industrialist who insisted on treating us to tea in the hotel proper, while he expounded his utter pessimism for his country's future, and his view that the only way out of the national morass would be to put birth-control pills in the drinking water. Tea ended rather summarily when he took advantage of my absence in the cloakroom to lay a paw on Elise's arm, gaze limpidly into her eyes and complain that his wife didn't understand him. She was also, one should realise, always tired...

If getting into India had been difficult, getting out was a nightmare. I still wake up in a sweat to think about it, and about the officials who have access to an endless armoury of spanners to throw into the works to bedevil the hopes of hapless travellers.

It began with booking passage on the only ship running to Africa, our enquiries initially taking the form of telegrams which took five days to be delivered; then direct questions to the agent. Would the ship definitely arrive on the date specified? "Oh yes, of course." It came three weeks late.

We were to purchase our tickets from the venerable firm of Hari Singh & Son, Travel Agents of Esteem. Before we could do that we needed permission from the bank, which took six hours and four banks. We cleared that hurdle, only to find that Elise had been taken suddenly destitute and could not pay for her ticket. Certainly, we had sufficient funds, but they were all in my name and we were not married, therefore Q.E.D. Elise could not buy a ticket. Surely I could pay for her? No, that would entail the transfer of foreign currency, which is prohibited in India...

The problem was batted about as officials contrived to find a difficulty for every solution. It ended in an expensive lawyer's office, where we signed an affidavit that we had been living in sin in our car for eight months and were therefore common-law man and wife. Back to the bank to cash Elise's fare-share of cheques into rupees which were issued to me in a welter of paperwork; I handed the rupees to Elise who signed various chitties acknowledging my gift. She handed the rupees to a teller who gave her more forms and some dollar travellers' cheques. She signed them, he filled in the complete paperwork, then he demanded back the travellers' cheques, checked to see they were genuine even though he himself had just issued them, converted them into rupees at a swingeing rate and deducted a whopping foreign travel tax, and we had permission for Elise to buy a ticket. Our troubles were only just beginning; it was to resemble a Wagner opera directed by Charlie Chaplin before the week was out.

Came the day before departure and we trundled our car down to the docks for loading. The paperwork took forever, officials backed several cars into ours, a tractor drove over some of our luggage, and at midnight when the car was finally being swung aboard, an adjacent crane began loading and our car was headed for an aerial collision only averted by our shrieked "STOP!"

At least the car was on the ship, but we weren't, and weren't destined to be either when it was discovered someone had screwed-up the booking. "Your car must now go but you'll have to wait for the next sailing," shrugged the clerk. There were heated exchanges of opinion and the threat of everything short of British gunboats, and we were on. In theory.

We woke the fateful day of sailing to find we had been massively overcharged on our tickets. Angry dashing from office to office in search of retribution and a refund brought only the stonewalling "Why don't you write to the Government about it, sir?"

By this time Elise had struggled aboard manfully with our baggage and I prepared to join her. I had reckoned without the rulebook.

The previous night we had been through the mill of a complete Customs overhaul, with each and every item checked against the passports. As many an unwary traveller found out to his cost, India then even insisted that every spare tyre be marked into the passport, and if you wrote one off in your travels you were still required to carry the carcass with you and out of India. Our finances no longer tallied - how could they, when I was several hundred dollars short (the money which had been "given" to Elise) while she had a ticket apparently bought with nonexistent funds?

All that was finally history as I presented myself at the last Customs hurdle, with Elise waving worriedly from the deck and the ship gathering steam.

"Where is your car, your typewriter, your tyres....?" asked the officer. I explained that it had all been cleared, and loaded, the night before. No good - that had happened during the previous shift and it was his duty to lay eyes on every single item listed in my passport, or I simply could not go. But the car was now several decks down and distinctly invisible.

We began a Keystone Cops chase through Bombay in search of last night's Customs man, from one office to another and take away the office you first thought of, and finally out to his home. As Elise grew frantic (she was no more allowed off the ship than I was allowed onto it) I begged, pleaded, reasoned and cajoled, and finally did what no traveller should do in India, something very un-British which I hadn't done in years: I lost my temper, shouted and ranted and caused the worst of all possible scenes, and was finally ushered on board in a palpable lack of Commonwealth cameraderie. For three days afterwards I was unable to speak, rendered totally hoarse by our last encounter with the quagmire which is India.

8
PASSING THE BUCK

The truth can now be told. We helped eighteen penniless Europeans to enter Africa illegally, by lending them each our $500 cash for three minutes at a time. It was the least we could do.

After all, throughout the voyage aboard the rustbucket SS Karanja, they had consistently passed huge wadges of their meals across the dining-hall to "the tall thin guy with the red beard." It was a touching humanitarian gesture, to avert the ravages of the chronic dysentery they were sure was going to put me over the side in a Union Jack. I ate like a horse; indeed, if rumours about the ship's cuisine were true I ate horse, shovelling down up to four meals at a sitting in an effort to put back the one-sixth of my body-weight which Asia had claimed.

The Karanja is rumoured to have sunk soon afterwards, and may it rust in peace, but the zoo-like conditions in which it transported human steerage between the Indian sub-continent and Africa will hardly be missed. There was something barbarous about the way herds of uncomplaining humanity were packed in tiers of bunks in one cramped, claustrophobic, sweltering shed-like area below decks, the single women protected from male predators by being locked in a cage for the duration.

Passengers in the lowest deck-class often went hungry, having to queue for up to an hour and a half for a handful of food. Excreta was everywhere with simple village travellers unaware of the purpose of the toilets, so that you stepped carefully throughout the ship, women raising their skirts, and the showers were unusable. The more refined of the passengers blew their noses on the ship's curtains - while the freshwater drinking fountains were soon swimming in mucus, used as the final target for the earth-moving rumble of an Asian hawk and spit which never failed to raise the hackles of nearby Europeans. (A favourite trick among some foreigners was to stand out of sight above the "European" promenade deck and imitate the volcanic imminence of an Asian expectoration aimed below. It could clear the deck in seconds...)

The atmosphere in the steerage section of the ship was asphyxiating, and those who could, opted to live on deck rather than endure the emetic conditions below. We were more fortunate.

For the few dollars extra which the pathetic majority of the Indian passengers could not afford, we could claim a cubbyhole in a cabin, sharing the foetid sleeping space with five others. My companions were Moslems determined to perform their five daily prayers at the correct time. Their resolution was thrown into fabulous confusion by the daily zonal time-change announced on the ship's noticeboard which few could or would read.

The clock moved by an hour or half-an-hour each day, and by the fourth chaotic morning my companions were waking in the dead of night convinced that sunrise prayers were upon them. The heated chatter of argument drove out further dreams of sleep, and once out on deck the anarchy was compounded. Well-prepared Moslems had their own compasses to ensure they aimed their bowing and scraping correctly towards Mecca, but what few understood is that a hand-compass wielded in the metal body of a ship is no more use than a sun-dial in the Arctic night. Needles spun like roulette wheels and the arguments raged on, leaving believers facing everywhichway in their devotions, while the scruffy European contingent looked on in delight.

Africa finally hove into view, a panorama of palm-fronded beaches and Immigration officials. After its two-week hiatus reality had returned in the form of a bureaucratic grilling, and it quickly became obvious that those Europeans who could not produce proof that they had the means to support themselves in Kenya were going to be sent straight back. An instant straw-poll revealed that about ten per cent of the assembled twenty Westerners could meet the regulations by being able to produce the required $500 in cash: Elise and I.

A conspiracy was hatched within seconds and intuitively grasped by its conspirators. We took our place at the head of the queue, answered the questions, displayed our $500 and were stamped into Kenya, passing the cash surreptitiously to the person next in line. It never occurred to officialdom to wonder at the exact amount tendered by each of the twenty in the exact same denominations bearing the exact same serial numbers, and one hour later I was delighted to have repaid my moral debt for meals rendered. We had arrived in Africa.

How can you describe the wondrous feeling of freedom which washed over us as we stepped ashore on the Dark Continent, after months of flailing around in the morass of India? No gawping crowds, no beggars tugging at our clothes, no reeking hordes of jostling, stumbling, meandering, obstructing people. Few people accosted us; when they did the results were often unexpected.

"Hey, mister!" a painted lady of the night sashayed at us in broad daylight. "How about you and me go jigajig?"

"No thanks, I'm with my wife," I grinned as Elise leant on my arm.

"That's okay," shot back the tart. "She can come too!"

Within a day our worries had devolved into one simple concern: whether a coconut might fall on us from the waving palm above, as we lazed and loved on Mombasa's beach, in the grounds of a simple hotel offering sun, sea and hot and cold running monkeys. The monkeys were often a nuisance, and were as skilled in theft as we were finding the locals to be. They were intelligent, too. I can hardly blame the sceptics for disbelieving what my diary tells me is true: the spectacle of a troop of monkeys forming a chain from their tree while one of their number unzipped an unoccupied tent, crept in, opened a packet of biscuits and passed them out along the line one by one, closing the packet and the zipper before moving on...

Africans, we discovered, were even more adroit at practising this national sport. Street mugging and handbag-snatching were childs' play, and woe betide any traveller who tried to change money on the black-market without several sets of friends' eyes to follow the cash. A German tourist was even mugged while swimming in the sea, relieved of his waterproof watch by two waterborne assailants. Countless bathers would hoist themselves out of the ocean to dress again in clothes which no longer existed, and one over-confident swimmer even had his garments lifted by a fishing-line lowered over the high, sheer cliff under which he had installed himself with a misplaced sense of security.

Another reality of Africa was brought home in Nairobi's City Park, when two overlanders were murdered one night on the way to the campsite's ablution block. City Park was closed to travellers after that, but not before we had experienced the sensation of living in a scrapyard.

For years, City Park campsite was the crossroads of Africa, the one place where you could be sure of meeting everyone travelling north or south. It was packed way beyond capacity with overlanders, many of them waiting like Billy Bunter for the postal order which never came, while they stripped their tired vehicles to repair the ravages of Africa or sold what bits they could to survive. To live amongst the detritus was closely akin to life in a breaker's yard, though the atmosphere was amicable. Living like sardines it had to be, with hardly enough space between vehicles to swing a mosquito let alone the proverbial cat.

Privacy became a relative term, emphasised the night Elise had to rummage around an inaccessible region of my body to find the cause of an irritating itch.

"You've got a tick!" she squawked in surprise. And from all over the campsite came the echo: "Guy in the Citroën's got a tick...."; "He's got a tick, the fellah in the red plastic car."; "The Brit's got a tick...."

The raw Africa was different, replete with its signs warning "Beware of Elephants and Wild Animals" and "Animals have Right of Way."

Nonsense, you think, and then around the next corner you stand on the brakes as a herd of giraffe stilt across the track. A little further and a cloud of dust signals that a mountain is moving up ahead, and you wait at a respectful distance to allow elephants to rumble on. You pass the buck, literally and in profusion. A short-sighted rhino tries to size you up for target practice in the Tsavo National Park, and you hold your breath and the gearlever, knowing full-well that your plastic tortoise in reverse has no hope against the top-gear of a rhino, and true stories flash through your mind of rhinos charging Land-Rovers and winning or storming trains and losing.

Today Kenya clings desperately to its image as one of the last havens of embattled wildlife. In all of Africa, elephants are down from 1-million to just half a million in the short space of a decade - and 75 per cent of that drop has been in East Africa. Hardly surprising, perhaps, for when we started travelling ivory was $7 a kilo, while now it fetches $200. In Kenya today, tourists are quite likely to see poachers being gunned-down by the army - as happened just metres from one horrified American group.

Things were a little more relaxed in the middle of the Seventies - certainly more relaxed than we were when an enormous whoofling, snuffling sound sent us careering into the imagined safety of our car. It turned out to be a honey-badger, playing havoc with our possessions left outside in its forage for food. The next morning we awoke in the car to stare up at an obscured sky through our wire-mesh roof; the obstruction was a lynx staring back at us from his vantage-point atop the vehicle. We dared not imagine the consequences of anything heavier wandering across our flimsy ceiling. What availeth the two thin panels of supporting hardboard, if a lion should drop in for tea and two people?

Months before, we had decided to try and crack a particularly difficult nut in Africa: we would hammer on the door of Ethiopia, a country not renowned for its welcome to overland travellers. The reason was as much personal as it was geographic, for we had friends working in Addis Ababa. Looking back we realise they must have been good friends indeed, for us to tackle 3,200 kilometres of the worst road we had ever encountered, a road which did more to mature our car and our ideas of adventure than any other we had driven so far.

We had been warned, but those warnings only struck home as we bumped, crashed, slid, jarred, juddered, crunched, and scraped day after day through the 1,600 kilometres of nothing between Nairobi and Addis Ababa. The frightening toll on our car mounted, as we threw away two wrecked tyres and their shredded inner-tubes. The steel panzer-plate underneath the car took on the appearance of a cheese-grater as the lava-desert rocks did their worst, and as the days of jarring progressed we constantly asked ourselves just how much more pounding we and the car could take.

Getting the visas had been the easy bit, despite the fact that the Ethiopians were enmeshed in a revolution and were not overly keen on any outsiders - let alone journalists - witnessing the lack of niceties involved. Confusion may have helped, for the officials at the embassy in Nairobi were more concerned with crossing out every mention of the word "Imperial" on our stamped visas and their forms, than checking to see whether I was indeed the innocuous teacher which my passport claimed.

Off we went across the Equator before they could change their minds, and reality hit us at the police-post in remote Isiolo, where civilisation suddenly stopped. "You can't possibly make it in that small car," warned the friendly police-sergeant. "Only trucks, Land-Rovers, sometimes Volkswagen buses with high ground-clearance, and once an old Citroën DS with suspension-height set on maximum, have been known to get through. See you back here in a day or so!" And he waved us on, certain we would turn tail once we saw what lay ahead.

He probably did us a favour. For though the thought of retreat did cross our minds, pride and a misguided determination to prove him wrong prevailed as we left the last piece of asphalt we were to see for days to rattle along the Great North Road.

"Road" is a euphemism; it consisted for the most part of heaps of stones laid out denoting a route across the treacherous lava desert. Trucks scattered the sharp stones during their infrequent passing, leaving a giant and lethal ridge in the middle, a ridge it was impossible to skirt. For mile after punishing mile our car became a lightweight grader, its belly scraping over the heaped stones in a cacophony of machine-gunning noise. The dust was all-enveloping; closing the windows kept out some of the dust, but it also kept out the air and kept in the heat. Within minutes of starting out each day we would look like mobile sand-dunes, resigned to the knowledge that there was no point in removing the dust, which would speedily settle again. We couldn't, even if we wanted to: on the seven-day run (if we were lucky) with no water available on the way we had only what we could carry in our two jerrycans. That meant a strict ration, besides what we needed for drinking and cooking, of two "luxury cups" of water each per night. We could choose what to do with this luxury, whether brushing our teeth or cleaning our faces and hands. Love maintained the bond of attraction between these two pigpens of people, but I shudder to think what strangers met en route would have thought. Or perhaps they wouldn't, for they would hardly have been truffles for the senses themselves.

(Years on, back in the bosom of respectable society, we told a muddle-headed banker friend about this brief stage of our travels and the rough-and-ready hygiene it entailed. Later he created instant social pariahs by his enthusiastic introduction to guests at a plush cocktail reception: "This is Terence and Elise Kennedy, who drove through Africa and they didn't wash for months!" Our corner of the room cleared within minutes).

Back on the non-road north, we were having tyre trouble at the rate of three punctures a day. Before setting out from England it had taken four hours to change our first tyre ever, much to the exasperation of our mentor. By the time we hit Ethiopia we had it down to an exact art. Using a spare wheel only doubled the labour, so it stayed where it was as Elise scrabbled for the patches while I raised the car. Off would come the wheel, with only vigorous bouncing up and down in hiking-boots necessary to break the bead thanks to the smallness of 2CV tyres. Out with the old tube, a quick check for any protrusions inside the tyre, and while I stuffed a prepared tube back in, Elise would be at work glueing a patch onto the damaged tube, allowing it a few hours to cure before the next puncture. Leaping on the footpump 60 times would have the wheel quickly inflated, and it was up and away once more in an average elapsed time of 11 minutes.

Sometimes the process was quicker than at others, notably when the car once went into its familiar slew with three armed Somali tribesmen approaching about eight minutes away on the horizon. Discretion being the better part of valour where the often-notorious wandering Somalis are concerned, that was one pit-stop which would have done a Grand Prix proud.

Sometimes the process was more painful than others, notably when I didn't remember to put tools not currently in use under the car, out of the sun. Blistering my palm with a tyre-lever turned searing by the sun often elicited a very heated "Good gracious me" or words to that effect...

It wasn't long before our shock-absorbers retreated in shock and our wheel-rims resembled stone-age man's first attempts at transport, but still we smashed on through wild, lonely desolation. Locked in our cage for the night we would look out at the animals roaming free: elephant, antelope, ostrich, warthog, hyena. The silence was so intense that relieving ourselves sounded like the onset of the monsoon, and whole days would go by without seeing a soul. When we did, as often as not it would be a solitary walker appearing from nowhere, sometimes walking for days on end between scattered settlements, sleeping rough and eating from sparse trees or a small bundle of wrapped food.

That food was as unidentifiable to us as ours was to them, and heaven knows what they would have thought of the enormously-appreciated luxury Elise gave me as a birthday present on that long and grinding road: a jar of mint sauce, imported from England. For weeks it was savoured by the rationed spoonful, but we were less selfish when an old warrior came to investigate our pineapple.

We had bought the fruit days before in Mombasa, before setting off, and were just starting into it when he appeared, dusty and respectful. Elise cut him a slice and passed it across. He took it with a grizzled hand, turned it this way and that, sniffed it, prodded it, squeezed it and uttered a little yelp of surprise when it leaked. He watched as we ate, then mimicked our movements with half of his own slice, nibbling cautiously and with obvious delight. The other half he carried carefully back to the village to display.

We would have missed the border if our Michelin map hadn't warned us it was there. Just a dusty shack set off one of the several vague tracks north, with a tattered flag atop a bent pole. Yet there was patriotic pride in that flag. For at six o'clock precisely by Immigration's watch a whistle blew and the scene looked like a still from a film. Everyone froze. Not just stopped what they were doing - they actually froze in mid-movement, with arms or legs raised in mid-stride while a soldier lowered the red, yellow and green colours for the night. Arm over arm he brought it down as though being watched by thousands instead of a dusty dozen. Then he blew the whistle again and life's projector resumed running.

The last 900 kilometres from the border to Addis Ababa was immensely trying, and not just because the ill-defined track often ran parallel to a gleaming new asphalt road which was barred to traffic because, rumour had it, the contractors hadn't been paid. Many times the track would peter out, or splay into a confusing tangle of directions, and we would have to stop to reconnoitre on foot, often climbing the foothills of the astonishing four-metre-high anthills to search for a landmark.

The gradients were daunting, sometimes forcing Elise out of the car to walk or push while I coaxed and swore through ditches and awful inclines. In one steep village a policeman waved to us to stop; I didn't dare, for I knew we would never get the car going again on that ridiculous hill, and for hours afterwards we expected police retribution around every bend.

At Mega a huge moonscape of a hill loomed, studded with boulders and there was no way we were going to make it. Two swarthy Ethiopians were happy to push Elise pushing the car, and we did. Further on we took a run at a long morass of a muddy hill and slithered to a stop within a few camel-burps of the top. We floundered around ineffectually in the slime, taking on the look of swarthy Ethiopians ourselves, but were only ultimately rescued when an earth-mover with tyres each twice the size of our car came splattering upwards towing a bulldozer. We were allowed to attach our tiny towrope to the train and up we went with no payment asked.

It took us seven days to reach Addis, having encountered hardly that number of other vehicles. We were happy to be there; less happy knowing we would have to struggle the same 1,600 kilometres back again.

Today Ethiopia is infamous and pitied as a cradle of world famine; then it was still a showpiece, the headquarters of the prestigious Organisation of African Unity, with its capital playing host to more embassies than could be rustled up in most of the rest of black Africa put together. The revolution changed a lot of that, as the country's planning degenerated into a one-armed bandit incapable of delivering all three oranges at once. The new Marxist-leaning government hiccupped along as its policies deteriorated into octopus flailings, leaving scars all too evident today.

The seeds were already being sown as we arrived, with the former Emperor Haile Selassie, "Lion of Judah, King of Kings" and several etceteras, locked in the now non-Imperial Palace as the endless war in Eritrea ground on amid rumours of appalling atrocities on both sides.

The tragic consequences of Ethiopia's political turmoil were still just beginning as we trundled into Addis Ababa, a sprawling metropolis offering more contrast than most of Africa's new capitals. Here indeed were the glittering skyscrapers, the wide boulevards, the trappings of Westernisation. But here too, cheek by jowl with the luxury, were the dismaying vistas of tin-shanty roofs, the shacks, the ghettoes, the beggars and the disease. Here were the children imploring you on every street corner, hands outstretched: "No mother, no father, no sister, no brother!" Here were the police whose corruption caused expatriates to carry a ten-dollar bill folded in their driving-licence as insurance against endless harrassment. Here, also, was the frequent night sound of gunfire. It didn't do to enquire too deeply; safer simply to accept the odd reports of nightly executions of those summarily found to have betrayed the revolution.

Our friends were in an invidious position. Barry and I had gone hungry together in London years before, counting out our coppers to see whether we could nurse a coffee-bar cup together by night, writing literally scores of media job applications by day. I finally returned to the music business and went on to become the object of Elise's luckily-brief "hate at first sight." Barry's destiny was more straightforward, as he and his wife Sue and children headed for Ethiopia.

He had landed a news-editing post which was to bring him into conflict with his conscience, his employers and the authorities, as he grappled daily with the complexities of getting out to the world the true story of Ethiopia's agony. Sometimes he was more successful than others, resorting to subterfuges which involved anything from using one of half a dozen pen-names, to spy-movie midnight meetings in deserted car-parks with conspiring embassy staff. The subterfuge was necessary, as many a deported journalist found in a tightly-controlled atmosphere where outgoing telexes were almost openly read by the authorities, and where journalists who had photographed riots in the middle of town were told by officialdom in hardly-veiled terms that there had been no riots and that was that or else.

Barry's local employer was the improbable Radio Voice of the Gospel, a Lutheran station set up at a cost of millions of dollars to spread The Word to Africa and abroad. The Swiss backers soon realised that Godspeak on its own was hardly a crowd-puller, and so journalists were brought in after considerable heart-searching. It was an uneasy marriage at best; journalists by their nature tend not to be deeply religious human beings, drawing their solace more often from cynicism and a well-written expense account than from any higher force. But sugar was needed on the gospel pill, and an efficient team of multinational, even agnostic hacks was excused the compulsory Morning Devotions to run what became a highly popular news service; highly trusted, too, for its balance and impartiality in everything except the restricted Ethiopian news.

Overall, though, the station's modus operandi could occasionally reduce the audience to stunned disbelief - or just reduce the audience. When one programme failed to take the air on time, a harrassed announcer grabbed a microphone five minutes later to apologise breathlessly for the technical difficulties which had been caused by, er, technical difficulties. When tapes had to be edited it was not always done by the usual method of dubbing back and forth between machines, but by young know-all Ethiopian technicians actually cutting the tape into unmanageable spaghettis - which could often never be put together again.

On one occasion the powers decided that a "hard-hitting listeners' problem programme" would boost audience figures, and listeners were invited to send in their personal problems to have them discussed on the air by an eminent team. Old hands feared the worst, and they were right:

"Our first question on the programme comes from a young Moslem lady in Sudan, who writes that she is in love with a Christian man who is already married, and that she is pregnant with his child. She is at her wits' end - her parents have thrown her out, the boy's parents vow murderous revenge on her family and she has contemplated suicide. What should she do?"

"The answer is quite clear," declared the most grise of the Lutheran eminences. "She should pray to God, and He will help her. Next question."

The programme had a predictably short life, and Evelyn Waugh, who set - and wrote - his insultingly hilarious media novel "Scoop" in Ethiopia, was vindicated once more.

On our second week in the heavily-guarded, machine-gun-patrolled compound where the expatriate staff lived under the constant and suspicious eye of revolutionary guards, I was taken to meet the architect of it all, the Scandinavian-born station head and local agent for Himself Upstairs.

He approached across his office, tall, immensely reverent and with an expression which was not so much a smile as a crack in his face. The outstretched hand pumped forward like a piston, his heels clicked smartly together and he bowed from the waist as he snapped the local Amharic greeting: "LUNDGREN!"

At least I assumed it was Amharic and a greeting, and so, very carefully, I shook his hand and returned: "Lundgren."

"No no, LUND-gren!" he repeated. I did the same.

A colleague rescued us from further silliness by pointing out that I had just been introduced to Mr. Lundgren. Surprisingly, I was still offered a job - which had I only known it in that climate of imminent disaster, would have been a little like qualifying as an airship pilot the day the R101 crashes, or taking passage on the Titanic after it hit the iceberg. I was ultimately spared the well-paid martyrdom of the rest of the staff by ending-up, after a paperchase lasting weeks, as the first foreign journalist to be refused a work-permit by the new government.

I was by no means the last. Particularly unfortunate was a British "fireman," or roving reporter, who joined our bunch of hacks out at Addis airport when the infamous German Baader-Meinhof gang had hijacked a Lufthansa jet called "Afrika" which was rumoured to be heading our way.

After hours of standing about we heard the sound of an aircraft, far too high to be more than a dot in the sky.

"Look, it's a German plane," said the wise-guy English scribe. "I can see the name clearly on the side: Afrika, with a k."

His remark was overheard, and Afrika with a k had him severely grilled for making fun of the continent and gross disrespect.

RVOG was nationalised by the revolutionary government not long after we left, and today as Radio Voice of the Revolution can boast the finest equipment in Africa, thanks unwittingly to the Lutheran Federation. One of their radio-evangelist associates has since offered me a long-term contract or six on the understanding that I first spend several months touting my cap around Europe to beg my own subsistence salary from well-off believers, no foreign coins please.

Unsurprisingly, they are consistently short of journalists, and at last count the rough tally was one.

Pausing only to offer condolences to an expat who had waited eight months for delivery of a Citroën 2CV similar to ours, only to see incompetent harbour crane-operators drop it into the Red Sea, we moved out of Addis for a quick fix of reality. We got more than we bargained for.

"Go to the Awash Game Park - if you can," said Addis expats. We couldn't, as we found when the road became a rutted slalom and we slithered and slushed in mud up to the axles, often with the car at a 45° angle and Elise taken suddenly religious. We forded several streams and rivers, then finally squelched to a sticky halt as a lake of slime gulped and swallowed with us as its morsel. The car settled to the chassis, and we were marooned in an Ethiopian bog.

Pushing, shoving and digging only made things worse, and then the warriors arrived, looking distinctly as though The Natives Were Not Friendly. With painted faces and flowing robes, each carried a spear, a dagger and a scowl. Only capitalism could save us, and I pulled out our wad of Ethiopian dollars.

They rejected these vehemently and with jabbing spears, and now it was my turn to be taken religious. As Last Rites loomed, Elise had a brainwave, and dug in her purse for coins. Of course! That was just the trick, in an environment so remote that mere paper money meant nothing but the tangibility of coins was richness indeed. No need for brown trousers for us after all, and even more astonishingly they hoisted up their robes, laid aside their weapons and began to push the car.

The show went on all afternoon as we guided and worked, all becoming more and more mudcaked as the day got hotter. Then the jack broke and we could have screamed in frustration. We probably did, but, finally, the engine coughed and sputtered once more, the car moved, the warriors slackened thinking the feat had been accomplished, I bellowed English obscenities which they understood perfectly well, they pushed again - and we were free. The cost: eight Ethiopian cents after they had refused $20 in paper; a pouch of tobacco and the prize of it all, a little packet of Austrian Pez sweets we had discovered wandering in our baggage. One or two of the warriors wanted the first ride they had ever had in a car, and when that was over we spluttered off into the afternoon towards a painful non-bath. Our water was limited and we were caked in mud - an unhappy combination of circumstances which left us both wincing through the unkindest depilatory of all, as we hacked and hewed at our limbs.

We finally reached a town now once again cut-off from the world as it was the century before we arrived, when that fabled overlander Richard Burton, daringly disguised as a local, was one of the first to rediscover it: Harrar, almost on the Red Sea next to a country of which few have heard, Djibouti or the Territory of the Afars and Issars. Crouched as unobtrusively as possible in a dusty corner of the bazaar we snapped and spied, revelling in a scene which has hardly changed since biblical times. Amid the camels, the merchants squatting on the ground with their colourful goods, the women balancing huge gourds and pots on their heads, the potters at their wheels, the basketmakers weaving, the ladies drawing from the well, only one aspect jarred: a film being advertised in a local cinema, and a South African film at that though it would never have dared to say so.

(In years to come we were to discover so-called "boycotted" South African goods in the strangest places. Usually their origins would be crudely over-stamped with a legend attributing them to Botswana, Lesotho or Swaziland or somesuch improbable place whose manufacturing capacity could be contained in a teabag. The strangest find in the strangest place was undoubtedly the South African Cadbury's chocolate-wrapper we stumbled across in a disused, semi-sand-covered Foreign Legion fort in the middle of the Sahara Desert. We carried it 30,000 kilometres all the way back south again for luck and sent it to Cadbury's in the Cape with an explanatory letter - a P.R.-person's godsend. Not even their computer bothered to reply, and we've eaten Nestlé's ever since).

Back in Addis with our friends we were treated by their Ethiopian helper to the national dish, Injera and Wat. Ethiopia's current starvation could hardly be worse, surely, as we persevered gamely at strips of Dunlop foam-rubber dipped in effluent? Our subsequent picnic far north along the Blue Nile would have tasted better, had we been allowed to enjoy it. We weren't.

The six of us had unpacked our hamper, spread on a blanket looking out over a magnificent gorge. Above us, a lone bird circled.

I raised a hamburger to my lips. Whoosh! Talons raked my hand and the hamburger sprouted wings, borne high as more birds attacked in a scene which could have been straight out of the Alfred Hitchcock thriller "The Birds." Kites, as we later found them to be, swooped and dived on our picnic, ruffling our hair, flapping in our faces, even drawing blood once with their talons as they clawed us out of the way of the food, dive-bombing Barry and Sue who struggled to save their children and the food. We made it to the car in unbelieving disarray, hurling stones in rearguard defence.

Ornithologists later dismissed our harrowing tale. "It simply couldn't have happened," they assured us smugly. "Kites, however hungry, would not attack people."

Months afterwards we had a printed letter from Kodak explaining that a "technical hitch" had caused them to destroy one of our Ethiopian films. The single free film they sent was mean compensation for the disappearance of once-in-a-lifetime shots of an event which could not have happened. Now you have only our word for it. And Alfred Hitchcock's.

9
TOWARDS WHITEST AFRICA

The Camping-Gaz stove sizzled out its aromatic promise of our 365th dinner on the road, as a meandering African paused to look on. With obvious bafflement he studied our cooking arrangements, fascinated by the blue gas cylinder and its two simple burners.

"Eh - what is this?"

We explained: our stove on which to cook food, an answer which worked its way into his understanding like a locomotive slowly gathering steam. After an eternity of ruminating, he was still bothered on one point.

"Where," he puzzled, "do you put the firewood in?"

One year and 50,000 kilometres on, we were in the heart of East Africa once more, survivors of the helldrive road back down from Addis Ababa. Over the Equator we had bounced again, past the milestone denoting the halfway point between the Cape and Cairo, heading through Tanzania and all stations beyond. One year, on a trip planned to last upwards of eight months, and we were still thousands of kilometres and hurdles away from our South African goal.

At this stage we had more will than wallet, but we had survived everything from dysentery to Bradbury's drinking-chocolate so what was mere financial embarrassment? Had we but known it, that liquidity problem would threaten a wedding in the African veld, courtesy of a flying magistrate and a backdrop of hippos, but that lay two months into the future. For the moment we were happy enough sitting in the bush supping our simple meal, basking in the glories of transcontinental gypsy life in a plastic car.

The week had not been without its trials. Sixteen hundred gruelling kilometres we had lurched back down the notorious Addis-Nairobi road and just when we thought it was safe to go back on the tarmac, a policeman built like an armoured car and looking just as endearing stepped out in front of us, a face like a well-kept grave threatening all the friendliness of a kick in the teeth as he ordered us to halt. We stopped, hardly daring to breathe, certain this was to be a shakedown which would hit us hard where it hurts: in the purse.

He scowled malevolently, studying the car, his expression promising service with a snarl. "What kind of car is this?" he barked, his right hand Clint Eastwooding over his revolver.

"Citroën," I ventured, cautiously.

"Okay, I was just curious. Have a good trip!" And he waved us off with a smile like a Steinway keyboard.

We had been incredibly lucky. Only later that day did we discover why all the petrol-stations on our route had been closed. Tanzania, desperately short of fuel and foreign-exchange to pay for it, had decreed Sundays to be car-free days, when driving was punishable by whatever arbitrary retribution local policemen cared to inflict. Today was Sunday.

Much has been written about Tanzania's famous Serengeti Reserve, one of the last real bastions of wildlife. To Tanzania's credit, despite crushing economic hardship and the political pressures which have nibbled away steadily at other reserves, Serengeti has survived largely unscathed, causing the title of one of the most famous wildlife films to be almost prophetic: "Serengeti Shall Not Die." Where Uganda's wildlife is now down by a staggering 90 per cent in two decades, and with other African states on a similar if less-spectacular downhill, Serengeti has lost only one major species in recent years: tourists. The crippling economic morass which is Tanzania today has left its game-lodges without facilities, its tour companies without fuel, its game-parks without resources to pay qualified, dedicated staff. On our last trans-Africa jaunt, some of the lodges could not even offer the visitor any water, so dire were their straits.

But the game is largely intact, and the world's most famous migration still occurs each year, when up to two million animals trek from the south to the north of the isolated park, a distance of some 200 kilometres. To be caught up in that migration is one of the wonders of the world, and neither words nor photographs can begin to convey the sensation of driving through open rolling plains speckled with thousands upon thousands of wild animals: zebra, wildebeest with their young who can and must run within just minutes of being born if they don't want to be a predator's fast-food outlet, antelope, gazelle, giraffe, buffalo - a horizon of animals stretching to infinity.

Here the motorist has no choice but to yield right-of-way to the animals, for there is no way through once they begin to take fright at your presence and begin a mass stampede across the track. The urge grips them in their thousands, and a cloud of dust begins to mushroom skywards as they pound across the veld - a wall of panic ahead of your car, following blindly those who started the stampede. Finally when one demurs, there is a gap and you creep onwards, lost in the magnificence of the wonder you have witnessed, and still the horizon is thick with animals.

At five one morning, still bleary with sleep as we breakfasted beside a river under one of those quite unforgettable African sunrises, we were surprised by two hyena, who were as surprised and possibly as bleary-eyed as we were. They slunk off quietly, much to our relief. Not so the Masai tribesmen later on the rim of the Ngorongoro Crater, who are now so used to tourists that they demand to be photographed in their impressive robes and daggers, and then, unsurprisingly, demand to be paid, as handsomely as their regalia suggests. Our often self-defeating determination never to pay for a picture prevailed, but two Germans following us tried for and took a photo without paying and were beaten to the ground. One does not trifle with the Masai.

Today Mount Kilimanjaro owes its romantic image more to Ernest Hemingway than to reality, thanks to aberrations like the sea of litter intrepid climbers might find when they reach the summit. Like many of life's wonders it was best from a distance, but two young Danish hitchhikers in a nearby campsite had no eyes for the mountain, after parking for the night in the lee of our car for safety. Their eyes were filled with tears the following morning as they described how expert thieves had slit open their tent with a razor while they slept, removing all their possessions from around them, down to rucksacks, passports, money and toothbrushes. Volunteer aid workers, they had served and saved for a year for this trip, which was now just four days old - and over.

Offering hopeless comfort for such despair, how can it be possible to feel sorry for thieves? Yet twice we were caught up in the committing of crimes in Tanzania, and twice we felt pity for the perpetrators.

In Morogoro, a man grabbed a shirt from a washing line and ran. Within seconds a rabble congealed, setting-off in hot pursuit which didn't, couldn't, last long. The thief was run down and set-upon with animal-like vengeance, beaten, pummelled, thrashed and mutilated to within an inch of his life before police arrived to take away what was left of him for round two. Later, as we camped beside a police station in Kerogwe, the sound of a police whistle shrieked out and, as one man, the town emptied as a blood-lusting horde set off for fun in the direction of the whistle, filled with that passion for violence which seems so much part of the African character. Even the police station was abandoned, and when we asked what was going on a man shrugged: "Oh, nothing much. Somebody has done something wrong..."

The severely-beaten wretch was dragged in soon afterwards, dripping blood. And people laughed. To laugh at misfortune is an African trait which has never really been understood by the non-African. Old hands will explain confidently that Africans laugh at the afflictions of others as a form of relief that it has not happened to them. That seems too simplistic by far, and the innate sense of cruelty often found in African humour is another facet which is beyond the grasp of outsiders. Nowhere was it brought home more vividly than in the "joke" which happened on a building-site whose European foreman had given us hospitality.

"Some of my workers," he recalled, "decided to play a prank on a colleague. They heated a bolt over a fire until it glowed red, then used tongs to lay it across the neck of their dozing friend. As the ambulance took him away they were still laughing fit to burst. Some joke..."

"Welcome to Zambia, the friendly country!" it said at the frontier redolent with the sour, dour faces of officials peeved to have their nap disturbed by travellers during working hours. Some travellers bribe or bully their way through borders and everyone has his own technique, none of which works consistently. We call ours the "teeth-and-eyes" approach, smiling and joking very simply as we did when we reached the gloomy office marked "Health Check."

"Ho ho, you don't have to worry about us," we beamed. "We are very healthy people."

No reaction. Then, after an age: "Huh?" So we try again, slowly, and the definitely sub-Einsteinian official decides this is the White Man's strange way of saying he is involved in the health service. He writes me down on the form as "Profession: Doctor." Sigh.

Good old Zambia, which since the story reported worldwide about Zambians being rolled down hills in barrels in training as astronauts, has become to Africa what the Irish are to humour in the Western world. You know the sort of thing: jibes about the Zambian abortion-clinic with a ten-month waiting list, or the Zambian who bought waterskis but was unable to use them because Zambia has no lakes with a slope, or the Zambian firing-squad standing in a circle, or the Zambian kamikaze pilot who is writing his memoirs, or the karate-enthusiast who joined the Zambian Army and killed himself with his first salute... A friendly folk on the whole, they are often their own worst enemy, and do their reputation no good whatever by the sort of blunder which had them arrest an entire expatriate dance-band at the height of the Rhodesian débacle for playing what they construed as a racist-song: "Bye Bye Blackbird." No sooner was the band released than it was rearrested for playing a song obviously in support of the hated Rhodesian leader Ian Smith: "For Ian's a Jolly Good Fellow." At least that's what the secret policeman sent to cover the dance swore it was called.

President Kaunda is regarded as one of the few Good Men of Africa, but he has his blind-spots. Who outside Zambia would not chuckle to read that KK (as he is known) was livid when he arrived on an official visit to the U.S.A., to find the American President himself was not at the airport to greet him? On an evening when all the world's news-bulletins were reporting the end of the Vietnam war and Israeli gunmen on the streets of Johannesburg, Radio Zambia's News was a ten-minute speech by KK decrying the fact that Man has drawn further from God.

Yes, good old Zambia. Back at the border, to cross just 50 kilometres of Zambia in order to reach Malawi you get hit for everything and a bit more. Elise needed a visa, the car needed a month's insurance for a one-hour drive, we had to have a health-check, and needed to put up our £2,000 customs guarantee for the car.

Elise's visa was the worst. The paperwork was fine and tedious, but there was a problem with the payment, the sum of one Kwacha twenty-five, payable only in Zambian money. We had none. Why? Because the official rules specifically prohibit the traveller from bringing in Zambian money. So, without Zambian money which we were not allowed to have we could not enter Zambia, Catch 22 and Joseph Heller would have loved it. (Years later, by way of a postscript, we anticipated the same problem aboard a Zambian Airways plane and decided to sneak some Kwacha aboard, to avoid dehydration when the bar trundled past.

Wrong - on Zambian planes they did not accept their own money under any circumstances, which must say something for its worth. But to return to our visa):

We would, finally, reluctantly, be allowed to pay for it with a sterling travellers' cheque. Now the pantomime was primed. We tendered £5, having agreed that each pound would buy us K1.55. Question: how much was our £5 worth in Kwacha?

Immigration's finest could not do it. The Chief Immigration Officer, drafted in for authority, pondered and willed a solution to appear on his piece of paper which it stubbornly refused to do. Two Customs men filled a sheet with figures, and still no success.

Could we do it, they asked? We already had, in our heads, but wrote it out carefully to salve their pride. They looked at the answer, K7.75, and decided we were trying to cheat them, so the Chief Customs Officer was dragooned. He couldn't do it either. Thus we entered Zambia on grudging trust, and were out an hour later.

We went into Malawi looking as neat as a new pin. How could it be otherwise, when the country enforces a strict but outdated dress code which excludes all but the most respectable of tourists? "Respectable" in their eyes means short-haired and long-skirted or narrow-trousered, and even in the "punk" period when fashion had come full circle and those with short hair were the nonconformists, Malawi went its own sweet way with bits of string at the borders. In case of any doubt whatsoever about male hairstyles, out would come the string to be looped around the head at the victim's mouth-level. Where it met at the back was where hair had to stop, and if it didn't the unfortunate traveller had three choices: a partner or friend could cut it off, Immigration would hack it off with all the finesse of Sweeney Todd the demon barber, or you didn't go to Malawi. Interestingly, my excessive beard which at the time would have won prizes at Crufts, was quite acceptable - a sign of wisdom, they explained and I've never shaved it off since.

Dress rules are similarly eccentric, dating back to the London days of His Excellency the Life President Ngwaze Dr. Hastings Kamuzu Banda (whose mouthful of a title and name must be reproduced in full, as above, at every mention, even in newspaper reports which may never even follow a full first mention with subsequent He said's or The President did's...). His nibs practised in Britain as a doctor just before the momentous Swinging Sixties days of peace, love, Carnaby Street and - in his eyes - total moral degeneration which was not to pervade Malawi under any circumstances. Hence the ban, not only on long hair but on fashions as innocuous as flared trousers.

Like many a traveller in those days I fell foul of the Flared Trouser Squad, which stopped us on the road and examined the pants which Elise had so carefully pinned into improvised drainpipes. Out came the regulation tape measure and printed rules stipulating that the hems of the trousers could not be more than six-fifths the measurement of the knees, and I failed. Elise set to work with needle and thread once more and the threat of a criminal record receded.

Elise, during all this, was sweltering in the Central African heat in a skirt the regulation 20 centimetres below the knees, short skirts - and female trousers - likewise outlawed as a sign of moral decay. That the rules began to look like something out of Lewis Carroll was apparent in the number of scantily-clad and occasionally even naked local lasses we passed on our way through Malawi. It did rather uncharitably cross our minds that this was all a convoluted plot contrived by His Excellency in retribution for perceived wrongs done to him at the hands of the British all those years ago...

I can't vouch for the veracity of one anecdote doing the rounds at the time, but it sounds improbable enough to be true. It had a very forthright tourist turned away from a Malawian bar for wearing a short skirt. Argument with the management revealed that she would only be allowed back if she donned a long skirt. Which she did, and was duly permitted to sup cocktails once more with civilised people. The fact that she had returned topless was neither here nor there, for African women have not always kept abreast of the Western passion for bras... Perhaps it should have been, in a country where kissing is excised from films and where even the line-sketch drawings in knitting patterns, and bits of innocuous Giles cartoons are painstakingly covered by the censor's black felt-tip pen if they display those ultimate symbols of our moral turpitude, legs.

So this was the peculiar little country into which we had slid from Zambia. Slid is the operative word, with not an inch of asphalt to be found anywhere in Northern Malawi at the time and the rains having turned the tracks into fairground rides. We pointed our Méhari at the lake 100 kilometres away and prayed, with the engine screaming in reverse much of the way down in a vain attempt to slow the muddy pull of gravity. Citroën used to offer a free car to anyone who could roll a 2CV in normal conditions, but these were hardly normal conditions and we weren't inclined to test the offer. We slithered sideways into a ditch, but stayed miraculously upright, then hit a mudbath and went careening off into the African jungle.

Our labours were rewarded in Karonga when a local expat stared at us in surprise.

"Where on earth did you appear from?" he asked, knowing Karonga had only as many vehicles as he had fingers.

"Chitipa, the Zambian border," I said, trying to be as nonchalant as possible about it all.

"In THAT??" he exclaimed, pointing at our mobile mud-pack in almost-disbelief. And shaking his head: "There haven't been buses or trucks on that road for weeks, and even Land-Rovers have been finding it impassable." Our car glowed with pride, albeit invisibly under the mud, where it was the same bright red colour taken on by Elise several days later when she found herself struggling alone and forever up one of the region's most notorious, sweltering mountain passes.

The object of the exercise had been simple: to continue heading south.

"Impossible!" declared the same friendly expat. "You'll have to wait for the weekly steamer down Lake Malawi, because you'll never manage the road ahead in that toytown car of yours!" A red rag to a bull has somewhat the same effect, and it wasn't long before we were off on the non-road south, where all went bumpingly well until we hit the Livingstonia Pass.

Scottish missionaries built the road in 1805 and rumour has it it hasn't been maintained since. With a perverse sense of humour they included in its impassability some 24 hairpin bends helping to take you up the mountain at a gentle 45° angle over a moonscaped seven kilometres What could we do but try, and within a few hundred metres it was obvious that our game little car was simply not up to this ridiculous challenge. There was only one thing for it: Elise would have to go.

I said a prayer, whispered sweet nothings to the car and the loss of Elise's modest weight was enough to claw it up the first few rugged inclines. On the third it slithered ignominiously back down, all the way to the beginning for yet another push from Elise. Half-an-hour later the exercise had taken on the appearance of a motorised snakes and ladders game. All caution was thrown to the wind while the car charged ahead at blind corners, scrabbling for a tyre-hold while I wrenched at the steering-wheel, aiming, yelling, pleading, swearing and actually having the time of my life, imminent destruction of our house or no.

Willpower, luck, tenacity and a seemingly-unburstable 28 horsepower grappled us to the top. And Elise arrived two-and-a-half exhausted hours later looking like a sad tomato in ketchup. She only found out that the pass was seven kilometres and 24 hairpins long once she reached the top; she had trudged around each bend expecting the sight of her home. One hour on she had switched to auto-trudge, and when she finally staggered to the top, waterless, she was on the verge of severe heat exhaustion. The expedition sweated on.

Malawians are known as the nice people of the region, and truly they are, as hospitality and friendliness we were to experience on this and the subsequent trans-Africa trip were to attest. But they were also, then, among the poorest, certainly in the neglected north where we had trouble buying even the most basic of provisions. Eggs? Yes, you would be told by someone with a wistful look in his eyes, there were some eggs in town a few months ago. And in Nkhata Bay when we asked whether we could buy meat: "Oh, I'm sorry sir, today is Saturday and they only kill a cow on Mondays." This in a town of 7,000 people. Not that we could have bought much had it been available, for we needed to change foreign currency and the bank only drove in every second Friday. When the road was passable. Which it wasn't except for lunatic 2CVs. Once, though, we came across a sack of oranges, and bought it - the entire sack, for the equivalent of 15 English pence and the merchant was unbelievably ecstatic about his good deal.

We moved on southwards, ever southwards being our simplified goal for the rest of the trip. We had reckoned without the knowledgeability of the Nkhata Bay police.

Michelin makes wonderful maps, but in Africa roads can disappear almost overnight in the rains - witness the infamous and grandly-named Pan African Highway which is supposed to be the main arterial through Central Africa. A decade hence we would find it to be just the nightmare memory of a highway, which enmeshed us in foliage and breakdowns both mechanical and (almost) mental. Malawi had a road like that, placed on the map with unarguable certainty, guaranteed good by the Nkhata Bay police whom we made a point of asking, and turning out to be about as passable as a rat ingested by a python.

Trouble was, we only found that out 140 difficult kilometres down the track, after crawling and clawing our way through mud sometimes up to our knees. A major bridge was down, and had been for months and damn the Nkhata Bay police. No side roads, no detours, no alternatives, nothing for it but to turn and crawl all the way back, often with the sympathy and physical assistance of local people who would do anything to help up to and including walking miles bearing wood which, unasked, they would stack under the car's rear wheels for grip, despite my explanations that this was something they hadn't seen before, a front-wheel-drive car.

A deep breath and eventually we made it back, having covered an average of minus-90 kilometres a day. Then, by a circuitous route, on to an uneventful run through Zambia and down to the fabulous Victoria Falls at Livingstone. "The Smoke That Thunders," the locals call it, and for us it was the pot of gold at the end of a very impressive rainbow as we contemplated the awe-inspiring spectacle of some 25-million litres of water a second, and a kitten, crashing over the precipice.

We did a classic double-take. A kitten, for god's sake? But there it was, being pushed towards the edge by a troop of baboons which were having a grand time of it, batting this tiny bundle of ginger fluff and its tabby brother back and forth towards the chasm.

Had we thought about it longer than a microsecond we would never have done what we did: charged the baboons at full tilt, bellowing and threatening. Baboons can be bad for your health, and have frequently been known to maul and kill people. Our charge was only marginally less foolhardy than the Light Brigade at Crimea, surprising the baboons as much as it did us and yielding fewer casualties - namely, one tabby kitten which they dragged along mewling in the general retreat. The ginger had been saved at the cost of several days' supply of adrenalin - but what to do with it? A pet does not fit in at all with an overlander's rough-and-ready, cramped, travelling life filled with bureaucracy which makes the forms you need for your car look like a paper-shortage compared with those you need for a cat. We did the only possible thing - kept the cat, and for the next two years we were three thanks to our aptly-named companion Victoria, hurriedly renamed Victorio when adolescence made several facts of life saliently obvious.

It quickly became apparent that we would be unable to take a cat of that young age through all the approaching borders legally, so smuggling was the only avenue open. At first we enlisted the help of a local vet, who joined the conspiracy by giving us some special sleeping tablets. They worked wonderfully - had they been pep-pills. Within minutes of eating them Victoria/o went into overdrive, hurtling around the car like a demented helicopter. Mass destruction of property proceeded at a dizzying pace and the border loomed along with our despair. Then, miraculously, as we approached the gates, our supercharged moggy suddenly ran out of puff, crawled into the concealing box we had prepared, and fell deeply asleep. She remained that way as we rocked across the Zambesi River on the famous Kazungula Ferry linking Zambia with Botswana, and stayed cocooned and invisible as we headed for Civilisation.

At least that was how we planned it. With Rhodesia still a bastion of White power suffering the labour-pains of its destiny as Zimbabwe, we had reckoned on an easy entry marking the end of the long, 60,000 kilometre haul through unknown territory, and the beginning of a relaxed, coasting holiday amid the trappings of Westernisation. It had been a hard road we had travelled, but we had persevered, and conquered, and here came the payoff, our cherry on the top.

"PROHIBITED IMMIGRANT." The stark reality on top of the form swam before our disbelieving stares, as delusions of justice crumbled and the White Rhodesian immigration officer boxed us in a cage of rules as effectively as a rabbit trapped in headlamps. We just couldn't grasp what was happening, so unprepared were we for this utterly unexpected turn of events. Could this really be happening after having struggled so far? Just when we thought our troubles were over could they really be just beginning? "P.I.'d" out of the one country where we had fondly imagined, if not brass bands and a mayoral reception, at least a hand-pumpingly warm welcome? All the way through dozens of Mickey Mouse countries and problems up to our eyeballs to reach southern Africa, and then THIS?

I'll swear Officer Bryce almost enjoyed it as he sank to the occasion, rubbing salt in the wound once more as he laid it out for us with childlike simplicity.

"You are not married. That is your own business," though his disapproval was obvious. "Not being married, you carry different passports. The British one is acceptable, the Dutch one is not without some guarantee that the said Dutch citizen will actually leave Rhodesia after her 'holiday.'"

We produced our £2,000 international customs guarantee on the car, normally accepted in lieu of a return ticket by even the most backward of countries,

Now and then - *Above:* an embarrassment of awards for long-distance travel beyond the call of wanderlust, during a recent gathering of thousands of international 2CV fans. *Below:* In the Beginning, preparing the first plastic-and-hardboard Méhari 300,000 kilometres, 74 countries and several filled passports ago.

Above: one more extremely flat tyre, of the 36 on the first African trip. The four hours it took in England to do the first tube-and-tyre change came down to eleven minutes somewhere around Ethiopia.

Left: ever-present carpet-sellers are an irritation during stops at Turkish caravanserais. This one was less irritating than most; it was Elise.

Below: the Africa of everyone's imagination, where animals have the right of way and roadsigns warn "Beware of Elephants."

Above: bespattered with mud after hours of Méhari-unbogging, Ethiopian warriors claim their reward - a handful of "real" cents after they rejected fifty times as much when it was offered as paper money.

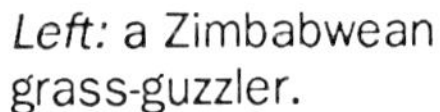

Left: a Zimbabwean grass-guzzler.

The Pan-African Highway on a good day.

Oh the romance of it all, amid a Saharan sea of sand so silent you can almost hear the sun setting. But oh the hard work, when the car prefers to make its way through the desert instead of over it.

for it's perfectly obvious that someone who drives in in a foreign-registered car will have to drive out again and not fly. Not to Bryce, nor to his rules. Only a return ticket to Amsterdam would suffice - or the cash equivalent.

We breathed a sigh of relief at this last way out. Our wallet was emptied, our piggy-bank pillaged, our emergency dollars brought into daylight for the first time in 14 months. An Amsterdam ticket needed the equivalent of 375 Rhodesian dollars. We did our counting, and we had 350.

"Nope, sorry, no good, I'd like to let you in but it's more than my job's worth," he smirked. Discarding the last vestiges of our tattered pride, we pleaded, we begged, we offered to make up in any way possible the tawdry 25 dollars which was all that stood between us and the vital home-stretch. It was like arguing with an Easter Island statue.

The impasse lasted six days as we languished in no-man's-land between countries. We could not go on - but had no new visa to go back, and so we hovered, non-persons living nowhere, while a sympathetic Scots samaritan on the Botswanan side checked regularly to see whether we had enough food and water. Telephone calls and telexes whizzed back and forth, depleting our capital still further. Finally it seemed there was only one solution, and a drastic one at that: marriage.

Elise's Dutch nationality was the sticking point when the mess was boiled to its basics. Were she but British, even nominally British, civil service logic said she would be less likely to be a penniless burden on Rhodesia. I can scarcely pretend to understand the reasoning, but if wedding bells were what it took, wedding bells it would have to be. We weren't exactly wallowing in a sea of alternatives.

Trying to get married in an African nowhere isn't that easy, we quickly discovered. True, there's a magistrate who does it if you can persuade him to fly in, and if the weather allows, and if you can produce the necessary references (we had trouble in that non-national wilderness just producing a meal, never mind references), and so the obstacles mounted as we began to see ourselves as a non-Flying Dutchman of the road, doomed to moulder forever with no port in sight.

And on the seventh day they rested and saw that it was good - thanks to contact with two wonderful friends in the Rhodesian city of Bulawayo, who moved heaven and earth and dollars from their savings account to put up a guarantee for us, and we were in, little the worse for wear and renewed in our faith in the basic goodness of human nature with the exception of Mr. Bryce.

On the Rhodesian side of the Victoria Falls we met our first South African. A caricature cartoon could not have been more typical, and he slopped over to us looking like a one-man slum, rough enough to strike matches on, with his hand enveloping the inevitable can of beer as he addressed us in an accent so thick it could break rocks.

"Hey man, where youse people from, hey?"

His enthusiasm for the idea of overland travel knew no bounds once we had explained where we had been.

"Ja, ach no, 'ell man, you know I wish I could blerry-well go through Africa!"

A little difficult, which is to say impossible on a South African passport, we pointed out. He pondered this for some time, then hit on the solution.

"Ach no man, I knows how I could do it!" he proclaimed, strangling himself on his Afrikaner accent, his mutilated vowels and crashing consonants sounding like a man walking across gravel. "I could get a blerry British passport, an' then, an' then - they wurr'nt even KNOW I were Syeowth Effrican!"

So we meandered through this splendid penultimate country on our trip while a delegation of family and friends prepared to welcome us in South Africa. A job worth sixpence slightly marred our arrival.

We had stopped in Salisbury to drink a final cup of coffee before setting out on the last leg. Mindful of the welcoming party, I was proud of the way the car looked: immensely authentic, the true battered and splattered veteran of 60,000 grubby kilometres, replete with the impressive mud, dust and dirt which told much of our story for us. That was before the coffee.

As we left the coffee-bar, a young black lad stood beaming at us, palm outstretched at the end of an arm on which dangled a bucket.

"I cleaned your car very good, boss!" he smiled. "You give me sixpence!" I wanted to give him much more, but Elise restrained me.

All that was left was to end as we had begun - in chaos, when we picked with a pin the only border into South Africa which turned out to be washed-away in the rains. "Welcome to South Africa," said the sign - on the other side of a raging torrent of a river, with no bridge. Back we went for yet another day of minus-90 kilometres.

Were we doomed not to reach our goal intact, I wondered the next day as a Transvaal policeman waved us down after an intersection?

"Man, didn't you see that sign back there?" he demanded. "It said clearly S-T-O-P, stop. If it had wanted you just to slow down like you did it would have said so: P-A-W-S."

But we were in, and nothing remained of the trip but for Elise to be stung by a bee, then for us to spend time coming to terms with the static life in a generously-donated Johannesburg apartment. Inevitably, depression set in, the low at the end of 14 months of constant highs. The trip of a lifetime had suddenly stopped and we were at a loss how to cope.

It's a hell of a thing at the age of 25 to realise that's it, the end of the road and, to all intents and purposes, the dramatic part of your life is over with about half a century left to kill time. For this was the trip which was supposed to work out our wanderlust for good, leaving the way clear for pastoral suburban existence, mortgage and all. Only trouble was, we didn't feel very suburban, and especially not in Johannesburg. Not even in South Africa, come to that, with its daft - and doomed - politics somewhere to the right of Hitler.

But we P-A-W-S-ed, long enough at least to get married, which had always been on the cards even if one upright member of our family sweetly believed we had slept in separate bunks - one upstairs, one down - in our cubic metre halfway around the world. The wedding was as prone to a touch of Murphy's Law as everything else we had done.

I suppose it was my fault for not warning Elise, still coming to terms with the vagaries of English as a very foreign tongue, that there was a verbal minefield to be negotiated before we were joined in matrimony. Hell, she couldn't even say "matrimony," so how could she possibly be expected to repeat that she knew of no "lawful impediment" why she should not be joined in it? There was an expectant lull while the magistrate waited for her to repeat the impediment he had just mangled in his thick South African accent. She looked at me in terror, then shrugged.

"I know no awful implement," she duly repeated, and another classic was added to the repertoir, joining the Fray Bentos she had discovered on the curtain of our car (a praying mantis) and the fine upstanding dinner-hosts whom she had once thanked for their hostility.

That we would live happily ever after there was little doubt, but where? It turned out to be Rhodesia, Officer Bryce's efforts notwithstanding, and it was less than two years' worth of ever-after before we realised we were no more ready to settle than jelly without the gelatine. The next continent beckoned, America, but ahead was an enjoyable taking-stock hiatus.

After living 14 months in the back of a tiny plastic car the idea of rattling around in a house like tiny peas in a giant pod filled us with horror. The answer was a caravan, still cavernous by Citroën standards, as we set out to earn the money we needed to buy our next travel-fix. Elise removed years and folding oblong from ladies in a beauty-salon, while I shamelessly wrote and uttered Governmentspeak for the national radio and television stations. The good days were made even better by the hiccups and blunders which went with the territory.

How many TV newsreaders can claim to have read a bulletin while an escaped cage-full of wild birds from the preceding wildlife programme flapped and squawked around the single studio, threatening to attack the announcer or at best deface his script? Or to have made entirely the wrong sort of reputation with on-air clangers like omitting the letter "m" from West German Chancellor Helmut Schmidt's surname?

All programmes were live because of the economic sanctions on Rhodesia which blocked the import of video equipment (though one complete transmitter did get in while I was there, breaking the sanctions by being consigned, improbably, to a fish-and-chip shop in Mozambican Beira). The scope for blunders was thus immense, and during a live sports programme a colleague flung his lapel-microphone onto his chair during a commercial break as he rushed to answer an urgent call of nature. He made it back to the studio just in time to fall into his seat and waffle once more. There were puzzled looks in the control room at the lack of sound until the penny dropped and a grinning technician waved a board at the announcer: "For God's sake don't fart!"

Our travels were put firmly into perspective during one of the talks and slide-shows we were pressed into doing for everyone from schoolchildren, usually an immensely rewarding audience to address, to womens institutes who would often have been happier with a Tupperware demonstration. Before just such an ordeal, to the clatter of teacups and sticky buns, I was asked whether the talk I would give would be illustrated.

"Yes, with slides," I replied.

"Oh how lovely!" exclaimed our vacuous hostess. "I absolutely LOVE slides! I could watch them for hours!" Elise managed to disengage me rapidly before I started to suggest several types of slides she might just not absolutely love.

Over the years we've kept gleeful count of the accidents we have caused - totally blamelessly on our side; is it our fault that other motorists stare at our strange vehicle when they should be looking at the road ahead and have their cars remodelled for their inattention? In Rhodesia we chalked up something rather special, though: a police patrol-car which wandered over to the wrong side of the road, then onto the pavement, and finally along a wall which refused to yield to the law. Admittedly I might have done the same had I, like them, spied Noddy's little red plastic car (our stripped-down Méhari, commandeered for a yuletide nursery-school treat), careening along carrying Father Christmas ringing out his ho-ho-ho's, and driven by a red-bearded and rangy Little Noddy whose total height, including pointed cap with dingaling bell, topped two-and-a-half metres...

The nadir was without doubt my being arrested in Botswana as a Rhodesian spy.

A colleague in the newsroom, hot-headed to a fault, had been picked up by Botswana police for filming a border-post, never a good idea in the Third World. A humble apology might have been his salvation, for the Tswana are essentially good folk, but his ill-considered torrent of abuse, vitriol and racist slurs ensured that he and the two innocent staff-members who were on the assignment with him were put away for six months. It was a harsh and obviously unjust punishment, and the station's powers decided a futile gesture was called for. A couple of volunteers were needed to go and plead his case. Rhodesians would not do, and as there were only two British passport-holders on the station, the other being the chief engineer, we were volunteered with mixed feelings and an earnest pumping of hands while imaginary anthems played and colleagues promised to look after our wives, if. Cause enough for immense concern.

Tony and I set off in the Méhari the several score dusty kilometres to the place where our colleagues were held, Francistown, and were promptly arrested before we could plead their case. Three hours of grilling by a firing-squad lineup of policemen had us pleading our own case instead, endlessly fielding accusations that we were spies. We remained up against the whitewashed squadroom wall, under siege as the afternoon wore on and they gradually wore out. Elsewhere in Africa we would have had the scars to show, but the Botswanans are a cut better than that. As dusk settled we were ushered out exhausted, full-bladdered but free. The jailer put away his keys (somewhat reluctantly, we thought), and we had five ineffectual minutes to speak to the lawyer engaged to defend our colleagues. Then we were told to high-tail it back to the border, being arrested again on the way before a radio message said we were free to leave the country and indeed encouraged to do so, or else. Our jailed colleagues served the full six months and emerged a multitude of kilos thinner, with the black one of the three having been mercilessly and repeatedly mistreated as a white collaborator. The idiot who had caused the fiasco in the first place emigrated soon after, now a rabid racist to the core.

For us, too, it was time to move on, albeit reluctantly in what could have been one of the world's most convivial countries. Steinbeck's "hunger to be someplace else" was upon us and our incurable wanderlust beckoned - along with the fact that our two-year period of grace as immigrants was drawing to a close. At the end of it, I would be given an army uniform and a loaded FN semi-automatic rifle like all good white Rhodesians and told to go out and kill people, something I've never been awfully keen on, particularly for such a patently lost cause. (Rhodesians had their own variation on a famous American T-shirt slogan: "Join the Rhodesian Army! Travel the country, meet fascinating black people with interesting points of view, and kill them!")

The end which awaited our very first Méhari was undeserved, to say the least. In the climate of terror and suspicion which pervaded Rhodesia at the time, it fell victim to a terminal misunderstanding. Denied to a millionaire who wanted it for a golf cart, it had been sold instead to a TV producer who drove it home one evening and, in the still African night, heard it ticking ominously after switching it off. Paranoia ran rampant in those days; he leapt out of the car towards the house, shouting "A bomb, a bomb!"

Méharis are renowned for their contracting bodywork and we could have told him about the ticking. But as he crouched in his doorway waiting for his car to light the night sky, without the handbrake having been engaged it slowly gathered freewheeling momentum down his inclined drive and eventually, with a sickening crash, it consumed the solid concrete gateposts and was itself consumed in the engagement. At least it went with a bang, not a whimper.

On my final day at work I handed over to a painstakingly-trained replacement, an aspiring African announcer whose tremendous zeal far outstripped his dubious ability. His first task on the air would be to give the British football scores, and he did me proud as the red light came on.

"Now," he read out, "we have the English Facup results."

10
BRAVE NEW WORLD

"STAY INSIDE THE CAR WITH YOUR HANDS ON THE WHEEL!!"

We froze in the front seats, our feet poised above the Land of the Free as U.S. Customs' right hand Starsky & Hutched towards his holster.

"Lemme see your papers!" he demanded. "Yup, yup, yup," he went as he read them, then: "OK, you folks from Yurup, huh? OK. Well, in the Yewnited States remember never to get out of your automobile like you jest did at an official checkpoint, until specifically told to do so. Welcome to the U.S.A." His face cracked into a plastic smile like a silent scream. "OK. Gimme the papers for this-here Folkswaggon."

"Citroën."

"Huh? No kiddin', you built it yourself?"

"No, it's a French car, a Citroën. They've made six million since 1948."

"Say, is that right, huh?" He repeated the name, then wrote it on his form: Sitreon.

We filled in the basic details required for the twelve-month import of a motor vehicle into the States, right down to the engine capacity which I had converted from its 602cc to something Americans would understand: 36 cubic inches.

"Yup, yup, yup," went Customs as he ticked each detail. He stopped at the 36 cubic inches, thought about it, then added a zero to the figure. "Looks like you kinda made a mistake here, bud."

No I hadn't.

"Now that jest ain't possible," he persisted. "No such thing as a automobile with 36 cubic inches. I got me a rig with 350." On the contrary, we explained that ours was the large, high-powered version, that the standard 2CV had 435cc or around 25 cubic inches which is probably less than the capacity of the average American lawnmower, chain saw, food-processor or automatic toothbrush. His expression faltered, unsure whether he was the butt of foreign humour.

"Uh-huh? OK - how many cylinders? Six? Eight?"

"Two."

"No kiddin'? Horsepower?"

"Two."

"Yup, I jest wrote that. Horsepower?"

"I just said it. Two, by French rating. That's why it's called a 2CV: 'Two Horses' in French."

"Gas mileage?"

"About 16 or 17." I meant kilometres per litre; he wrote it as miles per gallon, four times worse, and nodded, "Yup, not bad. Automatic?"

"If you go too hard it jumps gears by itself."

"How many gears you got?"

"Four: slow, slower and slowest, with an overdrive more like an underdrive. And ultra slow backwards; that's the standard 2CV way of tackling steep gradients."

"Top speed?"

"Seventy miles an hour has been known. Downhill. With a following wind. At sea level."

"Uh-huh. Air-conditioning?"

I paused, not sure how far we could go. What the hell, strike while the irony is hot... "Er, yes, if you turn this knob on the dashboard it opens a flap which lets in fresh air."

He ticked the box marked Air-Conditioning, then looked at the push-pull gearlever sticking straight out of the dash. "What's this?"

"Works the windshield wipers," I suggested, and he nodded comprehendingly.

"Power-steering?"

"Runs off the speedometer cable."

"Fuel injection?"

"Every 250 miles."

"Turbo boosting?"

"Downhill."

"Assisted braking?"

"My wife hauls on the handbrake."

"Generator?"

"Creates a lot of interest, yes."

"Emission control?"

"The gas pedal."

"Cruise control?"

"My size 11's."

"Collapsible fenders?"

"In an accident."

"Rear-wheel drive?"

"If you put it in reverse."

"Padded dash?"

"Soft tin."

"Adjustable steering?"

"Comes off with three bolts."

"Occupant restraints?"

"Our budget."

So far he had ticked everything yes, heedless of reply, yup yup yupping all the way. "Looks like it meets all U.S. federal safety requirements, huh?"

"Er, yes, in the year it was designed."
"Seating?"
"Two. Eight if everyone breathes in."
"Convertible?"
"With a can-opener."
"Any anti-theft devices?"
"The Citroën gear-shift pattern."
"Reversing lights?"
"If you turn the car around."
"Safety-glass windshield?"
"Except if it breaks."
"Automatic windshield washing?"
"When it rains."
"Winter tyres?"
"Summer, too."
"Shocks in order?"
"We're prepared for the worst."
"Muffler?"
"We'll buy a couple if it gets really cold."
"C.B.?"
"'Or not C.B., that is the question.'"
"Huh?"
"No."
"In-Vehicle Entertainment?"
"On rainy days."
"Vehicle fully insured?"
"Except against fire, theft or accidents."
"Spare parts?"

"Standard 2CV stuff: baby-powder for the gear-shift, castor-oil for the springs, Vaseline for the points, mashed bananas in case we lose our gearbox oil, office elastic-bands for the seats, a knitting needle to set the timing, oily paint-brush and an old hypodermic for the suspension pivots, couple of beer-cans for the silencer, chewing-gum for the gas-tank, half a brick to remove the fan, lots of string, and the addresses of 200 American enthusiasts."

His gaze fell on the burglar mesh-wire with its five-centimetre holes, fitted to every window. "Pretty big mosquitos you must have in that there Yurup," he mused, and it was my turn to wonder whether he was, so to speak, extracting the Michael. Finally, with formalities complete:

"Yup, real neat shopping rig you got here, fellah," he complimented. "Does it fit inside your Recreational Vee-hickle or do you haul it behind on a trailer?"

"Neither," I said. We're crossing the States and heading for South America in it."

"In THIS?... Oh, yeah, sure thing," he belched with laughter, pleased now to have realised this was all some kinda weird Yurup-ean joke. "To South America, huh? Yeah, that breaks me up. OK fellah, enjoy your vacation in our fine country." We started to leave.

"Say, one more thing," he stopped us.

"Yes?"

"Have A Nice Day."

I want to lay my hand on my heart or indeed anyone else's and swear that's just how it happened. But I cannot tell a lie. Still, for the most part we did have just what he wished, a Nice Day, and a total of some 250 Nice Days in a country where, as someone once said, anything is possible but most things aren't very probable.

The seed had been planted in Rhodesia the year before, then germinated by months of hard work in Holland as we accumulated the six thousand dollars we thought it would take to get from Canada in the North to Tierra del Fuego, Latin America's southernmost tip. We're still trying to get there, but that's another story. Back in Holland I had regressed to the one trade where I would be working for our trip and not the taxman: playing atrocious wedding and hit-parade music, excellent cash-in-hand and no questions asked, with a group of well-meaning if happily tone-dim Dutchmen. Elise's salary-spinner was just as unsavoury: working nights (so that we both had the days free for preparation) in the kitchen of one of the region's top restaurants, coming home each midnight smelling like the plat du jour.

The car, naturally, was another little Citroën, this time a delivery-van version of the 2CV with corrugated-iron bodywork and the same innards as our trusty Méhari. Again bought tax-free from Paris it was soon gutted as we worked at transforming it on the basis of our previous experience, thereby ensuring we made the same mistakes twice. There were differences. It was nowhere near as high as the Méhari had been, so that putting on pants in the morning moved from a six-stage operation to eight. It had less storage space, so we ended up taking more. But it had real windows, seats consisting of canvas stretched over rubber-bands instead of the foam-covered buckets of the Méhari, and it had one enormous advantage: there would be no more people tapping it at all hours of the day or night saying the same thing in virtually every language of the world: "Plastic!"

The intention was to go to America and keep going until we fell into the Atlantic somewhere just north of Antarctica. If not, we would simply take up our savings and drive anywhere, taking our time about it, and when we had arrived nowhere, we would think about coming back. In an odd perversion of geography our road across America ultimately led to the middle of the Persian Gulf, but that lay 250 Nice Days into the future.

Filling-in the forms for our visas, I pointed out a change in the questions since the first time we had tried.

"I don't see the old question up front here, asking our race," I mentioned to the friendly consul.

"Nope, you got it," he replied. "Things are easin' up on that front, and we can't do that no more."

Indeed. Commendable, I pondered - until I stumbled across the crunch of question 19: "Complexion." Had I only had the courage, or the foolhardiness, or perhaps just the fame, of Peter Ustinov I would have written "pink." That had him waving a mirror at unamused Immigration for three hours in New York's airport...

So by early 1978 we were finally ready for lift-off with the two good friends who were to join us on the first and later parts of the trip, driving an identical 2CV van.

The leaving of Liverpool involved first the obligatory steam-cleaning of the cars so that they would not pollute America, followed by a drive back across Liverpool to replace the germs just removed. Once the cargo ship set sail, we were left on land with two weeks to kill. While our companions wound up their affairs, we decided there was a sufficiently offbeat way to get back down to London and our eventual flight from Heathrow: like Jonah in the Bible we would walk through Wales.

A week later, our aching muscles had opened up whole new vistas of masochism for us, to be saved as a travelling last resort for The Day The Oil Runs Out. Breathing like a tyre-pump with our puffing, panting, willpower-stretching 12 miles a day up hill and down dale over the Offa's Dyke footpath, I reckoned we could walk around the world in five and a half years. Something to be borne in mind... At least we would surely do better than the two Irish hikers we met on the trail, staggering under the killing weight of their backpacks. We asked if they were okay.

"Ah sure we are," one said, resting his awful load against a rock. "We'll be alright once we've eaten some of these 20 pounds of potatoes we found on special offer in the last town."

Our meals were simple - so basic that on one stretch we even proved you CAN make tea over two candles. Wondering only briefly whether sheep could read ("Sheep - please close the gate" the signs often said), we covered 64 miles towards London, and then we were aboard the standby-fare £60 one-way trip to New York in a two-thirds empty jumbo; so empty, as companion Cliff remarked, that if we'd known we could have booked a few seats for the cars.

New York, the Big Apple, was everything the movies said it would be and more, littered with human debris, alive, vibrant, noisy - and foreign. Just how foreign we discovered when we crawled, wet and miserable from too much rain-soaked sightseeing, into a coffee-bar for shelter and hot liquid. We ordered four hot chocolates, happy at the prospect of nursing them in the warmth for the next hour before plunging out into the wintry melée once more.

"Tugow?" demanded the waiter.

"Er, four hot chocolates," we repeated.

"Yeah yeah sure - tugow?" he barked.

When in doubt, agree. Cowed, we did - and ended up back on the shivering street with our hot chocolates in a brown paper bag. "To go" means take-away in Queen's English, not that the Queen ever had a take-away. Later in a pizza-house opposite advertisements for nude fortune-telling, we were more successful. Pizzas are not really native to Italy, so history has it, but were invented by Italian-Americans and must be the closest the U.S. gets to a national cuisine, if you discount items like the "Kosher Hot Dogs" we saw in New York, or the "Government-Inspected Frankfurters," or naturally the mouthfuls of pasty nothing which constitute MacDonalds, Whopper Juniors and all the others notable only for being not notable in the slightest. Our pizzas, true to American form, were not only good; they were warrantied for size if not flavour, each bearing a little flag on a toothpick proclaiming "This Pizza is Guaranteed Twelve Inches Across."

Are New Yorkers as friendly as they're made out to be? "As long as you don't make eye-contact," runs the gag. There's a famous bumper-sticker which says simply: "Welcome to New York. Now go home." Sure they're neither better nor worse than most that we met - with the exception of the young, macho street-cop spoiling for a fight up ahead of us as he provokingly, and wrongly, accused a young black of bumping into his truncheon, while we reflected that it's only in the movies that the cops are invariably the Good Guys.

Word came through that our cars were about to land in Halifax, Nova Scotia, just a matchstick-length away on the map. That matchstick turned out to be 1,600 kilometres long, and we had to book a Greyhound bus-ride or four to get there, stopping for some reading-material at a news-stand advertising "Foreign Papers On Sale Here." I asked for something British, and was met by incomprehension.

"Your sign says Foreign Papers," I said.

"Sure we got foreign papers," replied the man. "From L.A., Chicago, San Francisco, hell, we even got some from as far away as Texas!" It was an oft-repeated concept of "foreign" which was to make us, to some Americans in the months to come, as odd as if we had landed from Mars.

Our first sight of Canada was a Greyhound bus-station toilet, a man sitting quite unselfconsciously with his pants around his ankles, there being no door. Elise was luckier in the Ladies; at least hers had a door which stopped half a metre from the floor. Someone had written on it in lipstick: "Beware of Limbo Dancers!"

As we waited for the car to be cleared in Halifax we popped into the local automobile club, flashed our British membership cards and as good a helpless-foreigner smile as we could manage, and asked if they had a couple of brochures to help us with our touring. They gave us five kilos - a pattern to be repeated throughout North America which is awash in free printed material. At least the Canadians discussed routes with us, unlike the Americans who invariably answered every question with yet another pamphlet or map, each of which had to be defaced by the statutory green felt-tip pen. Even the strip maps showing only one road had to have that road green felt-tipped in case you might think the edge-of-page border was your Route 66.

"So what's England like, big city?" asked the traffic policeman who gave us our first ticket in North America, for driving too slowly on a freeway. (The minimum speed was 40 miles an hour, a physical impossibility for a laden 2CV going uphill. Even with a following wind. Even at sea-level). But we were on the road again, having Nice Days, so what was a mere ticket especially when the address you had given was the time-honoured 12 High Street England? Both vehicles had survived the ocean voyage unscathed, apart from some dirt and salt-spray which we washed-off by breaking an automatic car-wash not designed for tiny, sharp-edged French vehicles.

Where a ticket couldn't dampen our spirits, the bugs did. Canada has four million lakes, according to its brochures. What they don't add is that each spot on each lake has four million bugs: blackflies zooming, buzzing, settling, biting, driving you totally and utterly gibberish. The first hour is fine - you swipe constantly, then think maybe if you ignore them they'll go away. They don't. The second hour you become somewhat agitated, and by late afternoon you're almost delirious, trying to hide under a towel or eating on the trot or running up and down the road to try and outdistance the hungry varmints. By Day Two you're almost reduced to tears.

North Americans, true to form, even make their insects bigger and better than anywhere else. They bite by day and night, even flying around in bucketing rainstorms and howling winds which would splatter lesser breeds into ex-bugs against trees and mountains. By night, trapped in your car, you can swat and murder with black bleak despair, but the Battle of Britain drones on with things going chomp in the night. They dive-bomb, they gnaw through the sheet and eventually, in utter hopelessness, you dress, scramble outside and pace up and down - at two in the morning. Finally, exhausted, you fall into a restless sleep for the last hour to daylight, and awaken looking like a napalmed Vietnam battlefield. The Canadians recommended a net and a powerful repellant. Both worked; you could hardly expect the repellant to do otherwise when the first thing it repelled was the lens of my wristwatch which dissolved instantly.

In the small town of Truro we had our first taste of the typical, trusting North American hospitality which was to overwhelm us all the way, when a lady got to talking, took us to her luxurious lake cabin, then gave us the keys telling us she had to go away for a few days but make ourselves at home. In 17 years of travelling elsewhere that happened only rarely; in North America it happened so often we almost felt guilty whenever, not wanting to be picked up and taken home yet again, we would slink into a forest hoping not to be "discovered."

We had hoped the Frenchness of our car would be a help in stubbornly Francophone Quebec. But the first Quebecois it attracted spoke English.

"Yes, I spent a lot of time in your country as a prisoner-of-war," he revealed, and we mulled that over for a moment, digesting the revelation that our parents had stooped to imprisoning their allies.

"Where?" we asked.

"Oh, somewhere over there. Germany."

He was almost the last Quebecois from whom we extracted spontaneous English. This was the period that nationalism ran rampant under the leadership of a fiercely partisan, separatist "Free Quebec" state government, and with our French then restricted largely to the name of our car and some pungent cigarettes, we were in trouble, in shops where staff refused on principle to serve anyone speaking English - which they all spoke perfectly adequately. We solved the problem as we had done in Greece, by entering spouting a loud babble of Dutch nonsense. As long as they realised we were not the chauvinistic English Canadians, we were okay, and they dusted off their English for an airing.

"Welcome to the U.S.A.," said the sign, more visual muzak among the sea of billboards which was to drive us crazy as we headed ever onwards, deep into a country which it is almost impossible to describe without lapsing into stereotypes. Here were the people who precisely resembled the cardboard characters of American movies: recognisable as types, but with neither depth nor complexity. Yet here too was the warm, trusting hospitality which would eventually almost swamp us.

To discuss anything beyond the ken of most people (which in America most often means anything outside town or state or not covered in the 60-second "sound-bites" which TV news offers) was to offer linguistic Valium, an appalling lack of knowledge of the world around them endemic to so many Americans. A depressingly materialistic society, too, where people insisted on telling us what they had; where they asked questions no European would dream of asking like how much we earned; where in some cases we were first-judged not by our appearance or even the eccentricity of our car but by the answer we gave to the status-setting question: "What year is that car?" (Later we watched a realtor - or estate-agent - friend in Arizona struggle to make ends meet because he was forced to buy a new car every year. "Americans won't buy real-estate from you if you don't drive the latest automobile and look prosperous," he explained).

Every American deems it his constitutional right to dump at least one dead car in his yard, just as he sees it his right to be armed. One restaurant we encountered even had a counter selling firearms, and in a campground a typical mobile-home owner was horrified when we revealed that we carried no gun.

"I got three in my rig," he said, proud of his status as a mobile combat zone.

"One in front, one in the middle, one in the back. YOU NEVER KNOW WHERE YOU'RE GONNA BE WHEN THEY COME FOR YOU!"

Even U.S. museum guards are armed to the teeth, something which could never happen in Britain. Most of our guards have no teeth.

Houses can be put up in one day, as we saw with fascination in Maryland, and homes (Americans always own homes, not houses) can be filled with everything from electric can-openers to the ultimate which we still can't quite believe, an electric fruit-ripener. Food isn't prepared, it's processed, and even their bread is different. All our lives we've managed to struggle along on a mixture of flour, water, yeast, sugar and salt, poor undernourished Europeans that we are. Here's the recipe printed on the first U.S. loaf we bought:

"Enriched flour, Niacin, Reduced Iron, Thiamine Mononitrate and Riboflavin, Water, Whey, Whole Wheat Flour, Sugar, Bran Yeast, Molasses, Butter, Vegetable Margarine, Partially Saturated Soybean Oil, Liquid Soybean Oil, Partially Saturated Cottonseed Oil, Salt, Wheat Gluten, Oil of Soy Flour, Calcium Sulfate, Calcium and Sodium Stearoyl-2-Lactylate, Polysorbate 60, Caramel color, Vinegar, Nonfat milk, Mono- and diglycerides, Calcium Propionate, Malted Barley, Ethyoxylated Mono- and diglycerides, Ammonium Chloride, Potassium Bromate, Azodicarbonamide" and give us this day our daily chemicals.

It tasted like turd.

Yet though only one in a thousand Americans might know what joie de vivre is, most of them have it to a degree Europeans would envy with their stiffness and rigid social codes. Imagine an English wedding, everyone very formal, very polite, and the usual inane toast to the bride and bridegroom. Good insipid stuff as it is and always has been amen. Now relish the American wedding we were sucked into as though in a whirlpool.

Irish-American, in fact. The bride's father, Murphy, sat next to us. At odd stages he would jab us in the ribs, proclaiming: "Say, this beer glass looks like a piss-pot, Holy Jesus!" Then the toast. The best-man stood up. "I'd like to-propose a toast to the bride and bridegroom. May they have a happy life together and all that bullshit." Or the bride's father to us: "Have you eaten?" "No, not yet, thank you" we reply with our old-world politeness. "Well, there's the food," he gestures with a thumb. "Move yer ass!"

Some things are as American as mom's apple pie and bankrupt railroads. The huge roadside billboards urging you simply to "Eat!" - an injunction dear to the heart of many in this land of extreme obesity. In North America everyone is "on the road" at some time or another; it's the world's most mobile society as they trundle back and forth in their pickups, with their caravans or in their unbelievably outsized R.V.'s ("recreational vehicles," the euphemism for multi-roomed houses on wheels in which owners get away from it all by taking it all with them).

A black taxi-driver leans out of his car to shout a long conversation at you in yours quite normally - though you're both doing 60 miles per hour on a murderous six-lane freeway. Other, more typical conversations with "nice" people prove only that deep down, they're really quite shallow; talk comes from no deeper than the mouth, leaving you as bitterly frustrated at the end as a hungry diner who is offered a two-hour meal consisting entirely of hors d'oeuvres. And there's the apparent inability of most Americans in what is a surprisingly prudish country to say the word "toilet," leading to euphemisms ranging from bathroom and washroom to the diabolical "comfort station," and the lady remarking that her doggy "wants to go to the bathroom."

Read an American newspaper. Better still, watch its abysmal television for if television corrupts, commercial television corrupts absolutely, in a lowering of intellectual content to a degree which makes Britain's tits-and-bums tabloid press look positively intellectual. It's little wonder the average American's horizons are so small. Just how small was brought home to us unforgettably in the town of Newburyport, Massachussets.

"Where you folks from?" came the inevitable question.

"Great Britain. We're driving through the States."

"Is that right? Say, how long did it take you to drive here from Great Britain?"

"You can't drive; there's an ocean in the way."

"Yeah?"

Never mind international geography, a lack of knowledge often excused by the very enormity of America itself. Many Americans don't even know the geography of their own towns, towns they may have lived in for years. A typical exchange, again in Massachussets:

"Excuse me," we asked a wayward pedestrian. "Do you know where Walker Avenue is?"

"Walker Avenue?"

"Yes, Walker Avenue."

"You wanna go to Walker Avenue?"

I already knew I'd picked a loser, one whose light shone only dimly in his attic. "Yes."

"Walker Avenue, huh. Yeah. Hmm. Right. OK. Well.....Walker Avenue, huh?"

Despairingly: "Yes."

"OK, you just go down that street, turn right at the lights and you're there in half a mile."

Had we done so in that coastal town, we would have ended up doing a passable impression of a bathyscape looking for the wreck of the Titanic.

Oscar Wilde described the Niagara Falls as "simply a vast unnecessary amount of water going the wrong way and then falling over unnecessary rocks." And Steinbeck just said: "Nice," wisely leaving it at that. I know how he felt. Still, what could be more American than Niagara, that magnificent spectacle which, as one American told us, God had not seen fit to equal anywhere?

I can't imagine he would want to. Not the way it is now, anyway, with the "subtle" development boasted by the brochures. They're about as subtle as a brass band falling down a lift-shaft: a plague of observation towers at every scenic spot, a Viewmobile for people too lazy to walk (i.e. most Americans), rashes of souvenir shops, restaurants, an elevator to take you down into the gorge, boats which ferry consignments of black-raincoated human ants to and from the bottom of the falls, helicopters droning, even an elevator actually bored out of the cliff to take you into the bowels of the earth and deposit you at the bottom of the falls where you may cluster, gaze not too long because further hordes clamour for their turn, snap a blurred picture on your Instamatic and then return bleating with the required ecstacy to dry ground. God may forgive the enhancers of his architecture, but I would advise him against it.

Our foray to the headquarters of the American Automobile Association near Washington left us more underjoyed. There we had hoped to arrange our travels all the way south towards the Antarctic. And there our hopes were dented. Not only would that travellers' bane, the dreaded and obligatory "Carnet de Passages" or car customs guarantee, be unaffordably expensive for South America, but by all reports we would have to ship at exorbitant expense around the infamous Darien Gap, where the grandly-named Pan-American Highway suddenly ceased to exist for several hundred swampy and impassable kilometres in Panama.

Just how impassable remained in doubt until years later when we read the book by round-the-world cyclist Ian Hibell, "Into The Remote Places." He and two companions got through - by hacking aside the jungle a few hundred metres a feverish day, endlessly through disease, heat, insects and snakes, where even a professional army-backed team of Range Rovers and a Land-Rover only just made it by an alternative route with a multi-man backup team. We had the will but not the wallet, so this time round on our limited resources, South America would have to wait, put on hold. Plenty of time yet; 17 years on we've hardly begun and there's a lot of world left - possibly to be seen in our current 2CV, which owes its ludicrous form to a chance encounter the very day we left the A.A.A. in quiet disappointment.

There, coming towards us was the weirdest "Folkswaggon" we had ever seen. The Beetle had been chopped in half, with the front end grafted onto a lumbering double-storeyed motor-home. The sight reduced us to helpless laughter. Then I started thinking about it, and Elise stopped laughing as the sickening realisation of what I was germinating sank in. She was quite right, of course. Our next-generation double-storeyed Méhari WAS gloriously unsuitable for the Sahara and the gulleys masquerading as roads in the jungles of Central Africa, as a subsequent chapter in our travels and this story reveal. One day, we'll get it right - but not too soon, I hope. It might lessen the fun.

American eccentricity unrolled on like a carpet. Some experiences were more pleasant than others.

Why settle for disaster when a calamity will do? Two teeth-rattling weeks of bouncing, crashing, juddering and flying over punishing desert rocks left the vital Saharan trailer pushing up sand-dunes, R.I.P. (Resting In Pieces).

Algerian warning - bumping into dunes can damage your health.

Bath-time on the non-road, sinking luxuriously into water up to the ankles...

Above: Casimir, hand-pedalling to California via Africa, on his homemade two-wheel-drive bicycle which was often impossible to steer thanks to a small design fault - no handlebars.

Below left: Namibia's awesome 34-metre "Finger of God" stood for tens of thousands of years. Two weeks after this picture was taken it fell down. "I swear we hardly touched it, M'lud."

Below right: shipping across the Gulf to Saudi Arabia aboard a rickety wooden dhow. Passenger peace of mind is not enhanced by the knowledge that the crew occasionally dump cars overboard in treacherous weather, to lighten their vessels.

Above: an oddball idea for a Bahrain newspaper feature saw the author spending a day as a circus elephant trainer, doing everything from riding the tusks to lying on the ground while several tons of potential suicide stepped over him. The punchline picture showed the only job with which, ultimately, he felt at ease...

Rural Oman, a mysterious and fairy-tale country closed to outsiders. It took six years to get a visa.

Rebuilding the Méhari by a true professional method: using a prototype model cobbled together from cornflake boxes. The resulting pop-up doll's house may appal and bemuse the Citroën designers even more than its predecessors did - but it's still almost capable of climbing trees.

We enjoyed the spectacle of a Blue Ridge Parkway hiker whose cocker-spaniel had its own backpack, and the man in the middle of the highway standing on a pedestal red-flagging us to slow down. We slowed, only noticing as we passed that he was a labour-saving mechanised dummy.

Less fun was the encounter with the law in the Shenandoah Park. Not at first, when the talkative ranger agreed that we could, indeed, sleep in our car on the "Scenic Overlook" where we had parked even though it was technically against the law. Next morning his colleague came along to give us a citation and like good Anglo-English speakers we were unsure why we were thus to be honoured. But "citation" was not the recognition of meritorious services as the dictionary has it; this was yet another traffic-fine, time once more to trot out 12 High Street England.

Even less enjoyable though we hoped it would be otherwise was the day we went to pot. Picked up and taken home yet again, we were offered a joint, something we've never been good at despite what a rock-music background and months along the Asian "drug trail" might suggest. What the hell, maybe this time it would work, and we puffed our way straight into oblivious sleep. Where others giggle into technicolour trips in strange and magnificent worlds, we snore on sonorously. As the old song might have said, "Yes, We Have No Nirvanas."

By the time we hit the South our budget had taken a battering and we knew we'd have our spending cut out just to get around the States, let alone the continent. There was nothing for it but a ruthless trimming, a careful costing of each item bought in southern supermarkets, where we had to keep leaving every ten minutes to recover from the sub-Arctic air-conditioning. By Alabama we had it down to a fine art, and Elise was probably the only person spending more time in supermarkets putting things back onto the shelves from her trolley than taking them off, as we juggled with the figures. I shamed us both deeply by engaging in a heated row with a cashier over a ten-cent discrepancy in our bill. My excuse was as feeble as our budget: "the principle of the thing."

The disagreement would have been minor without my English accent. Once the cashier became convinced I was trying to be funny by talking like "some kinda weirdo kook" it was downhill confrontation all the way and police were only narrowly averted by our tail-between-legs departure.

As Americans love to say of us: don't we talk funny, and many's the time we were taken home so that friends and family could also revel in the hilarity of our daily speech, incredulous that people actually talk like this outside Alistair Cooke and the snooty English actors seen on the highbrow Public Broadcasting Service. British travellers are always welcome because they speak English real good, for foreigners. Not many Americans, though, showed the erudition of the Alabaman treated to my more-or-less neutral Britspeak and Elise's slight but obvious Dutch accent.

"Hey, I know where you guys are from!" he declared. "Yeah, I have a cousin talks just like you two.

"He's also from Australia."

11
AMERICAN DREAM - OR NIGHTMARE?

For every American Dream there's a corresponding American Nightmare. Just occasionally they meld into one, and that's what happened when Southern hospitality started on the wrong end of a firing-squad of shotguns.

It began innocuously enough, as we drove along a Louisiana dirt track looking for a quiet spot to lay our two heads and cylinders for the night. Outside a remote farm fence we switched-off, nibbled our way through a desultory meal in the sweltering summer night, then crawled under our mosquito nets in the back of the van in a vain attempt to sleep.

Suddenly it was broad daylight at ten in the evening. Spotlights bored into our car to the revving of multiple engines as a voice shouted at us to come out with our hands up. I grabbed instinctively for the tear-gas spray - then realised it would be about as much use as a water-pistol against a Sherman tank. Up went our hands as requested and had they been any higher we would have hung on the clouds, as we tumbled out of the van to find ourselves staring into the most ominous black holes of all: the massed barrels of uncocked shotguns.

"Who are yuh, and whaddaya doin' here?" a voice demanded from the operating end of two holes.

"We're ...." I started to say, but no words came out as we stared into double-barrelled oblivion, waiting for them to start squirting lead. With an immense effort of will I reined in the galloping adrenalin and started again.

"We're tourists from Europe, driving around the U.S.A.," I stuttered, pleased for once to have an English accent and forcing it for all our lives were worth. They asked more questions, we stammered in reply. Only after an eternity did the lights go off, safety-catches went on and the leader approached to press flesh with us.

"Saw you near our land," he explained as he pumped my hand vigorously. "You kinda scared us."

Scared him? In a tiny 2CV, which must be about as intimidating as a custard-pie to Custer's brigade? But I held my tongue. Like the old gag replies when it asks what you call a man holding a gun: "Sir!" - and he could tell us he thought we were General Grant reincarnated and come to wreak vengeance for the 300,000 dead Yankees for all we would argue, just so long as he kept his finger off the trigger.

It ended in beer and invitations, and made us wonder yet again how so much schizophrenia can overtake a country. Strangers are so often automatically assumed to be enemies until they prove themselves otherwise, yet when they do they can be smothered with hospitality unequalled virtually anywhere, for in no country in the world is hospitality practised so fervently as in America.

A tad unnerved by the drama, we decided to move somewhere safer. It was, in any case, the start of the local hunting season, and every year at this time Americans kill or maim several thousand fellow-hunters instead of the intended wildlife, which says not a lot about the average gun-toter's judgmental abilities. Waiting to become another statistic in the badlands of Louisiana had little appeal, and we went to a campsite instead - where we met the most contented garbage-collector we've ever seen.

Frank Schmitt rattled around happily all and every day among his trashcans, singing country-music as he went.

"Yeah, when ah get in of a mornin'," he beamed at us, "ah feel right proud to see them trashcans full. Makes me feel good, knowin' folks is usin' my cans to keep America be-yootiful. Real proud." I started to tell him the story of the old, battered 2CV we saw on a French campground with all the doors and seats removed and the roof taken off, driving from litter-bin to litter-bin as an assistant tipped all the garbage into the car, filling it to malodorous overflowing. Before I could get to the punchline, where four Frenchmen at the disposal pit simply flipped the car onto its side to shovel everything out, Schmitt was off in angry pursuit of a camper who had dared to deposit his Hershey-bar wrapper beside, instead of in, his beloved trashcan.

In Gadsden, Alabama, we met the biggest family we know: the Warners. There were only two of them, but they made the Michelin man look undernourished. They met us in a tidal wave; we were paddling in a lake when they plunged in and hippopotamussed towards us, several hundred pounds of ballast threatening to swamp us as they stretched out pudgy hands to shake ours in mid-swim. If America's policy often seems like one of Survival of the Fattest, the Warners were a waddling example as they guzzled through their life in the fat lane - and whatever they weighed in pounds or kilos, it was hard to think except in terms of tons. They extended the inevitable invitation, and there began what seemed like a permanent diorama of eating. We hadn't a chance of keeping up as our trenchermen hosts shovelled it in by the spadeful while revealing they were on a diet. Some diet... The Little Green Book reveals that the average Westerner eats a ton a year and consumes, in his lifetime, 56 sheep, 36 pigs, eight cattle and 550 poultry; I couldn't help thinking the Warners would manage that for breakfast.

By ten-thirty that evening, bloated on the junk food which was all they consumed, we sat talking after Pam had left for her second job in an all-night supermarket. Don grew gradually sleepier until, in mid-sentence, his head fell back on the chair and snores reverberated around the living-room. Our European courtesy left us in a quandary as it so often did in the easy-going U.S.A.

Did we get up quietly and slink off into the night with nary a word of thanks, did we do the unthinkable and wake him up, or did we sit quietly in our seats and hope for better times?

We sat, leafing through the contradictions which passed for reading matter in their lounge: Bibles, biographies of Elvis, and a heap of Playboy magazines. We leafed, and we sat, and just as we were reaching social desperation around midnight, Don awoke, looked around him, and picked up his topic in mid-sentence as though nothing had happened.

The next day they loaded our car with junk-food, convinced we needed fattening on a good U.S. diet. Disaster loomed when Pam, all 140 kilos of her, asked if we could give her a lift to her parents. How could we refuse? It was a long, slow run, and Pam was moved to remark that she didn't think much of the Citroën springing. I hadn't the heart to tell her she was the reason there wasn't any.

The question began to get tedious: "Didya build that rig yuhself?" Occasionally it led to greater things, to invitations and rewarding social contacts; more often the conversation petered as quickly as a third-world matchstick once initial curiosity had been satisfied.

Reactions could be infuriating. In the small town of Millry we took the trouble to answer the inevitable question from a gas-station attendant, with a complete routine (my cabaret, as Elise dubbed it), explaining that the car was a French Citroën, two cylinders, and all the rest. He listened, apparently absorbing it all. At the end, his face brightened, and he looked at me triumphantly.

"Volkswagen, huh?" And he went knowingly to the back of the car to check the oil, baffled when he found no engine there. Further conversation was superfluous and I knew I was finally licked. The next day I typed a notice for the window of the car:

NO THIS IS NOT A VOLKSWAGEN!

It is the van-version of the French CITROEN Deux Chevaux (literally "Two Horses.") In parts of Europe it is also affectionately known as "The Ugly Duckling" - for obvious reasons. Virtually unchanged in design since it was first introduced in France in 1947, it is front-wheel-drive, powered by an air-cooled two-cylinder engine of 602cc (36 cu. in.) Top speed from its 28.5 horsepower output is around 65 mph - or up to 90 mph going downhill with a following wind... One U.S. gallon of gasoline will take it more than 40 miles. We began our long-distance drive from London, England, in April '74, and since then have driven roughly 100,000 miles through Europe, Asia and Africa. We are now on our way through North, Central and South America

Terence and Elise Kennedy

"Say, that sure is interestin'," said the very next American we met after reading the sign. "What kinda car is this anyhow - Folkswaggon?"

Even newspaper reporters didn't do much better. This purple prose comes from "The Messenger," in Marion, Alabama:

"Terence & Elise Kennedy created a pleasant diversion in downtown Marion Tuesday afternoon as they stopped here in their unusual car which bears a strong resemblance to a Volkswagen. Terence comes from New England, and Elise is from Dutch, and they have no trouble communicating with people on their worldwide tour because they are both fluent in English and Dutch...."

Very useful on a world tour, Dutch. I can hardly bear to re-read the rest of the article, written with the benefit of neither insight nor correcting fluid. It tells how we liked America because people feed us, how the car was designed as a motorcycle on four wheels and that it seems to go faster downhill with a following wind than on normal roads, and ending on an indescribably awful punchline tail: "It was almost dark as the Kennedys left Marion, headed south through Uniontown towards New Orleans." Gripping, compelling stuff all.

The linguistic massacre of a New Orleans encounter left us with two new pronounciations which we, and even some of our friends, use to this day. With most French cars becoming rarer in the U.S.A. because of the strict emission and safety codes (our 2CV, though allowed in for a year under a tourist concession, was actually illegal in 27 different ways), we met few remaining dealers and mechanics for Citroëns or their stablemates. One was in the middle of a park near Lake Pontchartrain. There, the local dealer spent an hour quizzing people scattered on the lawn until he found the ones he wanted: the owners of the 2CV in the car-park.

"Hell, I'm sure glad to see y'all," he guffawed at last. "See, I'm the local agent f'rSightrones an' Pudgets."

Looking up a friend in the labyrinthine streets of New Orleans wasn't easy; he lived in his alley at Number 108. I was relieved to note that policemen didn't fare much better - not the two we saw, at any rate. Following an urgent call on their walkie-talkie they set off to investigate, then stopped, then backtracked, then set off in another direction, then, finally, came over to us as we studied our Tourist Office map. Which they borrowed.

Leaving the city with its over-ground graveyards (bodies buried underground would be swallowed into swampland) we paused to rescue a tortoise crossing the road at about 0.000001 kilometres per hour. Just in time, too, for moments later a house thundered past - a real one, hoisted in its entirety onto the back of a mammoth trailer to be moved to a new location. Only in America... Only in America, too, would we see a burned-out shack in the middle of the swampland, its charred embers still smoking, all that remained amidst the rubble being the memory of a verandah - on which sat two elderly blacks in rocking chairs, creaking back and forth in total normality. Also normal in the U.S.A.: signs outside car dealerships urging teenagers to shop now for their back-to-school cars. (And don't believe what they say about American cars becoming more economical, by the by. With U.S. gasoline still almost the cheapest in the world with the obvious exception of the Arab producer states, there's still almost truth in one of my favourite American gags - the filling-attendant in the gas-station saying to the driver of a huge gas-guzzler: "Say bud, wouldya mind turnin' off your motor? You're gainin' on me.")

By the time we hit Houston, Texas - a city which foreigners, mindful of expected American pronounciation, wrongly persist in calling "Hooston" - the natives were becoming super-friendly. So friendly in one home that they insisted we use their waterbed for the night. It was our own fault for having revealed we had never sailed in one, and so there we were, tossing and gurgling through the long, seasick night on the thing, trying vainly to find our sea-legs every time my hay-fever-sneeze started off the undulating, swooshing, nauseating tidal wave once more. By four a.m. we could stand it no more and disembarked, dragging our rumpled bedclothes onto the hard floor for blessed relief and to compound our discomfort, that's how our hosts found us in the morning.

Our meander across the South squeezed out cameos and clichés of The American Way of Life like toothpaste from a tube. None could be typical, yet all were typical of a melting-pot society with all the twists and wrinkles of unravelled knitting:

The unfinished new apartment-block in Phoenix which at least had the most important of all facilities already installed: the Coca-Cola vending machine.

The mail-box atop a 20-foot pole in Silver City marked "Airmail."

The rash of no-horse towns from which any self-respecting ghost would have long-since fled, with populations as empty as the prairie sands, all called this or that City.

The Arizona restaurant serving deep-fried ice-cream - rolled in a Corn Flake batter and popped into the pan. Quickly.

The restaurant chain called Der Wienerschnitzel which doesn't serve wienerschnitzels and quite possibly has never even heard of them. "We got hamburgers, hot dogs and french fries," said our tired waitress. "Whaddaya want?"

The "Wandering Wilsons" in their gargantuan Recreational Vehicle, who cut short their camping vacation in the Painted Desert National Park because the dishwashing machine packed up. ("Roughing it" means taking along a black-and-white television).

The backwoodsman who asked us whether we'd like him to cut us some irewood, and when we said yes out came the power-saw to decimate the surrounding forest and slaughter the open-air silence.

The tarantulas of Texas, swarming over the road in spine-chilling flocks, each round and furry and as big as a fist before being murdered, splattered or pulped by passing trucks; farmers say they can cover the plains like a blanket and that cows disappear under undulating horizons of them, but this is Texas and they would say that, wouldn't they.

Everywhere the signs, from the dizzying rashes of billboards and Jesus Saves in neon to the eccentricities like: "No trespassing without permission." (Is it possible to trespass WITH permission?)

The tourist guides who address even two people as though you were a public meeting, reeling off a human pre-recorded message bristling with every fact and figure you never wanted to know until you're knee-deep in statistics and superlatives, as they boast their attraction to be the biggest or the best or the oldest or the most expensive in the world in outrageous claims which any self-respecting tealeaf could refute.

And America's truly awful electronic media, the minority Public Broadcasting Service excepted. Television which is only Valium for the eyes on a good day, interspersing its programmes with endless commercials for everything from haemorrhoid cream to automatic autumn-leaf collectors. Radio like audio wallpaper, drivelling with inane chatter uttered through the nose, commercial exhortations delivered at maximum volume, assembly-line music for the masses, and a look at the weather every ten minutes in what must be a primal American obsession with climate. "At this moment in time there's an extreme precipitation possibility this p.m.," drones the announcer. It might rain.

Why, you wonder, do so many countries so envy The American Way?

Yet America is so perverse, so frustrating, so contrary, so contradictory, it's impossible not to warm to it, and wallow, savouring it a lick at a time then coming back for more. Our own addiction to America soon began to be equalled by our addiction to its ice-cream. We started as chance users, like the man puffing at a joint in error for a cigarette. Several weeks and ice-cream parlours on we were mainlining, injecting a sugar-coned fix into our systems at least once a day, and it wasn't long before we were armed with a printed list of dealers who would satisfy our craving in each town before withdrawal symptoms set in. Towards the West of the U.S. things got totally out of hand, as we found ourselves regulating our whole itinerary by means of the printed Baskin & Robbins dealer-list, while our creative budgetting became ever-redder and our daft accounting system said we actually owed ourselves several hundred dollars. We only finally came to our senses when we found ourselves ignoring almost everything in San Francisco's remarkable Chinatown, in our efforts to pick out which was the Rocky Road Chocolate, which was the Pecan Sundae and which was the Here Come de Fudge from the Chinese franchise-dealer's squiggle-filled menu.

Had our cravings been more conventional back in the strict Mormon stronghold of Salt Lake City, we would have been in trouble. No, we couldn't have a gin and tonic with our meal, warned our native friends. That was strictly against local law. But we could order a gin, and a tonic, and mix them ourselves... Cigarettes had to be extinguished in buses in transit, and even coffee was forbidden to the more devout.

Mormon towns were the quietest we had ever known, with visitors advised not to breathe too loudly on the sabbath, and where a policeman's job seems akin to that of a nighwatchman in Madame Tussaud's. In most, all that is heard on a Sunday is the sound of the weekend decomposing in peace, shattered occasionally by a cricket chirrupping all the way from the other side of town. Obviously a non-Mormon. The famous Mormon Tabernacle Organ in Salt Lake itself was considerably louder, and considerably more excruciating.

Naturally it was "The Greatest Organ in the World," and I felt like asking our plastic-pleasant guide whether he had heard of Errol Flynn. We flocked into the Tabernacle and took our seats. The master of ceremonies announced the concert with one proviso:

"Ladies and gentlemen, if your children make a noise during this recital, FEEL FREE to remove them," he said with menace. He needn't have bothered. The noise of squalling brats would have been infinitely preferable to that made by the unfortunate organist, who even managed a musical impossibility by playing in two keys at once while creating chords unknown in Bach's era. Lucky Bach. As the aural agony thundered on all we could do was sit bravely in our seats, like the besieged of Mafeking waiting for relief. It was one of those recitals which began at two o'clock and went on for four hours, and then you looked at your watch to find it was only 2.20. Had it been Milan's La Scala the organist would have been asked to leave the stage accompanied by yesterday's vegetables.

We fled Salt Lake for the wide-open, silent spaces once more, up through the glorious Rockies to the western wilds of Canada.

Picking apples for a living should have been a longer highlight than it was. In fact our working career in Canada lasted the grand total of one day.

"Work" may be a four-letter word, but it seemed a good idea when we saw the signs pleading for fruit-harvesting help all through the lush Okanagan Valley of British Columbia. Why not, we thought, and off we went in search of a salary.

We were rebuffed at the first orchard, whose owner knew full well we were illegal. The second was more desperate, with his fruit starting to rot on the trees for lack of picking-power. We were hired - provided we knew how to pick apples.

Us? Pick apples? Tush! Of course we'd done it before, nothing to it, we pooh-poohed nervously, then put on our apron-bags the wrong way round so that on our first load all the apples fell straight through and onto the floor. The owner must have been in dire need indeed, for he kept us on, and we picked until we couldn't see another apple. That filled the first bin and notched eight dollars to our slate. We started the next, and two hours, aching backs and chronic vertigo brought on by unstable ladders chalked up the same again.

That night, nursing the unaccustomed after-pangs of work, we chatted with a local farmer, who just happened to mention that Immigration officials were doing a sweep through the valley that week looking for illegal labourers. Us! We were wanted by The Law, and dire consequences unfolded before us, from simple expulsion from the country to the impounding of all our goods and our vehicle. We cashed our $16-cheque and ran, leaving our kindly employer's fruit to rot because of a ludicrous system which discourages Canadians from picking because they earn more on Welfare, while prohibiting foreigners from coming in to do the job.

Before we knew it we were back in the States, and in another home experiencing that wondrous phenomenon called American Hospitality. Admittedly this was an extreme example of the lack of formality (Europeans would say "manners," but in an American context that sounds patronising). We sat down to eat with this very personable, well-turned-out family - and it was every man for himself as they gobbled and grabbed while we sat picking in stupefaction as their meal was annihilated. Our host had finished wolfing his first steak before we had even served ourselves, and we were barely halfway through our first helping when they were into thirds and all the food was gone. But then finesse is just another funny foreign word in America, and their hearts were as big as their appetites. It did set us pondering, though, the many and varied concepts of "guesthood" we had encountered in our months across the States.

Usually we were happy to be taken home, for half of travelling is the people you meet, and in most other countries we would have given anything for the personal contact which overwhelmed us in the States but generally underwhelmed us elsewhere. Americans opened their homes to us in their dozens, from the southern senator who even loaded us with the freebie pens, hats and novelties he uses to "buy" votes, to the Seattle Japanese photographer who insisted we swallow his personally-prepared octopus tentacles despite our being taken unaccountably green.

Many, though, lacked what Europeans would consider the basic graces of host-hood. "Help yourself to beer and food in the refrigerator," they would wave, and we rarely could. It's not easy fighting the legacy of decades of strict cultural injunctions that say "you just don't do such things." On other visits, we would be taken into a living-room and talked to or with or at for hours with nary a cup of coffee offered and on towards imminent anorexia. Within a week we had that eventuality down to a fine art, when Elise would announce several hours on that she had to check whether she had left the gas-tap open on our stove in the car, or I would go out "to see whether the ignition was switched off" - in each case grabbing bread to shovel it down with quick spoonsful of that wonderful standby, peanut-butter, before plunging back, refuelled, into the culinary void once more.

"Jeez, that Rowt 101 sure is sump'n," the RV-er in his International Harvester baseball cap said of America's fabled Pacific corniche road. "Only thing is, you gotta make sure you drive it south to north. Run it the other way and you could run your rig straight off the edge and into the sea..."

Perhaps - in a five-ton mobile-home with the aerodynamics of a breeze-block, the handling sensitivity of a Chieftain tank and driven under the influence of several quarts of Budweiser. Drunk only on the sheer physical beauty of the spectacular coastline and barrelling along with less than a ton of narrow manoeuvrability, we had no such worries as we covered around one degree of latitude a day, chasing the sun down through Washington state, Oregon and on towards San Francisco, pausing only to have our fruit checked and confiscated at the California border. (Just like Pakistan all over again, but without the overpowering bureaucracy and with a "Have A Nice Day" or six thrown in for good measure).

San Francisco - with more weirdos, nonconformists, screwballs, loonies, cranks, freaks, misfits, deadbeats, winos, nut-cases and people just plain out to lunch or with holes in their ozone layers, than any other city. Nowhere else have we seen such a concentration of kooks wandering the streets, talking to themselves, acting out their own private fantasies, haranguing passers-by, bellowing the Bible on street-corners, or breathing alcohol over you as they stagger or slump past or down. Some defy logic - like the ragged citizen straight off skid row who sat down near us and was joined by a plain-clothes policeman. They mumbled and muttered with each other, then the policeman passed over $50 and was gone. The possibilities are legion, shortly to be a major novel. In a downtown bar a lady sat on a stool with a baby sucking at her breast while she sucked at a bourbon. Or the hooker on Broadway: out she would come from the crumbling doorway of the Delta Hotel, sally up to potential clients while we lip-read the inevitable "Wanna good time?" A good time agreed, off she would go with trick in tow, to emerge less than twenty minutes later. Average turnaround time while we watched was seventeen minutes, and the Guinness Book has been informed accordingly.

San Francisco, it is said, invented topless dancing, though our time spent in Africa leaves me with doubts. Never mind - it has enough going for it even without a trip down mammary lane. How about a jaunt across the fabled but automobile-clogged bridges - perhaps better-known as car-tangled spanners? Or the disco called "Dance Your Ass Off Inc."? Or the staggering hills, so steep that when you're tired of walking through the city you just lean on it? Or the Water Bar, where you can drink 15 varieties of "designer" water from Perrier to Evian while loudspeakers susurrate the sound of waves, and clouds and waterfalls waft by on video amid the liquid blue of the decor. Not an experience for those with weak bladders...

San Francisco is also the home of the leftover hippy, and there are plenty left over, harking back to the good old days of making love not war and the Haight-Ashbury area where it all started. That's where a slightly wilted flower-adult stopped short in the middle of the road when he saw us coming. Memories of

French vacations must have meandered through his brain as he stared dreamily at our car, backing-up traffic for a block. Then he smiled, gave us the thumbs-up and let us know he knew where we, and our car, were at, by a simple gesture: in the middle of the horn-blowing street of traffic he mimed the unmistakeable swivel-left swivel-right dashboard push-pull of the 2CV gearchange. Peace, man.

Small wonder that soon after leaving the fascination of one of America's few idiosyncratic cities for more normal pastures filled with commercialisation, pre-packaged Americana and California's beautiful people wearing perfect teeth, I was moved to write the following complete entry in our journal:

"November 13: Bored."

Sir Edmund Hillary would not have enjoyed Everest if he had gone up it in a cable-car. And so it was with us and always shall be, if our worst fears are realised. No challenge = no fun - well, not much, and America is all too easy. Everything organised, signposted, comfortable, regimented even though just occasionally we were able to break out of that regimentation - as we did when we defied Rocky Mountain park rangers who insisted snow chains were needed to climb a pass. Not for a 2CV they ain't, and once their backs were turned we churned our way happily upwards to the astonishment of drivers clanking past in their chain-ganged yank-tanks.

Yet America must be one of the most pleasant and easiest lands in which to travel, and we'll keep going back for that breather. To seek out its history you need only look for the signs marked "Historic Site;" to look at its views follow the arrows to the "Scenic Overlook." But sit at a beauty spot of note and what you will see is an endless parade of obese buttocks passing before you, the thousands of "other" holidaymakers cashing-in on the mobility of this, the world's most moving society.

It was time, as Britain's zany Monty Python comedy team had it, For Something Completely Different. And it doesn't come much zanier, or more different, or even more Monty Pythonesque, than Las Vegas.

The name means "the meadow." Some meadow... Up until 1931 it was a sleepy desert town; then gambling was legalised. A decade later the population had increased several hundredfold, and today the fun never sets as visitors stream in to be parted from their money at up to a million punters a month, waving millions of greenbacks, patronising more than a hundred casinos, two hundred hotels, several dozen wedding chapels and even a few divorce chapels, some of them automated. (Automated divorce? Sure - put your $50 in the slot, punch in your name, take out and fill-in the forms, feed them back and in 24 hours your annulment is ready for collection, though signed by a real human magistrate. Not that everyone recognises the city's semi-instant divorces, though few will quibble with the instant weddings - even when they're performed by ministers in the Universal Church of Life, whose advertisements can be seen in Las Vegas newspapers offering to ordain you immediately by return of post simply for a "donation.")

In one week amid the kitsch, the glitter, the hype and the holler of Las Vegas we lived stupendously at no cost to ourselves and even ended up making a few dollars' profit - without having touched a cent of our own money. We ate sumptuously, we watched cabaret, we were given gifts from an appalling plastic clock to packs of once-used casino cards. We even won money - and all on account of our passports.

Or to be more exact, our out-of-town-ness. Well-primed by two Las Vegas survivors we had met in Quebec, we knew how to play the system and win. Not spectacularly, like the punters splashed across the front of the free local rags each week amid the advertisements for brothels and call-girls taking credit cards, but modestly, at no risk whatsoever to our fragile finances.

For potential visitors to Las Vegas I offer the Kennedy System, free with this book and guaranteed not to lose you money. Not to make you much money, either, but that's another mess of plastic. All you need is plenty of staying power and a lot of shoe-leather.

You start at one of the several tourist bureaux, presenting your proof that you are, indeed, from out of town as you ask for the key to it all, Fun Books. Filled with coupons from scores of casinos, these start you off on the road to non-riches as you work out your itinerary. Let's see now - as an incentive to play the slot-machines, Casino A will give you six dollars' worth of small change for the five that you change with their Fun Book coupon. You change your dollars but pocket the coins, repeating the trick all over town while your partner's copious handbag starts to resemble Sisyphus' boulder. Hard work, but 15 per cent profit straight off, and changing several thousand dimes and quarters back into folding oblong every couple of hours requires only that you pick a busy casino, pretend you just won it and saunter happily to the cashier.

Up-market casinos have up-market offers in their coupon-books - books which are, incidentally, also given out in shops like Green Shield stamps, or at gas stations or even, ludicrously, on the counter of a Las Vegas undertaker. The trouble with the better casinos' offers is that they require military precision to yield a profit.

In the most common at the time, many would provide a free silver dollar to the coupon-holder every hour over, say, five hours. Their assumption is that you will insert said dollar into a machine thus feeding it straight back into the system, and needless to say you don't unless, as in some cases, you are forced to or your effrontery fails you under the penetrating gaze of the issuing cashier.

The catch is that you must present yourself at precisely the same time every hour, which is logged on the cashier's sheet, or the offer becomes invalid. The theory is that you will while away the intervening hour by tugging at their one-armed bandits - or for those who want double-value in half the time, two-armed bandits so as not to waste a limb. With a dozen or so casinos running the offer, all widely separated along the considerable length of the famous Strip, it pays to pace out and time the distance between each one. And then you're off: into the first, present the coupon, take the silver dollar, saunter to the machines as if to play then get lost, hurry to the next casino, catch your breath, repeat the procedure, eye on the clock all the time from casino to casino to be back at the first precisely an hour from the start and so on for the next six exhilarating hours.

The modest profits pay for a splendid meal - not that it's necessary to use your own money to eat or drink. Coupons will keep you going in some casinos, with free hamburgers, soft-drinks, beer, hot-dogs, even steak dinners and in one or two notable instances, three-course meals at tables which each have their own slot-machines. (Even the toilets - sorry, washrooms - have their own slot machines, some in the actual cubicle, so that's nothing too remarkable, and many of the city's normal shops have machines - although it may not be true that the sugar-cubes on Las Vegas restaurant tables have dice-dots on them). There are casinos which can't even be bothered with coupons - they simply advertise free food to all comers in an effort to pull in the punters. But Las Vegas law says that a public offer made without qualification (i.e. no coupons required) must be available to all, so you run the interesting possibility of dining alongside the low-life of the Strip, the tramps and deadbeats who must be served beside the dinner-jackets and sequins.

Free photographs, free three-minute calls across the States, free pens, free circus-shows, free strip-shows - it's all grist to the neon-lit mill in a city whose profits cascade from sheer turnover. Strict controls ruled that 97.4 per cent of everything which punters pour in must be paid out in one way or another. Millionaires are made on the other 2.6 per cent, so great is the volume.

But is it all honest? Two experiences offer food for reflection:

In the first, we answered a sign offering a free flight, meal and gift for anyone from out of town, with no strings attached. We signed on, climbed aboard the aircraft and were flown over a nondescript piece of land, then brought back and fed while our details were taken and a kitschy clock presented, Have A Nice Day. The scam? A simple form of money-laundering. With our names, addresses and passport-numbers noted and even a happy snap taken over lunch for good measure, we had just become a statistic on the "operating account" of a "property developer," who could write-off up to a thousand dollars in tax for having entertained us "lavishly" as potential land-buyers. Several flights a day, a dozen candidates per flight and it all adds up - but only one piece of land which no-one has yet bought. "Ain't surprisin' 'cos it ain't for sale," chuckled our host in a rare burst of candour.

The second scam was infinitely less profitable.

By the time we hit Las Vegas we had joined-up once more with our 2CV friends Cliff and Sue; we had parted early-on in Canada, and now they kept their rendezvous with us in Death Valley to accompany us all the way South. They, too, were loaded with Fun Books, and between us we worked out a system to beat the roulette table. Like all good systems, it couldn't fail. Like all good systems, it did.

The theory was simple: with odds stacked heavily in our favour - thanks to the bias offered by coupons designed to encourage you to make a profitable start at the wheel of fortune - all we had to do was enter the casino from different sides, neither couple acknowledging that we knew the other (even talking different languages for good effect), then bet on different colours. They bet red, we bet black, and as one or the other had to come up, between us we would win back our stake and the extra the coupons promised.

We didn't. With hindsight our naïve little charade was as concealing as a Las Vegas G-string to croupiers trained at sniffing out chancers with bloodhound efficiency. They saw us coming; and the only one of two unlikely results which would stop a payout was if the ball landed on zero, which it did, a one-in-36 possibility which should have been in our favour. We gulped, but laid down more dollars and more coupons. This time the double-zero came up and I'll swear the croupier smirked as she scooped up our chips and waved four more suckers goodbye. Fixed? If that was random chance, so is every morning's sunrise. As those less innocent than ourselves will know, the odds on the zeros coming up twice in a row must be phenomenal. Too phenomenal to be true and that's the only night we ate peanut-butter sandwiches, our grubstake wiped out.

Sleeping in hotel car-parks under the watchful eye of the finest security guards gamblers' money can buy (it would be fatal publicity for a punter to be mugged outside a casino, so that Las Vegas is, perversely, one of America's safest cities), eating free lunch at four in the morning, wandering past the brothel signs advertising "All perversions catered for!" (and though I can't vouch for it, not being the customer-type, hookers reputedly carry the little credit-card zip-zap machines in their handbags so that you can pay for your lay with plastic and that will do nicely sir) - for an exhausting week we revelled in the artificiality of it all among the glazed-eyed, noise-battered, bandit-addicted get-rich-quickers milling around us.

Bahrain put an end to it all. The threat of looming employment had hung over us like a Damocletian sword ever since the day we realised we were starting to owe ourselves money in a travel-budget gone daft. Central America we might just have managed, but unless a rapid molecular transfer machine was invented and quickly, Panama's notorious Darien Gap with its thousand-dollar-plus shipping charge made South America as much of a financial proposition as a trip to the moon. The Wheel of Fortune came up for us in Las Vegas, with a payout somewhat different to the state-guaranteed 97.4 per cent from the slots: a letter offering a well-paid and challenging job, thanks to a totally random enquiry I had once made of a friend working out in the Middle East. The locale was Bahrain.

No, we didn't know where it was either. Or even what it was. It was only days after we had accepted the job that we realised we had agreed to live on an island just ten miles wide and floating somewhere in the Persian Gulf. Mongolia, it seemed, might have been more accessible, but we had agreed, we needed the money, we wanted the experience, and it was a country we would never have driven to, for you tend to fall into the sea once you get to the other edge of Saudi Arabia.

The die was cast, and we had just two more months of freedom before descending, as one returned and jaded Arab-world expat put it, into purgatory. We decided to make the most of it.

First off, a farewell splurge with our companions. If Bahrain was as unattractive a place as legend had it, with journalistic jobs going begging, perhaps they might even join us there? (Eventually, they did). Meantime, we headed straight for a slap-up meal in one of the best restaurants in town. And for a change Las Vegas wasn't paying - we were, substantially. Even so, America blew it in that, one of the best eateries in town with prices to match.

"Hey lady!" squawked the waitress far across the table in a voice which sounded like a siren being played through an electric shaver. "Didya finish yer meal?"

"Er, yes," said a surprised Elise, hardly expecting to be foghorned in such plush surroundings.

"Okay," screeched the service-with-a-snarl harpy. "C'mon, pass me yer plate!"

Like a man given only weeks to live, we scurried to cram as much into our remaining time as possible. Amid bursts of sightseeing, within days we were hurtling from office to office gathering details and making shipping and flying arrangements in the well-known city of El Pueblo de Nuestra Senora la Reina de Los Angeles de Porciuncula - Los Angeles to the rest of us.

Awaiting us in the home of friends there was yet another job offer, this time in the romantic Seychelles. Damn! But we were already committed and wouldn't it just be our luck that it never Bahrains but it pours? We telegraphed no, swallowed more of L.A.'s notorious pollution (locals are pleased with their Air Quality if they can see more than a thousand feet, or about three hundred metres, during the course of the day...), and plunged on through travel arrangements mixed with Disneyland.

The travel arrangements were less enjoyable than old Walt's wondrous park, mainly because we tried paying everything with that old-fashioned stuff, cash. Plastic Is All in America, and the travel agent didn't know what to do with our wad of greenbacks offered in exchange for tickets and, finally, couldn't even scrape up seven dollars to give us in change. (On a later visit we would find it utterly impossible to rent a car using cash - all the major companies now insist on the security they get by knowing that if you make off with their car, at least they can holler abuse at your credit-card company). Phoning about shipping wasn't easy either, when it took an astounding 48 telephone directories to cover the L.A. area. But we managed, and within days had booked ourselves by air out of

L.A. to New York and thence on to London, Holland and Bahrain, while the car would go aboard an empty oil-company supply ship plying between the oil-city of Houston, Texas, and the Persian Gulf.

We made only one social gaffe in those last halcyon U.S. days, when we were invited to the home of a very refined draughtsman couple in San Antonio. We expressed an interest in their work, and they took us to the studio to show us their immaculate drawings. Noticing an amazing American device on his table I exclaimed in astonishment:

"Good grief! Now I've seen everything. You two even use an electric rubber!"

There was an embarrassed chasm of silence, then laughter when they realised the mistake was both innocent and foreign. "Two nations divided by a common language," said Churchill or Shaw or somesuch, and how was I to know it should have been an "eraser" in American, and that a "rubber" is a condom? To cap it all, his name was Randy...

We arrived to stop over with 2CV friends in Houston, and they managed a miracle by organising a standby fare for us without the necessity for standing by. All that remained was to stock up on all the things we thought we couldn't buy in the deserts of Arabia (how wrong we were!) and to find a way of hiding them in the car - which, officially at least, had to be shipped empty.

The solution was to hammer together a false floor to stow all our goods in the van, making it look empty on cursory examination. All went well until we added the last items and laid down the thin carpet-covered hardboard, to find that it "gave" in places.

"Needs some padding material to fill it out," I told our friends.

"No problem, help yourself; piles of old magazines in the garage." We grabbed the first dozen to hand and stuffed them in, with great success.

When the car eventually arrived in Bahrain, we were dismayed to learn that locals wandering the harbour had broken into it, discovered the false floor and netted a valuable haul. But not one of our possessions was missing - only every single scrap of magazine packing material, which was worth its weight in gold in punitively-moral Arabia.

Unthinkingly, we had padded with Playboy.

12
ARABS IN BLUNDERLAND

It's more than a decade since we and the Arab world first set foot on each other. Soon we found ourselves going back to Bahrain after each new overland trip the way a dog keeps licking open a wound. It was fun while three-quarters of it lasted.

Little did we know as we picked our way gingerly past the posteriors suspended above prayer-mats in Bahrain's airport, that we were entering a life's chapter straight out of Alice in Wonderland - or just as often Arabs in Blunderland.

From the air Bahrain is a drab blob of brown dotted with oil-craters, nestled off the equally-uninviting coast of Saudi Arabia in the Persian Gulf. Bahrain's heavily-underworked Department of Tourism calls the island "The Pearl of the Gulf," harking back wistfully to the days when it produced some of the world's finest pearls. Today it is a tiny, heavily-populated melting pot where more than 300,000 immigrant workers outnumber locals two-to-one, where the main industry is money with 200 banks in a country just 16 kilometres wide. Once it must have been beautiful, thanks to the underground springs which left it lush with vegetation like an oasis in the Sahara. Today most of what grows is building rubble, accumulating where it can amid the litter which is the legacy of a young consumer society.

A tiny kingdom with a tiny king, Bahrain was the most liberal of the Arab Gulf states before the Saudis presented it with a little $564-million gift: a 25-kilometre causeway linking the island to the mainland. Now Saudi morés and standards are bulldozing in - along with reverberations from Iran's Islamic revolution and post-Gulf War nervousness - and the nightclubs are all but gone, the veil is descending, and the alcohol is evaporating along with many of the foreigners who enjoyed an irresistible combination: high salaries, and high life as long as you weren't too blatant about it.

"A good reporter," said writer A. J. Liebling many years ago, "if he chooses the right approach, can understand a cat or an Arab. The choice is the problem, and if he chooses wrong he will come away scratched or baffled." As our years hiccupped by we suffered steadily fewer scratches and slightly less bafflement, but by the stage we decided for the third time that we were yet again leaving for good, we knew only that we understood the Arabs better than we had done, while sometimes understanding them about as much as we understood the Mongolian yak.

As a journalist, one soon discovered the aversion Arabs have towards Bad News. For any reporter to do his job conscientiously in Bahrain was to invite frequent retribution from the "Ministry of Truth," as information officials were sarcastically known. Inevitably, the result there as elsewhere in the press-oppressed world is that journalists ask of their stories not "Are they true?" or even "Are they right?" but "Are they worth the hassle?"

Magazines and papers could be censured or banned for the most puzzling of transgressions - like unthinkingly running a picture of the Ruler on the same page as that of a donkey (it happened), or referring to Israel when everyone knows it does not exist and that the territory involved must be called Occupied Palestine. Or the gargantuan row which blew up during the Iran-Iraq War when Bahrain and Iraq were still on speaking terms. Our paper ran, on consecutive days, news-agency pictures of Iranians taken prisoner by the Iraqis (good propaganda against the Iranian enemy), followed by matching pictures of Iraqis taken prisoner by the Iranians (official verdict: high treason). Our misplaced British sense of fair-play had the newspaper suspended for four days of official wrist-slapping.

In such a rigidly-controlled news environment you soon learn that all you can be certain of changing in a newspaper is the date at the top of the page. That shouldn't stop you from trying even if it does occasionally seem like simply tinkering with the mechanism on a hopelessly-faulty motor. Like many of my colleagues I had to resort to all sorts of ruses to have even the most mildly critical comments and observations published at home or abroad. Pseudonyms were the obvious way to go, and by the end of our stay I was rotating no fewer than five assumed names (one of them a woman's) in order to have anything worthwhile published at all.

When days could be wasted drinking tea with officials in the hope of a story, only to be fed a catalogue of blatant lies while they waffled as vaguely as one possibly can while still actually talking of something; when all you got from constantly bashing your head against an official stonewall was a massive headache; when the cream of the country's decision-makers turned out to be rich and thick and full of clots; when Arab colleagues believed that anything worth doing was worth doing badly and that on a hot story one should hasten slowly; when uncomfortable facts were ignored in the hope they would go away; when appointments made were rarely kept; when censors could even, you thought, find moral offence in a seed catalogue - it was hard not to become about as much of an Arabist as the Crusaders, ending up like the mentally-scarred friend who still goes out of his way at the top of escalators on the London Underground to stand on the hem of visiting Arabs' bedsheets.

Newspaper photographers regarded arrest as a normal professional hazard, and many was the time we would be called on to bail them out after their latest brush with officialdom. Even photographing road-accidents could be decreed illegal - they took place, after all, on government property (a road), to photograph which you officially needed a permit.

Our European staff-photographer proved to be too tenacious, when he got himself arrested for taking pictures of the airport runway and all its bristling contingency security during an Iranian hijack drama. After two days Paul was released; his Nikon, which had been impounded with its highly confidential security pictures, was returned to him - still with the film inside. "They didn't know how to open it and were too proud to ask," he still maintains.

TV censorship could be puzzlingly fatuous. One of the hottest properties for years on Bahrain's otherwise-bland TV screens was, unsurprisingly, "Dallas." Picture the screen scene: sweet little Lucy, preparing to depart, leans over to kiss granny goodbye. Booiing! A rubber-ball bounce, and the kiss is censored. Yet wander into a Mideast airport any busy evening and you will be engulfed in a sea of public kisses, as families peck away at parting's sweet sorrow.

Still, at least Bahrain was less silly than one Gulf state whose TV screened the acclaimed Yorkshire vet series "All Creatures Great and Small." Viewers could see Dr. James Herriot ministering away at animals for all he was worth, and Yorkshire being Yorkshire some of his best patients were pigs. Except in that Arabian state, which blanked out the relevant part of the screen at the merest hint of a porcine snout. (Pigs, of course, are unclean in the Moslem world, though rather puzzlingly The Muppets in general and Miss Piggy in particular are great sources of Arab joy).

Perhaps one of the most crass examples of morality run rampant concerned the tourist whose brochure of Rome's 450-year-old Sistine Chapel was confiscated by scandalised Arab airport authorities. Who would have thought, had they not brought it to our attention, that Michaelangelo was in the business of painting pornography on the chapel ceiling all those centuries ago?

Self-censorship is a particularly insidious result of Arab heavy-handedness. Within weeks of arrival Elise and I were banned from Bahrain's top hotel because I had dared to write a bad review of a concert there. "Julie Rogers goes down like the Titanic," my critique had been headlined and went downhill after that - fairly, I thought, considering that when she finally left the stage half the audience had already beaten her to it, and that when she came back for a 20-minute encore it was like asking the hangman to pull the noose a second time. I would like to think my fearlessness for "telling it like it is" remained undented by that and many other subsequent bans and brawls, but towards the end it was hard not to feel that all I was armed with was the courage of my lack of convictions, many scruples having melted in the heat.

But only once was I actually physically manhandled for doing my job, after rushing out late one evening to investigate a fire at Bahrain's nonexistent American naval base. (The base, with up to 2,000 U.S. Marines who wandered the town at weekends as conspicuous as walking stars-and-stripes with their crew-cuts, was probably the worst-kept secret in the Gulf, known to all but never allowed to be mentioned in print). As firefighters poured in I joined them to slip into the normally heavily-barred base. Two burly Marines wasted little time in academic debate over my journalistic rights as I was hoisted skywards under the armpits and deposited unceremoniously outside the gate.

The story had a sequel. Back in the newsroom half-an-hour later as I tapped out the details for the morning edition, the telephone rang.

"Hello Terence, this is the Minister here." When ministers use first names it's time to man the barricades, and I was right. "You've just been down at the naval base fire, I believe?"

True, I answered - I was writing-up the story at that very moment.

"Ah," he said. "Well, I'm afraid there was no fire."

"No fire?" I echoed, naïvely incredulous. "But the flames were visible halfway across Bahrain!"

"Really?" He pondered this for a moment. Then, reluctantly: "Perhaps you have a point there. I suppose there was a fire after all. What's next-door to the base?"

"The expatriate school."

"Excellent. That's what you'll write then - a fire in the school." Naturally one is free to argue the point - all the way to the first flight out. Pupils were puzzled the next day when, despite what the morning paper had said, their school remained disappointingly unburned.

Journalists less schooled in our Western way of doing things had an easier time with their consciences. One Thursday afternoon our Sri Lankan reporter was sent to cover the presentation of a prestigious football trophy. By seven in the evening he still wasn't back, and the Sports Editor was in the early stages of a melt-down over the large white space looming on the back page.

At 7.30 the reporter sauntered in. "No story," he announced simply.

"Whaddaya mean, no story?" yelled the hapless Sports Ed.

"There was no presentation," the Sri Lankan shrugged. "During the match the two football teams started fighting, the police were called, a general free-for-all broke out and the ambulances started arriving. In all the fuss the trophy was stolen, so it wasn't presented - so there's no story."

Can you blame him, in an environment where an eagerly-awaited announcement on television about future oil-production came out like this:

"The Ministry has announced that oil production will continue as it is, or less, or maybe more."

Publishing was made no easier by some of the local staff who were un-dismissable thanks either to local political sensibilities, or the whim of the employee's uncle who happened to be a second cousin thrice removed of the friend of the brother of someone who knew a director of the paper. One such liability on the first paper for which I worked was the photographer - a description which does the man more kindness than he deserved.

Every day Mohammed would lock his wife in their house ("so she will not waste her time talking instead of cleaning") to arrive in the newsroom at whatever erratic hour he pleased, to make his usual fornicatory mess out of the day's photographic assignments. Mohammed had a remarkable talent as a photographer. Who else would take the required picture of two Arab men shaking hands by placing them, in their sparkling white "thobes" or robes and headgear, against a sparkling white wall, and then overexpose the photo? All that we got was two half-moon faces and two disembodied hands in a sea of white.... He had 36 cameras including a gaggle of the finest Nikons, yet could come back with a picture of only the left half of a visiting V.I.P. taken out of focus at a 45-degree angle in semi-darkness, and all on old paper blotchy with ill-mixed chemicals.

His particular talent was for sports photography - he could disrupt any event by bundling its participants out of the photogenic action and against the wall for yet another firing-squad lineup picture. But he refused to take pictures of football matches because the players moved too fast.

It was Mohammed who caused an almost-diplomatic incident when he was sent to photograph the visiting chairman of the Japanese Sanyo empire. In the middle of the reception, Mohammed shouldered aside the minions surrounding the head of one of the world's electronics giants.

"Bahrain Sanyo dealer cannot repair my Walkman!" shouted Mohammed, and he started to prod the visiting dignitary in the chest. "Why, eh, you tell me why he no fix, why he have no spare parts, why my guarantee no good, why, WHY?" Hotel security men had to drag him off the stunned chairman, whose assistants looked as though they were contemplating public disembowelling - preferably Mohammed's.

On the home front all was well. While I wrestled with a job which was sometimes akin to swimming through clotted cream, or like trying to read braille with mittens on, or coping with the Sisyphean task of trying to get hard news out of a people whose mother-tongue is ambiguity, Elise had set up in business in a local beauty salon, smoothing away wrinkles, tension and lots of dinars from affluent and sometimes effluent local ladies. I have no idea what the salon looked like inside, for no man was ever allowed through its front door for fear of sullying its reputation forever. Occasionally she practised away from her base - on those days, a stretched Cadillac would glide up to whisk her away to the palace of the chic of Araby: some of the royal wives, where she would exercise her craft in tastelessly-opulent surroundings, and might be rewarded with a tip three or four times greater than the actual charge for the treatment.

Just like their menfolk, Arab women are notoriously dismissive of time. When they could be bothered to keep their appointments - their favourite excuse for turning up late or not at all was simply a shrugged and enigmatic "My sister..." - women would glide in dressed in the traditional black abha, the tent-like cloak which covered all and a good thing too in many cases, with a lot of the Arab women under it looking about as adorable and vulnerable as an armoured car. Bahrain may be a tiny country, but the women are not, in a society whose males like their women meaty. Many are four-score kilos and rising despite Elise's best efforts, and not a pretty sight. Even so, under their abhas many of the customers would be sheathed in the most expensive creation from the house of Dior or somesuch, while ladies would discuss with each other the different shades of black available for their abhas. The more prudish expected to be body-massaged through their several layers of clothing, and many expressed themselves infinitely happy to be wandering around enveloped in black.

The protection they felt under the strict Islamic tenets governing women kept them shielded from male-induced harm, they asserted, and some even felt sorry for Western women who were always being sexually assaulted if the American movies they watched were anything to go by. Few could, or would, admit that in their marriages it was their own husbands who often performed the sexual assaults - selfishly demanding, and getting, conjugal rights whenever and as often as they liked, even when their wives were patently unwell, unhappy or just plain unwilling. Few Arab women would dare to refuse, or even to suggest to their husbands that they wanted the pill, and one obvious result was an overall Gulf birthrate in excess of seven children per woman.

Our work, though sometimes resembling try-outs for the funny farm, was challenging when it wasn't head-bangingly frustrating. I moved steadily sideways from reporting the non-news, to running a features department with no feature-writers and then editing, under yet another nom-de-guerre, a magazine which purported to tell its 70,000 expatriate readers something this editor didn't always know himself: how to cope with life in the Arab world.

Though the telex machines were almost certainly bugged, freelance stories usually got out intact, though getting the papers which contained them back in again was another matter. Britain's Financial Times, for which I occasionally wrote, suffered one memorable ban imposed two hours after the paper had hit Bahrain's streets. The censor had lingered too long over his morning tea, noticing too late the paper's suggestion that the country's prime minister was becoming inordinately richer thanks to having a finger in an enormous number of development project pies. But when bribery has been legalised in the Arab world under the term "commissions," and when every thinking person in Bahrain knew all about the P.M.'s perks anyway, banning the paper after it had already gone out to several hundred banks and as many private readers seemed an exercise in utter futility. Nevertheless whole squads of police were mobilised to visit every bank, lamely asking for their F.T.'s back. Needless to say most had mysteriously "disappeared" by that time and photocopy machines were working overtime.

Newspaper work brings you into contact with more than the usual quota of oddballs, and we met our share. One was a model-railway fanatic who devoted every spare minute to building miniature rail networks in his living-room, while the stereo rumbled out an L.P. of a 1930's Mallard Pacific 4-6-2 locomotive thundering from the bedroom to the toilet at 200 kilometres an hour. Rather than be a railway-widow his wife elected to join him in the hobby; her favourite activity was knitting grass for the lawns of his miniature stations.

Interviewing celebrities could be far less interesting, with the exception of artistes like Charles Aznavour or Vanessa Redgrave, who really did have something to add to the Gulf's store of knowledge. Fallen stars were the worst, for local impresarios appeared to use the Missing Persons Bureau to dredge up entertainers to relieve the undiscriminating populace of its admission-charges. Cilla Black, Lulu, Lonnie Donegan, The Supremes, Freddie and the Dreamers, Trini Lopez, to disinter just a few - and they would stand on stage resplendent in their too-tight mothballed suits and mortgages, in front of bands who probably had trouble staying awake during rehearsals. Some had started out at 78rpm and were down to 33 when they hit Bahrain and sinking fast, and interviewing them was often about as much fun as a funeral.

Political animals like prime ministers were more challenging - though Pakistan's late and widely unlamented tyrant super-Moslem General Zia managed to add a bit of spice, when he protested at an opposition paper having had the disrespect to send a woman to interview him. U.S. astronaut and senator John Glenn spouted hyper-space waffle, while the coldest fish of all was black American presidential candidate the Reverend Jesse Jackson, a man who didn't so much smile as simply expose some teeth. He managed the singular feat of barking hackneyed political slogans at my notebook over coffee in the Hilton lounge as though I was a massed crowd of thousands.

Less odd except in the Arab-world context were the many European prostitutes in town for the easy pickings. As "Time" magazine reported and was banned for its pains, they earned up to $1,000 a night. Some that we knew shared rooms in the Holiday Inn, the Hilton or the Sheraton in eight-hour shifts, working to an up-market clientele who thought nothing of rewarding some of the more eccentric services rendered with a Rolex or a pink Mercedes. Many of the girls came in aboard one of the region's airlines as hostesses - a stewardess estimated once that about 50 per cent of her colleagues were "on the game," using their jobs as an introduction to the region's high-flying sugar-daddies. Fair-haired girls stood the greatest chance of success, and any woman who could cope with the rather peculiar demands of the job implicit in the Arab world, (taking things lying down was the least of their problems), could probably be up and about and away in six months, her nest feathered enough never to have to take up employment horizontal or otherwise for the rest of her days.

In an environment where every writing assignment was odd, some were odder than others.

Scraping the barrel for new feature ideas, I once spent a day disguised as a doorman in front of the Regency, one of the island's top hotels. The hotel's management showed remarkable courage in allowing it, for within an hour I had mangled one customer's Gucci bags in the revolving doors, had sent an arriving guest's bags to the airport, and had bowed and scraped subserviently to a man who turned out to be there to clean the toilets. Matters were not helped when our photographer sent to record it all for a centre-page spread was arrested, because three of the guests I had been ushering in as he snapped the shutter turned out to be undercover British security men preparing for a ministerial visit. Sportingly, instead of demanding the destruction of the film, they allowed us to develop it in their presence and then took away the incriminating shot.

Another bright idea had me as the only male at a females-only fashion show - a bending of the rules which took a lot of engineering in the strict sexual segregation of the Arab world. The resulting article ended on a fashion note parodying the sort to be found in "real" fashion reporting:

"For the show," it noted, "Mr. Kennedy wore an eye-catching number chosen for just such an occasion in 1971. The off-beige suit was by Oxfam Charity Shops of London, with underclothing and hosiery by Bert's Surplus. Trendily-scuffed shoes were by Bata, jewellery was by Timex, while no-one in their right mind would want to admit manufacture of the tie. Hair was styled by "Ma Femme" of La Maison after a disaster at the Al-Karim Hair-Cutting Establishment (Men Only). The pocketchief was by Kleenex, and Van Heusen would like it known that the shirt was definitely not one of theirs."

Certainly the oddest idea of all for a feature was the one which put me underneath an elephant when the circus came to town.

"You don't have to be drowning to have your life flash before you," I wrote in the article. "Two-and-a-half tons of towering elephant poised to turn you into hamburger can have somewhat the same effect. Was I scared? Not at all. Terrified is a better word as I lay there prostrate in the circus sawdust feeling like the spot marked with a cross where the accident was about to happen.

"'Relax, Anja won't step on you,' trainer Helmut reassured me. 'Not with her front legs, anyway, although she's not too good with her back ones...'

"Lying there as relaxed as a pneumatic drill, I wondered just why I had allowed myself to be volunteered for this ridiculous journalistic assignment, one which at that moment I was enjoying with all the enthusiasm of a butterfly contemplating a lepidopterist. At worst, this newspaper space could have contained an epitaph. At best, if the elephant moved just a little more forward and let fly, the paper would have a dry-cleaning bill of elephantine proportions. Knowing what was in store I had been to the Gents. But had the elephant?

"'Have a little rest now and I'll take Anja for a walk...' said Helmut, '...over you. She's never hurt anyone yet, but if she wanted to she could demolish the whole circus by herself.' What a comfort the man was.

"She walked. I died, mentally, several times, enjoying it all about as much as a lying-in-state, which is how it was surely to end. Miraculously, we both survived unscathed and at the end of it all I shook her warmly by the trunk and praised her intelligence and my good fortune.

"I learned later I was not the only one to have suffered stress from the experience. Anja had a headache and the vet was no help at all. 'Take a kilo of aspirins and call me in the morning,' he said."

(Later Bahrain's state vet lodged a complaint with officialdom because of that last paragraph. He had, he said, been grossly insulted in print...)

While we were so busy being Terence of Arabia and El-Ise, our car had survived relatively unscathed. Not only were we members of the 2CV Club of Bahrain, we WERE the 2CV Club of Bahrain. With Citroëns having disappeared years before because they were "too complicated for the Arab world," we found ourselves with the only one in the whole country. Achieving this unique status hadn't been easy.

The first time we came in, it took four days of grinding bureaucracy to legalise our car. The second time, after we had crossed Africa in another Méhari, it took 11 days and 26 offices to have our paperwork stamped, signed, scribbled on, stapled, separated, stared at, shuffled and sidestepped.

In the next stage of the snakes-and-ladders paperchase I spent three hours searching for one elusive rubber-stamper. I never did find him; he'd gone to Oman to watch a football match taking the stamp with him, and his subordinates only had authority to count paper clips, sharpen pencils and straighten rulers. Finally, though, I was out of the harbour and on my way to the Traffic Department. They refused to register the car in Bahrain.

"Car no good," said the friendly official regretfully.

"No good?" I protested. "But it's been the equivalent of twice around the world with hardly a squeak. What do you mean, no good?"

"Is plastic, yes?"

"Yes."

"Bahrain hot. Car will melt."

Photos of our car in the Sahara solved that impasse. On to the office charged with actually issuing the registration papers, and the next hurdle.

"To register your car you must have permission from the previous owner," read the decree. I tried explaining inbetween the constantly proffered glasses of chai, (the tea which after eleven days of this was sloshing far above my Plimsoll line), that I had always been the previous owner, that we had bought the car direct from the factory.

But I reckoned without the rule-book, That Which Must Be Obeyed. Another impasse, until my friendly clerk waited for a break in the tides of supplicants washing through his office, then shoved a virgin sheet of paper at me.

"You write a letter from the original owner," he smiled. And I did under a five-year-old date: "I hereby agree to sell Citroën Méhari chassis number ..... to Mr. Terence Kennedy." And I signed it with a flourish: "André Citroën," (dead these 50 years and never called me customer).

"Very good, Mr. André," chuckled the bureaucrat. He stamped the paper - and we were a two-cylinder family once more.

Three days later our car was shortened from behind - by a driving instructor.

"Sorry," blustered this errant bastion of motoring skills. "I was thinking about my friend that I haven't seen for two days." Humble with embarrassment and more mindful of the damage to his reputation than to either vehicle, the instructor offered repair and reparations. Anywhere else that ploy might have worked, with the aggrieved victim pocketing his rage and some compensation and going off in search of a "denting shop," as they are so quaintly known. Not in Bahrain.

The rules governing the round-the-clock crash and tinkle of motorists hitting stationary objects, pedestrians or each other didn't work that way. If after an accident you were lucky enough not to be pushing up palmtrees, your presence was required in innumerable offices for a protracted round of form-filling. In this case the guilty party was fined - as was the innocent, even though my vehicle had been stationary at an intersection before being attacked from the rear.

Could it really be, as cynics quickly told me, that anyone in an accident, whether technically at fault or not, is guilty of contributory negligence - in that he was negligent enough to place himself in the path of an accident looking for somewhere to happen? The earlier case of a colleague offered an insight into the local logic which is not so much twisted as utterly sprained.

His car, correctly parked in a legal zone while he worked in his office, was set upon by a runaway vehicle driven by a man who admitted total guilt. Yet my colleague was also charged a fine. Here's the stated reason: had he not been working in Bahrain at the time, his car would not have been parked where it was and would therefore not have been involved in an accident, so he was thus partly to blame. Geddit?

Back to our own car, and there came a stage when it suffered an electrical fault which, try as I might, I was unable to solve. Foolishly, I took it to our local hole-in-the-wall workshop. They kept the car for a week before announcing they had found the problem.

"The problem," revealed the turbanned owner, "is the distributor."

"But 2CV's have no distributor," I said.

"Yes!" he cried triumphantly. "That is the problem!"

The final injustice to our long-suffering vehicle had to be the day it became a permanent part of Bahrain's road network.

There it sat, outside our apartment, R.I.P. (Rusting in Peace), when a road-surfacing gang happened along. If I thought nothing could surprise me in the Middle East by this time, I had another think coming. When I emerged from the flat to go to work the next morning I stood rooted to the spot. As rooted as the car, which had been cemented into the road.

The gang, it transpired, could not be bothered to move it when they laid their new asphalt. And so for days, as I engaged in frank and meaningful discussions with officialdom (which only reached satisfaction when I published the whole ludicrous affair in the newspaper and they sent an apology and a pneumatic drill to my door), I had the only car in the country several centimetres lower than the road on which it stood.

Five days later a roofing team set to work to repair the top of our apartment building. Our car stood underneath - precisely in the spot where they spattered their surplus cement. I became the only owner out washing his car on a Friday with steel wool, sandpaper and a Brillo-pad.

At least I had a complete car to clean - unlike the colleague whose jeep stood parked in the very ethnic Arab village in which he had chosen to live. He came out to find the local goats had eaten his seats and were rounding-off the meal with the canvas canopy.

There are several things Arabs do well. Making money is one of them, and we cannot hope to compete with people who have been able for centuries to work out in their heads 13.25 per cent of 1,420 dinars compounded over 134 days AND convince themselves it didn't count as usury.

They are also past masters at obfuscation, the art for which their flowery language is so admirably suited. Unfortunately they do it in English, too. I remember sitting at a major Arab press conference in Kuwait attended by several hundred of the world's journalists. Speakers had waffled interminably about bilateral relations, brotherhood, Arab unity and all the rest of the verbal folderol trotted out so often, when what the world's newsmen really wanted to know was what steps were going to be taken about an escalating military crisis, and they said so.

The spokesman assumed an air of gravity. "I shall tell you..." he promised, and as the press sat up, pencils poised, he revealed all: "We shall not hesitate to take whatever steps are necessary. Next question."

They can also be marvellously self-righteous. A rather forthright Australian lady was walking in the bazaar when her bottom was pinched by a passing Arab. She turned to give him a blasting of which any sailor would have been proud, and he tottered under the verbal onslaught. Then he recovered his composure.

"How dare you speak to me like that?" he demanded. "You are a guest in my country!"

Arabs are past masters at hypocrisy. A small but telling example was the meeting of the anti-smoking committee, when ashtrays were provided. (All power to one of my colleagues, incidentally, who decided after reading so much on the dangers of smoking, to give up reading).

The Arab world is particularly good at producing fractured English. It is one of the more predictable consequences of the verbal morass into which their laziness has dragged them, for they have imported so many foreigners to do their work that most Gulf states now have more foreigners than Arabs. Not unnaturally, the lingua-franca is English, with Arabs reduced to having to use it rather than Arabic if they wish to get anything done.

It's not just the Arabs who are responsible for some of the more memorable blunders, some of which I've treasured in tattered notebooks for years. Here's a quick selection:

-The Bahrain paper which reported a sheikh visiting the Institute for the Blind on a "sightseeing tour."

-Classified adverts offering a Volkswagen with five new radios, or seeking a living housemaid.

-In the catalogue of an Indian-run video shop: "Atilla the Nun." And item 27 on the menu of a local Chinese restaurant: "shrimps balls."

-The Arab dance group presenting sketches from "Worst Side Story."

-The Jaguar Car Company whose attempts to re-enter the Arab market were not helped by sloppy translation of their advertising copy into Arabic, so that the car's "unbridled power" came out as meaning a vehicle you cannot stop, i.e. without brakes.

-The European journalist whose interview with a Minister was abruptly terminated when he said how pleased he was to be getting information "from the horse's mouth."

-The Bahrain newspaper guilty of lèse majesté when it raised the eyebrows of readers whose mother-tongue was not generally English, by headlining news of the Amir's trip to Australia as "Amir Goes Down Under."

-My favourite, when an English-language paper carried a feature-article on the history of the city of Jeddah. The article contrasted the city's non-stop traffic with the days when there were no cars, only donkeys. "When The Donkey Ruled Jeddah," read the nostalgic headline. The mayor demanded, and got, a printed apology stating unequivocally that he was not a donkey.

Arabs can be astonishingly generous to those they like. The day before we left we went to bid farewell to the Amir, the jolly little king known colloquially as Happy Jack or His Shortness.

Years before, we had had him literally doubled-up with laughter when our "Such a funny little car" first drove into his beach resort - the area he opens to foreigners and where he entertains the bikini-clad European ladies he particularly enjoys. He insisted on a guided tour and ended-up wandering around in the back of the vehicle, chuckling away and muttering "Good, good!" every time we demonstrated its features. On one occasion we motored to the beach along his narrow driveway to find him seated at a small table in our way, sipping tea while contemplating his prize camel opposite us. We stopped and began to reverse.

"No, no!" he called. "Come!" So saying he lifted his tea things and folded his table, holding all to one side while we passed in mortal fear of driving over a royal toe.

Now, at the end of it all, he implored us to stay as Arab hospitality decreed he must. This time, we replied with some genuine regret, we really did have to leave for good, but had enjoyed our stay. "Good, good," he beamed. "Take this little gift to remind you of us."

His "little gift" was one of those gold Rolexes most of us can hardly lift let alone wear, and another few thousand dollars' worth of solid gold bracelets.

Many expatriates in the Arab world have similar tales to tell, but few can cap the one we heard about a sheikh who bought a Rolls-Royce and hired an English chauffeur to ferry him around Britain in it for a fortnight. At the end of the time, as the sheikh was leaving from Heathrow Airport, the worried chauffeur asked what he was supposed to do with the Rolls.

"Keep it," said the Arab.

13
SAUDI - NOT A PRETTY SITE

The memory of our first venture into mysterious, Kafkaesque Saudi Arabia will stay with us to the crematorium. It began as we entered an Immigration office devoid of anything whatever - no tables, no chairs, no furniture of any sort. And no immigration officials.

A passing Pakistani eventually took pity on our baffled pacing in the doorless, windowless, anythingless room.

"Acha, you must be knocking on wall for assistance," he instructed.

Sheepishly, we did what he said. And open sesame, the wall parted - or a piece of it did. A hand emerged, groping, and I couldn't help thinking of one of those practical-joke plastic toys you may have seen, where inserting a coin in a slot of the innocuous-looking cube causes a little claw to dart out from a concealed trapdoor to snaffle your coin. Our paperwork disappeared, the wall closed, then opened an hour later to disgorge our passports containing the necessary stamps. A disembodied voice told us to proceed to the next two rooms - one for men, the other for women.

Happily there was enough light in mine to see what was happening before I felt it. But Elise blundered into her gloomy cubicle still blinded from the searing Arabian glare and knew instant panic when hands roamed intimately over her body. Her shriek of resistance elicited a stream of guttural Arabic from the old Saudi woman performing the required body-search, and for a while the cubicle sounded like a demented aviary until order was restored. On then to the customs hall, where bored officials grudgingly ceased their vital work (watching a newly-applied coat of paint dry) to tear our possessions to pieces.

No cursory check this - this was the four-hour mother of all customs searches, as Arabs piled into our car and ransacked everything. Nothing was sacred; even the petrol-tank was poked into with a stick and the air-filter was dismantled. Thus it came about that we were caught for smuggling a substance whose mere possession in Saudi Arabia carries a massive prison penalty: booze.

Not just any booze, mind you. We wouldn't be that stupid, and weren't. No, so insignificant was this alcohol that we had genuinely overlooked its existence in our much-travelled and rarely-opened first-aid box. Like many European travellers, we've always carried a tiny phial of a herbal remedy called either Underberg or Fernet Branca depending on its manufacturer. Ideal for stomach disorders, cramps, menstrual pains and more, though if the ailment doesn't do you in, the taste of the stuff probably will. Our tiny bottle had lurked forgotten in our medicine box for ages, but try telling that to a triumphant Arab elated with his latest "bust" - especially when he speaks no English.

As he sniffed the spirit and glowered a look which promised six months to a year of King Fahd's spartan hospitality, I grabbed for inspiration and our phrase-book. My fingers fiddled open the book's section on health, and I indicated the bottle while blurting out my mangling of the Arabic words for "I am constipated."

Not surprisingly, he didn't understand. So I passed across the book to let him study the word for himself.

"Aaah, zain!" he said - good, and deftly pocketed our phrase book as he repeated our constipation. Then he reasoned for a moment before doing the last thing we expected: he kneaded his own abdomen experimentally, uncorked the little bottle, raised it to his lips, and before I could warn him he was about to be kicked by a liquid dromedary, he drained all 20 potent millilitres in one gulp.

We held our breath, but hardly for the same reason that he had to hold his. Someone hit him with a piano, then, slowly, his ambushed look turned into the supporting programme for a heart attack, as the European fire-water slid almost visibly down the inside of his torso. His eyes settled gradually into their sockets again, and a beatific smile spread across his face.

"Ghalas!" Finished, he said, pointing to his ex-constipation. Then: "Na'am, rooh, rooh!" he commanded us to go with an exhalation of 88-proof fumes, and so we did in great haste before he changed his mind or the Underberg wore off.

Saudi Arabia was the starting-point on a long and winding road between the Persian Gulf and Western Europe which we were to cover three times before all was said and driven [illegible] gluttony for punishment we found hard to rationalise.

Several decades [illegible] ,000 kilometre run was a mighty slog, a duel between man an[illegible] time we did it, tarmac had eased the traveller's lo[illegible] the mentally robust. The Middle East still has a [illegible] motorists, not least of them the man-made mo[illegible] stance measured as much in miles per sheaf of pa[illegible]

Physically, [illegible] re boredom and itinerant camels combine in d[illegible] storms that can be devastating to car and constit[illegible] eal danger amid Arabia's genuinely burning san[illegible] re are no hotels, no refreshments, no garages, no [illegible] either. But there is also no finer way to sample a[illegible] idden to outsiders - for while countries like Saudi A[illegible] sts, a reluctant concession allows transit-drivers to c[illegible] a glimpse of the dusty texture of extra-ordinary everyday [illegible]

Not that it's everyone's [illegible], as friends made clear every time we announced yet again that we were hitting that uncertain road for "absolutely the last time." Neither was it the last time doubt would be expressed about ownership of our marbles, and there were occasions when we tended to agree. Especially when our travel-tales contained all the twists of a garrotte, including being trapped in a cloying sandstorm with Elise on the brink of passing-out from heat exhaustion and suffocation, or finding ourselves at the dead of night at the wrong end of six Syrian army rifles, or spending a whole morning driving painstakingly up a frozen Turkish mountain pass - only to slither ignominiously all the way back down again just a few hundred metres from the summit.

But such is the warp-and-woof of travel. And though it may be true, as some maintain, that we've spent the best part of two decades and 300,000 kilometres attracting mishaps like fleas to a dog, it's also true that travel and travail meld into the very stuff of which fine memories are made.

Saudi Arabia, like its women, shelters behind its veil. One of the world's last enigmas, it has opened the door only a chink in the past few decades so that outsiders can take a stab at imagining what life must be like for these people of the desert.

At least that's what they were, though their rulers have spent billions on providing enticements to lure the bedu out of the desert and into the rapidly-growing towns and cities. It's not always a happy transition, as the many deserted Saudi tower-block apartments testify. Renowned for their planning folly, many of these high-rise monstrosities stand in ugly emptiness, rotting in peace because the rural folk they were designed to house saw little future in hauling their chickens and goats 15 storeys into the sky.

Today's Saudis are much-maligned for the seeming arrogance which their oil-wealth has brought, yet scratch any Gulf Arab and underneath you will find a bedouin still bearing traces of the fierce desert ethics which pervaded his society. In less than half a century Saudi life has been turned on its head, and what the oil-boom has left is not a pretty sight, nor a pretty site as excavators rape the virgin desert to throw up garish concrete structures. The song of the cement-mixer is equalled only in volume by the roar of the lunatic traffic.

What happens when the oil really does run out, and with it the money? Theories are legion. Were it not for the huge financial reserves which the Arabs now have stashed away, ticking nicely under the stock-exchanges of the world, credence could be given to the pessimistic scenario suggested by one published Arab-watcher. In essence, his belief is that the curse of history will collapse on them like a tent, causing the Arabian peninsula to revert to a sand-covered landscape of desolation as the Arabs drift back into the desert from whence they came to contemplate their camels, their goats and their navels. Unlikely, but interesting.

Wilfred Thesiger was one of the earliest of the Arab-watchers, and his anecdotes bring home the flavour of those early desert days. When he paid for his provisions in the bazaar, or souk, the traders who took his money washed it to remove its Christian contamination. Once he was entertained by a bedu sheikh, who later destroyed all the crockery from which his guest had eaten, contaminated as it was by a non-Moslem.

Thesiger also recalls how, on a gruelling 1946 Arabian trek notable for the pitifully small amount of food his Arab guides had, they would regularly fight for the right to be given the smallest portion - a point of honour which few Westerners, then or now, would understand. After the food ran out they had days of hunger which finally looked set to be relieved by the capture of a desert hare. Amid joyous anticipation of the first meat in a month, the animal was cooked. But as the hungry circle squatted around the fire, dreaming of the delicacy to come, "guests" appeared on the horizon. Sick with disappointment, Thesiger watched as his companions uncomplainingly served the hare to these visitors - as decreed by the tradition of hospitality. The hosts went hungry...

Today's Arab is the archetypal nouveau riche, yet it's not too long ago that banks in the Gulf resounded all morning to the noise of coins being bounced on the floor to ensure they were genuine. Paper money was unpopular, and expensive items were as often as not bought with great sacks of coins. Until comparatively recently, too, the ruler of one tiny Gulf emirate kept the state's entire wealth in tin trunks below his bed. He would frequently summon his hapless British financial adviser in the middle of the night to count it. The practice only ended when rats consumed many of the region's paper money assets.

One of the many overseas cartoons which didn't make it past the omnipotent Saudi censor shows two Arabs standing in front of a rig drilling for water. "Allah has not been merciful," laments one to the other. "We've struck oil again." Indeed, Saudi Arabia is gazetteered as the world's largest country without rivers, and Arabs attach a reverence to water which is beyond foreign understanding. An English writer recalled years ago how he accompanied some very prominent Saudis, men of the desert, on a sightseeing tour of Europe. When they reached the imposing Schaffhausen waterfall in Switzerland, the bedu stood in awestruck wonder at the sight of so much water. After half-an-hour in which they showed no sign of wanting to move on, the Englishman cautiously suggested departing.

"No, no!" protested the Arabs. "We cannot possibly leave before it stops!"

Today the Arabs' water comes in expensive designer bottles, or is converted in hugely costly desalination plants which make a litre of water dearer to produce than a litre of petrol. Arabs have even commissioned the towing of a plastic-covered iceberg to the Gulf. (The experiment was adjudged a failure when much of their investment melted away en route).

Despite diminishing oil barrels, the staggering cost of the war against Iraq, and the rising cost of running the family Rolls-Royces, the Gulf states are still not exactly short of the readies. A cynical banker once told me that there's enough of it around to buy out America's top 20 corporations, settle the Third World's debt, keep Kuwait in roulette chips for years and still have enough change left to pay the Oxford Street shoplifting fines.

One characteristic which money has not dented in the Arabs is their remarkable non-work ethic and their innate inefficiency. Arabs, even the least observant visitor must soon notice, seem to regard work as the refuge of those with nothing better to do, and so they do just that: nothing. In a Bahrain newspaper editorial I once dared to suggest that the local will to work must inevitably go in the only direction left: upwards. It couldn't possibly get worse, I argued, when a poll found that Arabs spend only two per cent of their time working, while three-quarters of Saudi Arabia's civil-service employees arrive late for work and one-sixth of them do no work at all.

The article struck a raw nerve among the hard-pressed expatriates flown in wholesale (three million in the Gulf at the peak of the oil-boom) to do the Arabs' work for them. One reader, anonymous for love of his residence permit, struck back with a tale which experience makes me accept as totally true and lacking in exaggeration, guaranteed to restart the nightmares which any ex-Gulf expats reading this may think they have finally suppressed.

His saga began when he ordered a consignment of sheet-music from New York for his expatriate drama group. All they had to do was pick up the parcel. Now read on:

"Airport enquiries denied the very existence of the flight on which our goods had been consigned. The timetable said otherwise - so with the group chairman I set out for the cargo terminal anyhow. After being pushed around by sleepy and lethargic security guards we entered the office and joined the queue.

"We had just got to the front of the line when prayer-time was called and everything closed. When it opened, we were pleasantly surprised to find the documents pertaining to our parcel neatly collated in a folder. These we took to an office staffed by 20 tea-drinkers, one of whom we managed to rouse so that he could astound us with the following logic: (A) - Although the man to whom the parcel was addressed was there in person, with proof of identity, he would have to provide a letter from the chairman. (B) - As he was in fact the chairman, he could thus write the letter himself, but would have to go home for the paper on which to do so.

"We left, and decided to employ our Arab 'Mr. Fix-it' in the hope of a smoother passage. He insisted on an Arabic translation of the letter to be on the safe side then came back to report failure. He went again the next day. And the next. We began to despair, and took with us a man of influence to see a notable in the customs directorate.

"This eminence took 15 minutes to append his signature to the top copy of the waybill in-between reading the newspaper, drinking coffee and greeting all and sundry who entered the office with much shaking of hands and kissing of cheeks. Armed with our papers, we went to the designated warehouse - to be told the waybill was not acceptable because it was in English.

"Finally, an Egyptian labourer was delegated to locate our parcel, stopping only momentarily on the way for a chat or six, a bemused examination of parcels in an unrelated section, exploration of a facial cavity and a cup of tea. Having done his duty, i.e. passed the buck to a forklift driver, he returned with the coveted parcel. Opened...

"I signed the waybill for the umpteenth time and went in search of a customs officer. He consented to help after only half-an-hour, signed my waybill and came to look at my box. There ensued histrionics when he saw the parcel was open, and he demanded to know why I had done this. I hadn't, it arrived thus, I explained - but was taken aside to be searched just in case I should be hiding a pile of 50 x 35 cm. sheet music about my person.

"Finally satisfied the box had been opened by person or persons unknown, he then treated the music scores with infinite suspicion in case this literature with which he was obviously not familiar could be join-the-dots pornographic drawing or worse. The bureaucrat signed the waybill and sent me back to the customs director. He signed the waybill. His entire office staff signed the waybill. I was asked to sign the waybill. I was finally cleared and picked up the parcel.

"Five hours after entering on the final day, I was out in the bright sunshine with my box. At the gate of the car-park I was stopped by an old man - - who signed my waybill.

"If this is what progress means to the notion of the Arabs coming to terms with modernity then heaven help us all. As I have signed quite enough documents recently this piece will remain anonymous..."

There's no doubt Saudi Arabian life today has a degree of daftness about it which even the notorious liar Baron von Munchausen would have found hard to exaggerate.

Where else, I wonder, could a jogger out on an evening run be arrested by police with this justification: "You have obviously been doing something wrong because you are running away," they told him. "Don't worry, we will find out what it is..."

As young Saudis would show us with pride during our visits, the country had all the trappings of modernity, even down to universities which were nibbling away at doing the previously unthinkable: educating women. It's worth noting just how they were doing it.

No decent woman may meet any man who is not of her direct family (and incidentally there are precious few indecent women in Saudi Arabia, other than the odd freelancing foreign housemaid out for a discreet slap and tickle and a supplement to her salary). Therein lies a problem for the few women now allowed by their families to pursue a college education, for how do they learn from lecturers who are for the most part male, when society decrees they may not see that man face to face or even face to veil? The solution is typically Saudi - logical in their eyes, utterly absurd elsewhere: the lecturer sits in a separate room in front of a video-camera, expounding to the ladies next door. They in turn can communicate with him by microphone, though he is never permitted to see what his students look like.

The same warped logic pervades the new Saudi woman's desire to work, a recent aberration which is so typical of the East-meets-West dichotomy straining tradition at the seams.

Liberal-thinking employers (the term is hugely relative in Saudi) have set-up offices staffed by women doing mainly secretarial jobs. Yet their bosses are men, and how can the work bridge the gap to get from the bosses to the secretaries and back? The solution: married males and females may legally gaze upon each other - so such firms hire married couples as go-betweens. They meet in a sort of "air-lock" decontamination room separating the sexes, shuttling the paper-work and the instructions back and forth.

Naturally such anomalies cannot endure long as Saudi subscribes to more and more Westernisation, not least through its imported television fare even if this is often censored to the point of total incomprehensibility.

By the terms of our visas we were always given just 72 hours to cross 1,800 kilometres of desert. Take away formalities, frequent roadblocks, and any night driving unless you have unshakeable faith in the goodwill of Allah (dead cars and splattered camels almost every kilometre of the way show that he's fairly selective about casting his mantle of protection), and you're almost left with the makings of an impossibility for a laden 602-cc car which hardly manages 60 kilometres per hour against a desert wind.

We were at least better-off than the trio of disconsolate round-the-world Swiss cyclists we had met. As tourists they had somehow managed the impossible by obtaining Saudi visas, but their elation evaporated when they learned at the border that they, too, would be allowed only the standard 72 hours to cover the distance. Pleadings availed them naught, and all that was left was the anticlimax of hiring space on the back of a transiting truck for themselves and their bicycles. They saw little of Saudi, and had lots of bruises to prove it.

Four flat tyres on during one of our trips, we were actually within hours of beating the deadline when disaster struck as the alternator in our engine set up a banshee wail. As we stopped to investigate, so did an Arab motorist coming the other way - the "Help other travellers" rule of the desert holds good, even in motorised camels. He peered knowledgeably under the bonnet as we assessed our chances of making it to the border with a rapidly-seizing alternator. Then he reached into my unwrapped toolkit for a screwdriver and prepared to be helpful, by inserting it straight through the problem part which was turning at several thousand lethal revolutions a minute.

His repair, had I not caught him in time, would certainly have fixed the alternator. Forever. Also much of the engine, himself, and us. The scattergun effect of a shaft of metal being jammed into a compact and charged spoked wheel turning at high speed should only be contemplated in nightmares. We thanked him sincerely for his assistance as we edged him back towards his car, then decided we would limp to the next village where mechanical help might be at hand.

Allah was merciful and there was a garage - one where the owner even spoke impeccable English, machine-pressed our spare bearing into the alternator, and eventually insisted we stay the statutory three days which the Islamic rule of hospitality decrees. Alas, our visa said no - and even worse, this being Saudi Arabia Elise had had to remain cooped in the broiling car away from male sight throughout the three-hour repair.

By the time we bounced back into the desert she resembled nothing so much as a terminally wilted flower, and worse was to come as the sun battered down. Within the hour we were in the middle of a fierce shamal, or desert sandstorm, reduced to a mole-like blind crawl amid the sound of a thousand maniacal Brillo-pads scouring the car.

As the atmosphere grew steadily more oppressive, we were presented with Hobson's choice: either we kept the windows closed to keep out the sand, thereby keeping out the air too, or we opened the windows to breathe and be sandblasted. The windows stayed closed, and the wilted flower slumped in the passenger seat drooped further towards the brink of hyperthermia, her condition made worse by the electrical charge of the storm. Our water was as good as useless. Not only was it as hot as we were, but it had come from a dubious well en route and was badly tainted.

As her breathing became shallower and her eyelids started to flutter, I knew the awful feeling of helplessness in a virtually hopeless situation. We were in the middle of the desert miles from people or help, carrying nothing which could serve as a remedy, and hemmed-in by a sandstorm which could last for days. At our present rate of travel we could struggle on for hours before reaching the border, but stopping would have been fatal, for it would have deprived us of that last little wisp of fresh-air we were able to coax from an almost-blocked air-vent as we drove.

No doubt you've seen many a cartoon where tattered survivors crawl through the dunes towards the mirage of a Coca-Cola machine. In Arabia it would never be allowed - how could it when Coca-Cola is banned along with 6,000 other products officially decreed to be Zionist-tainted in one way or another? But Pepsi's okay... And never more okay than from the little ramshackle shop which suddenly loomed behind a huge Pepsi sign in the middle of nowhere that frightening day. Even as we poured it down our throats we were still convinced it was a mirage, but Elise recovered and we carried the can that did it for months as a keepsake, so perhaps there is an all-seeing astronaut up there after all.

As quickly as it had sprung up the sandstorm abated. We arrived at the border 74_ long hours after setting out, fully expecting to be arrested for overstaying our 72-hour welcome. We would not have been the first. But our appearance came ten minutes before closing-time - and they just couldn't be bothered.

14
POSTERIORS IN A PERISCOPE

Great was our need as we headed into Jordan. We stopped the car in a quiet olive grove, pocketed our unisex toilet roll and set off for the nearest bush, there to squat contentedly, each to our own, jeans around our ankles. This touching scene of alimentary bliss was shattered by the sudden appearance of a well-dressed Arab.

"Salaam aleikum!" he greeted us as though nothing were amiss. What was amiss was that both of us had handfuls of fumbled loo-roll and trousers which refused to hoist fast enough as we hopped frog-like around the back of the bush.

He followed. "Sit, sit, please sit," he insisted as we crab-staggered further, flushed with embarrassment which appeared not to affect him in the least as he trailed on after us. "I wish to ask about your country," - and he did while we struggled with buttons which wouldn't, recalcitrant zips, and several centuries of European breeding which refused to concede that the scene was anything less than mortifying. The conversation was one of the shortest we have had.

Friendly people, the Jordanians, and possessors of one of the more interesting of the Middle East's drab landscapes. The "lost" city of Petra is the jewel in their crown of ancient legend, rediscovered hardly a century ago in all its magnificent desert isolation. Today the government has virtually won a controversial battle: it has evicted the bedu who have lived for generations in these splendid pillared halls and houses hewn out of solid rock, in an effort to turn it all over to tourism, leaving yet another lifeless monument instead of the living history it was.

We hiked through the fabled "eye of the needle" canyons at dawn to avoid the horseback package tourism, and were rewarded with a biblical vision: the bedu cave-dwellers coming to terms with another uneventful day, dressed as though they had emerged from a children's illustrated copy of the Old Testament, baking their bread, preparing their meagre wares for trade. The only disappointment was the unfulfilled promise in the local tourist office's pamphlet.

"From Petra's entrance gates," it had said, "you enter into the lovely valley, growing more beautiful as you proceed." Well, we did it, and I didn't.

With unbated breath we slumped in the detention-room at the Syrian border, marooned. This was how cultivated mushrooms must feel: kept in the dark, and every now and then someone comes and throws a bucket of manure over them.

The stalemate had endured all day and well into the evening, ever since a bored official had stopped excavating his nose long enough to forbid us to enter his country. As far as we could gather with our limited Arabic and his limited desire to be disturbed, on the second Monday of every fourth month containing three syllables or somesuch, the Syrians break-off relations with whichever flavour-of-the-month civilised government Allah or someone slightly lower in the heirarchy has chosen. This was one of those days, Britain was the favoured flavour, and we were the dupes.

Teeth-gritting supplication was futile as the immigration chief repeatedly put forward his ideal solution, requiring merely the loan of Elise. It became steadily harder not to recommend that he perform an anatomically-impossible exercise on himself, and the buttock-numbing hours dragged on.

Relentless insistence finally yielded a phone-call to a Damascus supremo.

"Of course, no problem at all, I apologise for the inconvenience, now let me talk to the chief there," he effused, and we marvelled yet again at the ease with which influential Arabs can turn rules on their heads. We were in. In theory.

We were waved to the first desk in the immigration hall, where a clerk squinted suspiciously at our passports as though we had made them ourselves, then spent forever copying-down their details. Where his form required "Place of birth" he wrote the address of the passport issuing office; for "Age" he gave us a 10-year validity. All that was missing was the experience which befell roving reporter Edward Behr in some equally desolate outpost: having my name copied from the passport as "Colouro feyes." Thence to the next desk for another scene in this farce without the laughs.

"Visitors to Syria?"

"Yes."

"Change a hundred American dollars each in the bank." Naturally at a rate only three or four times worse than that quoted weekly in the Financial Times, and naturally with the resulting Syrian pounds no more reconvertible at the end of it all than Monopoly money.

"Export plates on your car, my friend?"

"I'm afraid so."

"You are a truck. Change and pay more than 2,000 Syrian pounds for a truck manifest."

We paid. "Now may we drive through Syria?"

"Not yet. Pay another 200 pounds for insurance."

We paid. "Now may we...?"

"Not yet. Pay our handling and clearing charges: 600 pounds."

We paid. "Now...?"

"Not yet. You must join a night convoy through Syria. There will be 80 trucks, and each must pay one hundred American dollars. You too."

We paid. "...?"

"Yes - after the small matter of baksheesh has been settled to get you through Customs." It was - settled, not small.

Thence again to Immigration, where the very official who had just issued our new visas had moved to another desk. He studied our passports as if he had never seen them before, and discovered the visas he himself had just provided with mild surprise. Unable to be helpful by taking more weight off our wallet, he stamped us through reluctantly. And so for two nights in the driving rain we were buffetted and dragged slipstreaming behind 80 trucks.

At every rest-stop we tried to catch a little desperate shuteye, only to be hammered awake by members of the next escort group demanding papers. One insisted on seeing the engine-number in the pouring rain, so that when it came to start-up time again our drenched motor emitted only bubbles and no squeak of power. Breaking-down costs you another 1,000 pounds, but we were spared as the engine spluttered reluctantly into life only minutes before the convoy's departure, and we were able to continue our zombie-like push to the border, after three fitful hours of sleep in 48.

At the border travellers are besieged by the Syrian Youth Mafia, children in cahoots with Customs to ensure that if you don't part with some more of your folding greens to them (the kids aren't stupid - even they don't want Syrian pounds), you will be left to rot forever on the wrong side of the barrier.

More money changed hands. Lots more, in fact, but by this stage, sleepless, burned-out and beyond rational anger, you pay, pay and pay again. Anything to reach the sanctuary and sanity of Turkey.

When we got there the most incredible thing happened as we prepared to pay the expected round of Turkish entry-fees. There weren't any. And they gave us tea.

The convoy at least had the advantage of getting us through what is said to be the oldest still-inhabited city of the world: the utterly labyrinthine, belching, chaotic, unsignposted Damascus - something we had had to do on feel and a prayer the first time with only our 99-pence plastic windscreen compass to guide us. That partly explains how, on that previous trip before the authorities realised what a moneyspinner a convoy system could be, we came to find ourselves in front of six Syrian rifles late that night.

Blundering alone in search of a Turkish border-post which turned out to be a figment of the map-maker's imagination, we came to the end of the road, literally and possibly also terminally, for we found ourselves staring down half-a-dozen gunbarrels. The uniformed leader of the patrol barked at us in Arabic, and we stuttered back the few phrases of greeting we knew. It was enough, and that famed Arab hospitality came to the fore yet again as we found ourselves fêted, plied with tea and snacks as the evening wore on. By the time the candle sputtered its bedtime suggestion we were the firmest of friends and the captain insisted we share his bed. Firm friendship or not, I slept in the middle.

We took with us to Turkey an admirable Arab trait: the desire to hasten slowly. We felt we deserved it, and despite our own and others' horror-stories about Turkey it remains one of the finest of the region's countries as long as you don't mind tea. Lakes of the stuff, foisted on you at every opportunity if you show the merest flicker of friendliness. Turkey's is certainly the only border, in hundreds of frontier crossings, where we've actually been given tea by Immigration - and all because we recognised the inevitable portrait of their father-figure founder hero, Kemal Atatürk. Hell, you have to be blind not to see him - every tiny village has his statue, every shop and office and even home his photo in what seems suspiciously like a second religion.

With only the odd hiccup, we revelled in the delights of Turkey, wandering its magnificent Mediterranean coast under stark and unspoiled cliffs. Every hundred kilometres or so there would be a state campsite, and the temptation once inside was to linger, and linger longer. An idyllic existence, pottering around each day seeing only to the very basic wants, an idyll interrupted just occasionally by the odd passing Turk wanting to practise his English or sell you a carpet.

Why all the friendliness among a people whose country has for so long had such a poor world press? Part of the answer certainly lies in the march of progress, which has seen Turkey make enormous economic strides in the past few decades. Part, too, is a conscious effort to be more European, even down to applying for membership of the European Economic Community. But certainly the most visible reason is the all-out drive being made to promote tourism in a country replete with reasons for foreigners to part with their cash.

Turks are constantly bombarded with exhortations to be nice to tourists, to treat them well, to be honest with them, and it shows. One of the most public of the campaigns is a poster seen everywhere which, translated, bears a slogan something like: "Make one tourist happy and he will bring a thousand." A fellow-traveller learned first-hand just how effective that slogan is.

Locked in an acrimonious dispute with a Turkish trader, our traveller settled the argument with a metaphorical blow to the kidneys. "Listen," he told the arguing merchant. "You know what the government says about making tourists happy? Well, if you make me unhappy, you make a thousand tourists unhappy."

The trader thought about it - and capitulated immediately.

Certainly the increasing number of tourists could hardly complain about the country's prices. We knew Turkey was cheap, but just how cheap was brought home in the earthquake-ravaged town of Fethiye. One of Elise's sandals needed a major service to see it through the next 20,000 kilometres, involving the complete stripping of the sole to insert a new thong. We tracked-down a hole-in-the-wall cobbler, where the master and his four apprentices - none older than 14 if that - laboured in semi-darkness at a profusion of footwear which would long-since have been abandoned in our more prosperous countries. When we pantomimed our problem, the cobbler beamed at the opportunity to make another thousand tourists happy. Come back in an hour, one finger held over his non-existent watch intimated.

The repair was magnificent and worthy of the best hand-craftsmanship, finely-

stitched and immaculately finished. But could our wallet stand the strain?
"How much?" we asked with trepidation.

"One hundred lire," came the reply. We worked it out, then thought we had misheard and asked again. The reply was the same and we paid, disbelieving, the equivalent of ten English pence, for which we were solemnly given a receipt.

A local told us later we had been overcharged.

It happened again near the ancient port of Olympus, where we had exchanged greetings and one of Elise's cigarettes with a shepherd. The next morning as we unlocked the day with a cup of tea, there was a knock at the car door and there was our shepherd once more. Laid out neatly on the ground were six eggs, two green peppers, some sage, and two red roses which had been crushed in his pocket in the dawn journey from his village. The eggs were 20 lire each, or about two pence, and the rest was a gift to make another thousand tourists happy.

Of course it can't last. Already the towns along the country's western Mediterranean coast are beginning to resemble European rent-a-resorts, with their mainly-German holidaymakers driving huge motorhomes and armed with wads of the de facto Eurocurrency, Deutschmarks. With the invasion comes temptation, and another overlander was murdered by armed robbers during one of our trips. Turkish males become steadily more predatory, too, and can one blame them with topless European sunbathers and a rash of imported sex movies and magazines playing havoc with their notoriously restrictive Islamic morés? The surprising number of Western women arriving for a blatant good time doesn't help, either.

We saw it frequently: not-so-young fräuleins often looking like the northern aspects of a southbound bus, whose chances of being asked for a fling by a young man back home would probably be the same as mine. Turks are less choosy, when the conquest of a Western woman is a prestigious achievement, and they enter into the wooing with a marshmallow old-fashionedness found only on the most cloying of Valentine cards, roses, chocolates and all. So far from the gossip and strictures of home, the object of all the attention welcomes it with open limbs, and so the legend of the promiscuous Europeans is fertilised and grows.

It hardly makes life simpler for the travellers whose raison d'etre is not in their knickers, especially if they're the Turk-coveted blonde or, in Elise's case, redheaded. The very slick Osman of Antalya was a good example, a paragon of friendliness when we asked directions in his city. One thing led to another chai, and his smooth patter and like-mindedness allayed our naturally-sceptical suspicions, enough to bundle him into the car for a cosy trip together to the home of his seaside friend. It turned out he had more cross-culture fertilisation in mind than we did, as we discovered with the consumption of drinks which had been heavily spiked to eliminate both me, and Elise's resistance. The evening ended frostily with us barricaded in our car sadly sure of our prejudices once more.

Yet just when you think there's no hope unless your wife becomes a wrinkled centenarian or cuts off the hair which seems to have the same effect on Turks as catnip has on a moggy, something happens which turns your cynicism topsy-turvy. Mountain-top Mehmet coveted the red hair, but only to share with his village...

We had set off inland in the thick of a Turkish winter, and were clawing our way painstakingly up a snowed-in mountain pass. No sooner did we crest the penultimate ridge than our tiny wheels lost traction for good and we slithered ignominiously back down again, narrowly avoiding slewing into a bus which had had even less success. Mehmet was a passenger, on his way to his nearby village after two years of the most gruelling National Service which any country, surely, can impose on its young men. (Just one example: like his comrades Mehmet was dropped in the snow-clad mountains with a basic survival kit and rations for two or three days. He would only be collected two weeks later).

Turkey has a million of its people working in Germany at any one time, and so, like many, Mehmet spoke fluent German so that we had an open line of communication. He insisted we accompany him to his village; unable to go forwards or back, and contemplating the prospect of a night sleeping in our car in the middle of a frozen Turkish pass, well, why not?

The evening was informative, educational and a cherished glimpse into everyday Turkish life. But we certainly weren't prepared for what Mehmet had initiated the next day. By mid-morning a good half of the village's population stood milling outside the door of his parents' house where we had slept. First our permission was asked, carefully, then the visitors were allowed in, a handful at a time. Each would greet us smilingly, then advance on Elise's crowning glory to reach out and feel it, running the red strands through their gnarled fingers with expressions approaching awe.

"They are very happy that you are here, not only because they have never seen fair hair before," explained Mehmet as we wondered at the intensity of the almost-religious experience being played out in this spartan room. "To actually touch red hair brings them luck."

The generations-deep animosity between Turk and Greek leads to many anomalies, not the most inconvenient of them being that you could not take a ferry between these two neighbours. But Greek islands don't count, the charade runs, so that we could either drive all the way back around the Aegean Sea as we had done in the past to cross the sole land frontier, or we could island-hop.

Rarely have we been as pleased to see land again, as the rickety Turkish boat bucked and wallowed towards the sleepy island of Chios. With every wave our car slid inexorably further towards the open loading-ramp and the sea despite the inadequate wooden chocks and a blocked handbrake and gearbox. All hands were called once or twice to manhandle our house back to safety.

Chios had everything the non-tourist wants. No discos, no pubs, no fish-and-chips shops for the English bucket-and-spade crowd or beer-cellars for the

Germans. Not even a single campsite in its 60 kilometre length and 40 kilometre breadth. In contrast to its counterparts like Rhodes and Crete, Chios is so undiscovered that most mainland Greeks don't even know it's theirs.

The natives, as a result, are friendly, and in the tranquil weeks to follow we were greeted like brothers, plied with food, friendliness and 100-octane Greek coffee. The local yardstick of a good cuppa is whether the teaspoon stands up straight in the sludge at the bottom. Interestingly, in a local garage while having a small repair carried out, I was brought one of these potent treacles and Elise was not; it made us realise once more how close the Greeks (and the Turks) are to the Arabs in their male-orientated society.

Camping along the empty coast with only a foraging family of night-foxes for company, we would hear the throb and thrum of diesel motors, yet could see no source on land nor sea. The days drifted by and we gave it little thought, as we indulged in the luxury of throwing off all our clothes every hour to seek relief in the quiet ocean. When Elise and her binoculars, scanning the sea, spotted what looked like a bent piece of mobile plumbing studying my lily-white rump from afar, the penny dropped and we knew the source of the diesel-rumblings. I hope the Turkish submariners enjoyed that view through their periscopes. I can't vouch for the aesthetic appeal of my own rump, but perhaps Elise's lovelier curves at least brightened what must be a very boring watch or six for the sailors assigned to keep their glass eye on Chios.

Our record would be blemished if the next ferry took us to Greece without incident. True to form, this time it was a near-asphyxiation as dozens of truckers warmed-up their motors fully half-an-hour before landing at Athens' port of Piraeus - in a totally sealed, almost airless ship's hold containing, among others, the trapped and slowly choking driver of a tiny Citroën. A truck inching forward blocked the only door back to the deck and there was nothing for it but to stuff a handkerchief in the cakehole and hope for better days. Say what you will about Athens' appalling pollution - I've never tasted air so sweet, and was so intent on breathing it that I drove straight into the back of a car stopped at a red light. He shook his fist in friendly greeting, and we went on.

It should have been plain driving after that, but we reckoned without Albanian-border potholes.

As we bumbled flat-out down the busy road at a mighty 60 kilometres per hour, we were greeted by an amorous overtaking truck, which tried to embrace us as it passed. As so often before, we were pushed onto the verge. And into a massive pothole.

There was an horrendous crack as the car became an excavator with its whole right-front suspension collapsed. We looked at each other in appalled silence, before working our way methodically through our respective vocabularies of English and Dutch expletives. (Interestingly, there seems to be a far wider selection in English than in Dutch, or perhaps it's Elise's genteel upbringing).

What to do? We pushed the car with difficulty onto a nearby village track, surveyed the damage in the hope that it wasn't as bad as it looked and had sounded - it was - and then made tea. A born non-mechanic, I only have trouble with the very first part of any major repair: getting my hands covered in grease and slime. Once that's over the rest is easy as I scale new heights of mechanical incompetence. By the time even my elbows were thick with international grime and multigrade I knew it was hopeless but tinkered on in futility.

Jugoslavia's Albanian population is a taciturn race unto itself, and it would have been unthinkable for them to rush up to us brandishing help. But by the second morning they thawed enough to sidle closer as we worked. Once satisfied we were not the usual hated tourists who came raping their countryside and bringing the foreign currency which would never filter down to their poverty-stricken villages, the barriers came down, and by lunchtime on Day Two there were so many people working on our car I could hardly get near it and Elise was kept busy ferrying Nescafé back and forth. We had no common language, and no sophisticated tools, but they practised a mechanical philosophy dear to my own heart: if hitting something with a hammer doesn't fix it, use a bigger hammer.

Inbetween blows with ever-bigger hammers I was taken into the village to be fed and watered. The local grocer even opened his shop on the sabbath just in case we should require anything. Finally, slowly, amid a haze of pungent cigarette smoke our suspension was rebuilt in a fashion which would have had Andre Citroën spinning in his grave so fast it could have powered a small town.

At the end of it all I had my doubts about the durability of the cobbled repair.

"Inglaterra, okay?" - would we make it to England, I asked the 'chief mechanic'?

He grinned at me. "Ostraliya okay!"

They refused even to take the proffered gift of Elise's remaining French cigarettes. Our feeling of gratitude knew no bounds, even if the whole repair did collapse spectacularly eleven countries later and we're still trying to get to Australia.

Travellers come packaged in all manner of vehicles, but surely none stranger than the holiday tractor which reduced us to helpless laughter along the Jugoslavian coast road.

Snarling-up the hurtling summer tourist traffic was a gaily-painted blue and white Massey-Ferguson topped by a tassled and striped canvas canopy. Underneath it, singing away above the belch and roar of the diesel unused to this endless run flat-out at 28 kilometres per hour, was an Austrian farmer in holiday mood, heading for the beach several hundred kilometres distant. And why not? Many's the time we have longed for a tractor as we've struggled to extricate our tiny car from the clutches of Mother Earth, though the idea has less appeal in the middle of one of Europe's busiest one-lane holiday routes at the height of the season, with irate motorists reduced to a crawl and in no mood to appreciate the originality of it all.

Our mechanical problems multiplied, as we moved into Austria with a gearbox deprived of its fourth gear and sounding like something out of Bayreuth on a first rehearsal. The British 2CV club puts out a layman's repair guide which is filled with all sorts of original tips in its troubleshooting section. I looked up the one closest to our problem: What to do when the gearbox becomes excessively noisy. The solution - "Turn up the radio."

By the time we hit Switzerland there was no getting away from the fact that major surgery was required, and international 2CV-club friends came to the rescue when they wheeled in a fanatic for whom there was no life beyond Citroëns. He breathed, ate, slept and dreamed Deux Chevaux and had no social life other than long talks with his toolkit. It was rumoured that he once had a girlfriend, but the relationship crumbled when she sold her 2CV.

For three weeks we lived in a Swiss garage while Edgi rebuilt the car almost from the ground up, new engine and all, taking perfectionism to a degree more suited to a Rolls-Royce than our humble tortoise. It was not an easy restoration given the havoc that our oddball existence plays with vehicles, but he persevered with almost-Teutonic singlemindedness, polishing every bolt, every screw, every nut before putting it back.

The job was made no simpler by the omnipresent threat of police raids. These were initiated by long-suffering neighbours unsympathetic to his love-affair with 2CVs, in a quiet residential area echoing long and often to the screeching of his power tools. (And when the police did raid to confiscate any vehicle being worked-on which could be proved not to be his own, I never quite saw the logic of them ringing him openly the night before to warn him. "That is the way we do it in Switzerland," he told me later, setting back my Euro-understanding by decades).

There were many other less epic trips during our Persian Gulf sojourn, though the daddy of them all was still to come when we decided over drinks one evening to drive through Africa top to bottom - and then spent the next year wondering what on earth had possessed us as Life threw seven kinds of excrement at us and then some.

At odd times before that ultimate trial, I found myself clutching a notebook, a camera and a deadline in the strangest places, like sifting through the smoking wreckage of a crashed jetliner at Qatar's Doha Airport and trying to hold on to breakfast when I came across a severed arm. There was a memorable trip to Sri Lanka which must have been the perfect exercise in futility, because the idea of the laid-on jaunt was to promote tourism in that war-ravaged country - somewhat akin to luring holidaymakers to Vietnam in the 70's, Afghanistan in the 80's or Eritrea anytime. In Singapore I was shown countless golf-courses, something which was of less use to me than a corkscrew in Kuwait. I only found out why when I caught sight of the one-letter mistake in the telex sent from our Bahrain office. It warned the local P.R. people of the imminent arrival of a "Golf journalist."

In Kuwait I survived the mortification of being seen asleep on television by thousands when I should have been working. There were mitigating circumstances, M'lud.

The event was the immensely underwhelming summit of the Gulf Co-Operation Council, the local equivalent of the E.E.C. The summit served only to rubber-stamp decisions long-since taken by the six Arab leaders and was no more than a showcase spectacle for the cameras. Press statements were notable for being totally un-notable, and there was endless soporific waffle spouted about the usual Arab brotherhood, fraternity, bilateral relations and all the rest of the verbal camouflage at which the Arabs are so adept. Three days of this is a recipe for terminal boredom, except that on the final night I had the good fortune to stumble into an interview with the Saudi oil-supremo of the time, Sheikh Yamani. At three in the morning.

By the time the final press-conference started rolling at nine that morning I was in fairly bad shape, and as I slumped into my seat amid the 300 hacks present it took only a soupçon of Arab unity, brotherhood and bilateral relations to lull me into the sweetest of dreams. Kuwait TV chose that moment to zoom in on a close shot of the assembled scribes. Six hundred kilometres away in Bahrain Elise was among the thousands who must have chortled with amusement. To his credit, so did my boss.

Kuwait hadn't, in any case, been the easiest of assignments, and not just because the hotels served only six kinds of orange juice, or apple-juice bottled in pseudo champagne bottles right down to a pop-cork and a year of vintage on the label. The first day out we were taken by boat to the Kuwaiti island hardest-hit by the spillover from the Iran-Iraq fighting. The Polish news-agency correspondent turned steadily greener as the waves battered the boat. I reached out to steady him, and he threw up quite spectacularly over the front of my jacket.

Once that trauma was past we trundled off by bus to Kuwait's oil refinery, and the driver managed to wedge us under an archway which any self-respecting pedal-car driver could have seen was too low. When the World's Press finally got back into town the G.C.C. opening ceremony was about to begin and surly police refused to let us through the cordon, so that the opening itself went largely unreported by those who had been brought out at vast expense specifically to cover it.

(Years later the Iranians were even better at shooting themselves in the foot after the death of Ayatollah Khomeini. His successor called a huge conference of all the world's Press - and over-zealous security guards impounded every journalist's pen, notebook, camera and tape-recorder. The conference, unsurprisingly, was not widely reported).

Still, despite the frustrations of the Kuwaiti non-event, the statutory gold watch handed out to journalists later was some compensation. And I can say with some self-righteousness that I did not do what most of my colleagues did and sell mine the moment I got home.

Indeed not. I waited a few weeks until the market was less saturated.

We arrived to see friends in Qatar, doing what expatriates visiting other expatriates in Qatar always do: carrying a suitcase full of bacon. The stench in our spare clothing was awful, but we were luckier than the man who tried to bring in equally-unavailable Scotch whisky for a friend. Customs put his bag through an X-ray machine, spotted the banned bottle, and tapped the bag forcefully with a hammer kept especially for such occasions. The Arrivals Hall reeked for ages, not to mention his luggage.

Qatar had more of an ambivalent attitude to alcohol than some of its neighbours. Like them, it banned it - but accepted that its enormous expatriate population would be happier and therefore would work better if lubricated by the odd strong drink. So it evolved a farcical compromise in which all conspired. Only registered alcoholics could consume liquor, officialdom decided - but it was left to the expat population itself to decide who was and was not an alcoholic. And those registered were given a fulsome alcohol allocation which would have most bottled laboratory specimens turning up their toes within seconds.

Thus were new arrivals whisked off in their first days in Qatar to sort out their residence permits, their work permits, their driving licences - and their declarations that they were alcoholics who could not do without the demon spirit. Needless to say, virtually every one of the country's tens of thousands of Western expatriates was an alcoholic, nominally at least. And needless to say, "dry" Qatar had among the highest number of registered alcholics pro rata in the world.

For five years we had tried to crack the hardest Gulf nut of all: Oman, a country even more restrictive than Saudi Arabia in its determination not to allow in anyone other than the foreign workers it needs.

By coincidence the London couple who had helped us all those years before, through the traumas of Afghanistan when we had been stoned by local children and had later grappled with crippling dysentery, now turned out to be working in Oman - this mysterious and closed country we so wanted to see for its reputedly spectacular desert scenery and the unspoiled life in its hinterland. They offered to "sponsor" us as their niece and nephew wanting to visit their loving family.

The paperchase began and within weeks we were almost knee-deep in forms with no end in sight. We needed a visa, but the authorities would not issue a visa unless our local police provided a good-conduct reference. And our police would not issue a good-conduct reference unless we had a visa... When we finally submitted all our papers to the local embassy our photographs were too big and had to have the borders trimmed. But we were sent home to trim them, for the embassy of one of the world's richest oil-nations apparently had no scissors.

Finally came the big day as we arrived at Muscat's airport. There, neatly collated in a file were our visa approvals. But though we had submitted two passport pictures each, Elise's had been stolen and were no doubt now doing duty on some happy clerk's wall. He had got round the problem by affixing my own second photo to Elise's form - and the airport Immigration saw nothing unusual in the application of a female beauty-therapist who not only looked uncannily like the man she was accompanying, but who appeared to sport a luxuriantly bushy beard to boot.

In retrospect it may have been unwise to return to Bahrain aboard a creaky, leaky wooden "dhow" instead of by air. Britons may come and go at will in this ex-British Protectorate, while Bahrain's relatively liberal immigration policy allows most other foreigners to enter for three days before either moving on or regularising their situation. With her Dutch passport Elise had done this many times before - but never through the tiny, parochial dhow-harbour used almost exclusively by Arabs who, by definition, needed no visas. Though by Arab law she was no more than my chattel and should thus have been allowed to stay, they had changed the law for foreigners, and she was arrested on the spot as an illegal alien.

Police shepherded her off to a detention-room while I tried to sort things out with little success because in the early afternoon, the only people with influence in such things would be asleep for hours to come. A guard was posted at the door of her cell in case she should decide to plunge into the Gulf and swim 25 kilometres to the improbable freedom of Saudi Arabia, and I was allowed to shuttle food and drink back and forth while the hours dragged on. Finally I was able to buttonhole a sleepy minister, and she was out. But the experience left its mark and her loyally-Dutch defences finally crumbled. What the hell, she shrugged, "I'll be British and have done with it."

We filled in the forms, paid our substantial sums of money and booked the date when she would stand so patriotically before the Queen - or at least her portrait in the Bahrain Consulate - to vow that she would henceforth be a True Brit and would stand to attention at the first rumblings of the anthem Spike Milligan once rendered as "For God's Sake Save The Queen, Irene."

Elise's conversion had to be postponed when her passport disappeared in Bahrain's Immigration office. Repeated overtures and confused searching achieved nothing for three weeks. Then it reappeared - bearing a multitude of ring-stains on its cover. A clerk had been using it as a coaster for his teacup.

15
THE TROUNCE-SAHARA TRIP

The idea was hatched in a light vein which would eventually become varicose. Why not, we idly mused over drinks with some traveller friends, tackle the most challenging trip any of us had ever attempted: buy the new military 4x4 version of our Toytown plastic car and spend a year together noodling from the very top of Africa to the bottom?

The result was an unparalleled plethora of idiocy, and little did we know it would be the ultimate test of our travel spirit - but oh the romance of it all, the idea of finding ourselves in faraway places where the hand of man had never set foot, of blazing pioneering trails through the African jungles, of crossing a Sahara so silent you could almost hear the sun setting. Oh the occasional frustration of it all, when we were robbed, attacked, struck down by disease, charged by a herd of buffalo, saw our mobile home rendered frequently immobile, and even ran over a $150 chicken.

We wouldn't have missed it for the world. But for every highlight there was an accompanying lowlight, some of them times when we would gladly have traded our mosquito-infested, besieged and crippled car for even a fortnight's holiday in Beirut.

From the day we landed in Tunisia to receive our first parking ticket and wheel-clamp, we realised that things would be longer on reality and shorter on romance. Within just two months in Algeria we had chalked up an ignominious catalogue of catastrophe: all our emergency rations for the entire year's travel accidentally doused in petrol; our vital trailer wrecked; the back chassis of the car cracked; our front suspension gone and the the front of the vehicle smashed during a sandstorm tow; and three bouts of illness as harbingers of the health disasters which were soon to come. Everything was thrown at us but the proverbial kitchen sink, and even that didn't work in our camper-car anymore, clogged as it was with Sahara sand.

Farce, said Feydeau, is funnier the more truthfully you play it. Our farcical moments of truth came at us in droves, and most of the time we didn't so much rise to the occasion as trip over it...

The aftermath of our latest trans-Arabian jaunt had found us back and travel-itching once more in Bahrain.

Into the vacuum fell some good travelling friends. And as one thing led to another drink it gradually dawned that we had committed ourselves to a trans-African safari, largely through foot-in-mouth disease and the sort of planning used in those party games where players each write a segment of plot without knowing where the story is heading.

In retrospect our biggest mistake was the first one: anyone who is any kind of individualist should never agree to travel across town with friends, let alone to the ends of Africa. An invariable result, as we were to find, would be ex-friends; no matter how deeply democracy is embedded, there are few friendships which can survive the conflict of aspirations and expectations on a trip, never mind deciding who does the washing-up. Within the first few weeks our party of seven in two vehicles was down to three, then to just two - Elise and I. Years on we're all talking again - but never of travelling together.

Four of our companions had opted for a rebuilt Land-Rover, and while we gave that idea the careful consideration of about eight seconds' thought, there was never really any doubt that we would go for another plastic car. By happy coincidence Citroën had just announced a vehicle which was to become one of their commercial disasters: a military, four-wheel-drive adaptation of the Méhari. It proved virtually unsellable, because at a before-tax £5000 it cost 2.1 times the price of the normal version, and only 1,236 were ever made. But tests showed it could almost climb trees, and if we really wanted to go "where the hand of man had never set foot," this surely had to be the car to do it.

Essentially it was still our trusty little Noddy-car, but with a heap of surprises under its Acronitryl-Butadiene-Styrene co-polymer thermoplastic skin. The engine was still the robust two-cylindered 602cc workhorse, but it was coupled to a nine-speed gearbox with high and low range, driving either two or four wheels. The car could pull-off fully-laden on a 66% gradient, and would happily claw its way up a 1-in-1 hill. It had a rear differential lock which would prove a godsend in soft sand and mud, the chassis was strengthened, the suspension was beefed-up and adjustable for height, all wheels were still independent with an incredible flexibility and travel, and a smooth steel panzer-plate covered the entire bottom of the car so that we could happily belly-slide across the dunes. Which we would.

True to form, I ruined much of Citroën's good work by building an apartment block on the back, hitching up a trailer, and carrying a load which would have taxed a tank. With our experience you'd think we would know better, but it's almost as if every generation has to reinvent the wheel.

Overloaded with my partner's misgivings and underloaded with commonsense, I set about transmogrifying the little jeep until we had a double-storeyed house with all the aerodynamic finesse of a wall, on hopelessly overburdened wheels. No car of such a short wheelbase ever had the potential for so much comfort, not that that's a priority in the Sahara but on I hammered with all the fanaticism of the truly reasonable.

Like Frankenstein, I had created a monster. When I was finished, an aluminium house reached some two-and-a-half metres skywards, bearing an upstairs double bed, a downstairs kitchen, and a living-room in which Elise could even stand or walk around while we drove if she wished (she didn't) to prepare coffees and food. So spacious was our "lebensraum" that all seven of us were able to celebrate the Dutch pre-Christmas "Sinterklaas" on December 6 in the back of our 2CV, though mingling with the guests was only possible if we all breathed in.

If the Méhari was ludicrous, the trailer was an idea which should not have been tossed aside lightly; it should have been thrown forcefully. From any or all the guidebooks: "Don't take a trailer across the desert. It will not stand the pounding." So whadda they know? As it turned out, a lot, but for the moment it seemed the only way to accommodate the decision to carry three people with all their gear, a couple of hundred kilos of petrol and water, a trencherman's supply of food, half a car of spares, enough tyres to restock a Michelin supplier, sand-ladders, tools, clothing and 200 kilos of house. Barrages of warnings about the futility of a trailer were like the worms - going in one orifice and out the other and leaving little trace.

I tracked down one of Holland's better-known trailer-makers and we came to an understanding: for a reasonable price they would produce a super-strong "Sahara" trailer to my specifications, running on 2CV wheels for standardisation, with high ground clearance, heavy-duty shock absorbers, reinforced frame and more, and in return I would "road-test" their trailer across the desert and send them the photos for their brochures.

The photos would have done little for their sales. Disembodied bits of wood and metal half-buried in the sand tend not to be a great recommendation, and neither were the things I would have liked to tell them about their flimsy product. As it turned out I couldn't because they went bankrupt two months after we left. The news induced the only medically-certifiable bout of hysterical glee I have ever experienced.

But for the moment, with lift-off imminent and £4,000 in our pockets, all we still needed was half a passport-full of expensive visas as we form-filled our way around London. The paperchase fulfilled all our expectations, from the obtuseness of the Nigerians whose bloody-mindedness has sometimes led to fist-fights in their consulate, to the Upper Voltan consulate we had difficulty leaving; the travelling world was hardly beating a path to their door, and they were so happy to have customers that they treated us to coffee and cakes. On another consulate's application forms, Elise answered the question about her religion with "None" - and was duly awarded a visa, as a nun.

Our two-car convoy set off in the depths of a British December, groaning ominously under the weight of all its safari-gear, festooned with jerrycans, sand-ladders, shovels, tyres, chains and survival equipment. At Dover a bemused customs-officer cast an appraising eye over it all.

"So where are you heading with all that rough stuff?" he asked.

"Calais," said Elise.

We slushed to Sicily through a wintry Europe hissing down with rain, there to ruin whatever little springing the overloaded car had left. The plan called for us to take the wheels off the trailer and manhandle it into the back of the car to save ferry-charges, but sending a 2CV across the Mediterranean with the equivalent of another car on its back was not, in retrospect, a terribly wise idea.

With Europe behind us and Africa in front, our first African experience followed form: it was a cock-up, when the impromptu guide who pressed his services on us amid some historic Tunisian ruins, slipped on ice and broke his hip. With its long flat floor our car made an ideal ambulance, and we slithered and slid through the snow towards the nearest hospital, our patient's hefty groans increasing in intensity according to the sympathy-level of the audience (wife 10 on the rictus scale, daughter 6, hospital 8).

The next day we were adopted by a village invalid on a motorised tricycle; he couldn't do enough for us despite his obvious poverty. He plied all seven of us with the national dish, cous-cous, filled us with tea and sweets and insisted we cram into his ramshackle house to watch television with his family. Our faith in the essential goodness of man stood high when we left "Tricycle Charlie" the next morning, after putting together a small donation of clothes and some dollars.

The interlude had been brief, but the cock-ups were calling once more and we trundled several hundred kilometres south to the edge of the desert for a camel-festival which turned out not to exist.

The Sahara is the largest and most formidable desert in the world, spanning eleven countries and nine million square kilometres - roughly the size of the entire U.S.A. It is one of the last truly solitary spots where the eyes and ears can breathe, and its sense of utter desolation cannot be compared with anything else on earth. Temperatures reach in excess of 55°C, and sandstorms are frequent and can last for days. Much of it consists of vast "ergs," seas of sand containing dunes up to 230 metres tall, and driving can be a nightmare not only in the obviously-thick sand, but along tracks littered with huge thorns which play pin-cushion to your tyres.

Most treacherous of all is the "feche-feche," stretches of solid earth which look safe enough, but which can break up without warning and sink your vehicle deep into the powder-sand below. Years ago, Russian engineers thought they had designed the ultimate vehicle for Saharan oil-exploration: a monstrous machine on huge balloon tyres whose traction area had been carefully calculated to spread the weight and prevent it from sinking. One sizzling midday its crew followed the age-old desert tradition, catching several thousand winks in the shade under the truck. Their little sleep became forever when the truck broke through the feche-feche as they dozed, taking all hands down with it.

To anyone brought up on Beau Geste stories this is a world of infinite sand interspersed with murderous Tuareg bandits on camels. In reality there is more rock than sand, and though it's true that wherever you are the Tuareg may materialise out of nowhere, they are either friendly and hoping for a handout, or more often stand-offish and aloof. They rarely deign to be involved in the petty problems of European travellers, whose wish to cross the desert just for the hell of it seems utterly without sense to them. Their bafflement at our motives - or lack of them - is not all that strange, shared as it is by most Third World people of our experience, who cannot understand why we should want to go somewhere without there being any specific compulsion for our journey. We have our compulsion, but it's well beyond their struggle-for-simple-survival experience.

Contrary to popular expectation, the Sahara is not dead and devoid of life. All manner of little creatures scrabble for existence, from lizards and insects to the scorpions which we learned to accept as camping companions though never to love. It wasn't always so, and rock paintings still show the Sahara was once a fertile area filled with animals, from elephants to giraffe, ostrich to antelope.

Vegetation is sparse, and made even sparser by a drunken French truck-driver whose shame is recorded in the records book. He it was, years ago, who succeeded in the seemingly-impossible. One oasis tree, listed as the loneliest in the world and the only one for hundreds of kilometres around, and he managed to drive into it...

Into this empty Algerian world of utter solitude we crept, ecstatic to have left the real world behind us. We hadn't. In clouds of roaring, choking, fume-filled dust we were enveloped in the Paris-Dakar rally as souped-up vehicles and their hyped-up drivers hurtled past us at 120 kilometres per hour plus, shattering our silence and, as frequently, their own cars.

Murphy's Law shifted into higher gear the further we clawed our way through the scree and sand and across the murderous corrugations which loosened everything from screws to teeth.

Desert day one, grouped around the diesel-filled burning tyre which provided our nightly warmth: an acrimonious seven-sided row as we tried to reconcile the irreconcilable. For two of our group, "getting there" was the trip's raison d'etre, and they were tally-ho for pushing-on relentlessly, rising in the dark, prepacking coffees to avoid having to stop mid-morning, enduring picturesque marketplaces only as briefly as shopping necessity dictated, then driving till dusk for eight hours of sleep and on ever on. Three others wanted a compromise, while the last two wanted to stop and stare, frequently, drinking it all in and moving on only when the thirst was satiated. No prizes for guessing which we were and the row creaked on, insolubly and cancerously.

Desert day two after endless stretches of juddering corrugated track: our poorly-made trailer began to come apart. Algerian engineers in an oil camp near In Amenas came to our rescue with the offer of welding equipment and some friendly hospitality, and after long cold hours of round-midnight repairs by our never-say-die mechanic Bernie we rattled on.

Desert day three: the constant shaking dislodged the cap of a petrol jerry-can and doused all our carefully-carried year's emergency rations. Much was lost, including tempers and a few tears. Stubbornly, I refused to accept that even our precious luxury bar of Cadbury's Dairy Milk chocolate was now 97-octane poisonous, and gamely gagged on one foul square each night rather than throw it away with the rest of our provisions.

Desert day four: the trailer came adrift again, and now we knew in our hearts it was only a matter of time, as it deteriorated even faster than relations between the seven of us.

Desert day five: north of Fort Gardel on the little-used "piste" towards the desert oasis of Djanet, we were overtaken by a wheel which looked familiar. It was. The next instant the car slewed violently as bits of trailer launched themselves skywards. It had never been designed to fly, and after its ten-thousandth flight behind our madly-bucking, swaying and jarring car, its landing gear had given way spectacularly. R.I.P. (Rest In Pieces).

As was our wont, we never settle for disaster when calamity will do, and the realisation of the pickle we were in hit us with all the force of a sledgehammer. There was no chance of putting together the pieces, a task with no more hope of success than trying to reassemble a crashed Boeing with bubblegum. Only a demonic workshop could even begin to make sense out of the scattered debris, and we were patently short on workshops in a mid-Saharan nowhere. Still, at least someone was happy about the crash: those enigmatic Tuareg, who appeared out of nowhere and could hardly wait for us to move on so that they could salvage the wreckage.

But moving on wasn't that easy. The Land-Rover was full to the gunnels, and we had chosen the most difficult of the two Algerian Sahara routes so that there was scant chance of help from passing traffic. At the same time we couldn't simply ditch the several hundred kilos of irreplaceable gear now scattered across the sand.

"Oh well," we mused, "when one door shuts another one closes." After some purging melodramatics we shrugged as bravely as we could, and presented the remains of the trailer to the waiting Tuareg who disappeared over the horizon to nowhere bearing wheels, axle, side panels, frame, the lot. We threw in our towing-hook for luck, wondering while we did how they might attach it to their camels. Then we bent our backs to our baggage and piled it ever-higher in our car, which sank ever-lower. I couldn't help thinking this was all uncannily akin to rearranging the deckchairs on the Titanic.

Somehow I couldn't see us getting to the next sand-dune like this, let alone the Fairest Cape. Companion Cliff was suspended atop a mountain of impedimenta in the back of the car with no visible means of support, fending-off the shovels which kept attacking his head. Elise squatted on the front seat amid more detritus of desert travel, her calves saying hello to her chin while I changed gear and as frequently her kneecap. Our ground clearance was reduced to the height of a respectable pebble. Later that night I did some figuring and wished I hadn't; it showed us to be travelling in a 2CV laden with 14 people.

Something had to give as we lurched and scraped ever onwards to the next oasis, hundreds of kilometres distant, over terrain which looked like a napalmed Vietnam battlefield. Rocks machine-gunned the car's belly, the springs were unsprung as we rode on the suspension's protesting rubber buffers, the shock-absorbers soon didn't, the differential guard passed away with a spectacular whoomp and the stones cut treadpatterns in the sidewalls of our splayed tyres.

By Djanet near the Libyan border we knew it was futile, and our snail's pace 40 kilometres-a-day progress had been the last straw for our fretting Land-Rover companions. Appropriately in this desert oasis, we had reached a watershed.

The first decision was almost the easiest: our two groups would shake hands, wish each other luck and no hard feelings, and the Land-Rover would head south at its own rapid pace. (Which is just what happened and they reached South Africa months ahead of us, and in silence, for the rift had deepened even within their group and conversation was reduced to passing the salt).

The Djanet exit of the four left us more freedom to ponder our own dilemma. Now we were three, and even getting back to Europe would be a miracle in our present disarray, let alone thrusting deeper into the Sahara. Agonising finally yielded a plan for Cliff to fly to Europe, pick up another 2CV, then motor back to meet us in the Sahara's central travellers' rendezvous, the southern town of Tamanrasset. But before that we still had a hurdle, and a several-hundred-kilometres one at that, for with no other transport out of Djanet we actually had to reach Tamanrasset for Cliff to get that plane. With our car all but crippled and the track through the rugged Hoggar mountains notorious for its arduousness, our plan to save the trip was still no better than throwing a drowning man both ends of the rope.

The track was as rough as a street brawl and we crashed, crunched, jarred, smashed, ground and scraped onwards at an average 10 kilometres an hour, up through the Martian landscape and in low gear, low-range much of the way, our car taking a punishment we were sure had to be fatal. Surprisingly, we crested the steep and tortuous road up to the Assekrem hermitage of the famous Pater de Foucauld, a road at which even a German Unimog go-anywhere truck had baulked. We were rewarded with a breathtaking, cold sunrise which left us diametrically opposed to the acerbic and cranky Evelyn Waugh, when he said of a sunrise near Etna: "Nothing I have ever seen in Art or Nature was quite so revolting."

So, somehow, with a rapidly-ageing car we reached Tamanrasset and our troubles were over.

They weren't. Getting Cliff onto the plane and out of the Sahara became a bad joke, after days of queuing outside the Air Algerie office each morning to join the Arab rugby-scrum for tickets on the hopelessy overbooked daily flights. He pushed, he shoved, he clawed and elbowed with the best of them but was beaten to the desk every time and came back to our desert camp disconsolate.

Defeated, he finally slumped into a foetid bus and resigned himself to three uncomfortable days to the Mediterranean.

Our next month of waiting was little short of blissful, a chance to take stock, to unwind and to rekindle the travel-spirit which had been tarnished by the squabbles of the past ill-considered weeks. We parked under a thorn bush and were visited only by itinerant camels and their itinerant herders who occasionally joined us for one of Elise's cigarettes or a cup of coffee. Time passed with the timelessness of the desert.

Tamanrasset was a dusty jewel in the Sahara, a revelation with its profusion of little shops, restaurants, a bakery and even a supermarket - though in true socialist style there were more empty shelves than goods, and what goods there were bore no relation to the needs of the people. One whole wall contained baby food, another toilet paper, and a third, of all things, grease-guns. Buying bread at the bakery entailed the usual scrum, but with the bakery counter well raised and my long arms gangling from a 1.93-metre frame, I had a bread-buying advantage the shorter Cliff had missed with his air-ticket. Water was sold in this desert town at the equivalent of a dollar a jerry-can, and occasionally there would be the rumour of eggs, though this was usually enough to start a riot and we were rarely lucky. But there was rice and overpriced fruit and now and then a vegetable, and when we tired of our own cooking we could try a dingy restaurant. There, on our first visit, our query about the menu saw the waiter remove a half-eaten dish from under the nose of a nearby Arab diner to show us. We ordered it - how could we do otherwise? - only to find to our dismay that it was liver. Of what, we hardly dared contemplate as we chewed.

One memorable afternoon on a dune in the foothills of the Hoggar mountains, we watched with interest as a camel-caravan hove into view. A few hundred metres distant it shuffled to a stop, the camels were unloaded and hobbled, and the drovers pitched camp for the night.

They regarded us warily, and we could understand why, in the light of the unmannered way in which the more crass European travellers sometimes foist themselves on the Tuareg as though by Thomas Cook-given right. Having a strange vehicle can be a pain in the butt when you want privacy, but at times like this it's unmissable, and it wasn't long before their curiosity got the better of them. Their French-speaking spokesman wandered over with a careful "Bonjour, ça va?"

We returned his greeting with a cigarette, then some tea, and within a joke and a few minutes all reserve crumbled and we were invited to dinner.

It will long be remembered, and not only for the havoc it wreaked on our bowels. As guests of honour we were accorded the blanket on which to sit, as the four weatherbeaten, gnarled "voyageurs" squatted in a semicircle around the fire. Conversation was stilted yet warm. The oldest man, his face like a sandstorm-etched rock, pointed with glee to my old bush shoes, and then to his bare feet which sported years of desert-tramping callous far stronger than anything on my footwear. Elise passed around her home-rolled Dutch cigarettes, and we both began to reel under the onslaught of their strong-as-a-house green tea which kept coming in treacly draughts.

The ingredients for the meal were thrown into a large pot, though the old man had difficulty in deciding what to do with the turnips we had contributed, never having seen any. The meal's staple ingredient, bread, was being kneaded in an enamel basin, and finally its doughy lump was buried in the sand under the hot coals of the fire, just as it was.

We waited, heady with more green tea and basking in the desert camaraderie. After an hour the bread was judged to be ready; it was dug out of the sand, scraped, then washed. Surprisingly, the men who were to break the bread first rinsed their hands in the precious water, then crumbled the circular loaf into hundreds of small pieces in the basin. The contents of the pot were mixed in, along with some goat fat, and the dish was set down beside the fire.

Squatting around the dish, each brandishing a spoon, we all tucked in, spoonful by spoonful in strict turns, they careful to see that they didn't eat more, or faster, than we did so as to preserve the proper courtesy. Little was said as all attention turned to savouring the meal - a heavy, stodgy, bloating porridge which left us cramped for days, sleepless and wallowing in semi-hallucinations brought on by the vast infusions of caffeine in their flood of green tea.

We parted the best of companions, rounding off the courtesies with the pointless exchange of addresses and invitations - all part of the ritual of friendship. Yet what, I wonder, if one of these days a Tuareg camel-herder should turn up at Heathrow looking for us, or more boggling still, tether a dromedary at the front door of Elise's aged parents in Holland....?

Our desert idyll was interrupted by protracted bursts of car rebuilding as I struggled to undo some of the ravages of the non-road behind. The list of damage to be put right was truly daunting and could only be approached with that old Alcoholics Anonymous motto: one day at a time, until the 47 repairs and modifications were complete.

I patched innumerable tyre tubes, demolished the ridiculous upstairs bed, scrapped the whole back seat and put a temporary wooden splint on one cracked window. Our storage space had to be rebuilt almost from scratch, door-restraints remounted, a wing-mirror replaced. Brackets were cobbled onto the bonnet for the four petrol jerrycans which had been in the trailer, and I tried as best I could to reinforce the two cracked arms of the back chassis. The heavy sand-ladders designed to give traction when you sink, were wired onto the front bumper. The rear wooden floor joined the pile thrown out to save weight, the windscreen had to be remounted after shearing away from the bodywork... And so it went on, day by day with infinite patience born of our surroundings, as we struggled with our inadequate tools to put right some of the devastation of the desert. To save weight in planning the trip I had skimped on our toolkit - a false economy which was to prove disastrous in the tough months to come. For now, we drilled with a semi-plastic drill and sawed endless lengths of wood, plastic and metal with our worth-its-weight-in-gold Swiss Army knife. I "went for the burn," sawing and drilling till my muscles were on fire, then Elise took over, and so the days passed.

Five weeks on and there was still no sign of Cliff as our non-extendable visas ran out and our funds dwindled, in this expensive oasis town where everything was trucked in through the desert and bore a price-tag to match. Oasis food supplies often ran out, and we were rapidly demolishing the only supplies of protein we still had left, our lentils and peanuts.

Forays to the post-office were fruitless. When Tamanrasset postal clerks looked in our passports they invariably started searching all mail beginning with a T or a B - mistaking for our names the prominence given in British passports to the occupations, Teacher and Beauty-therapist. But even under our own initials there was still no word of Cliff and finally, as police started clearing overdue foreigners from the town in preparation for the President's visit to a local camel festival, the decision was made for us. We would have to set off alone, and hope to stumble across Cliff later. Anyway, we couldn't possibly miss him amid the Sahara's nine-million square kilometres, now could we?

Things were going swimmingly as we slithered through the sand, pausing only to prove our infinite capacity for getting lost and relocate our route with varying degrees of navigational incompetence. We revelled in the alone-ness of it all, stopping frequently for tea and petrol-soaked biscuits, or to strip-off completely for heat-relief and the hell of it, secure in the knowledge that any intending voyeurs would need a radio-telescope at least. The near-painful silence was almost deafening in the empty, endless nothingness that stretched to infinity around us. Still overloaded we were clattering along at a modest pace with all the grace of a fist in the face, but life on the non-road was simple and good and the next bureaucratic hassle was days away at the border.

Of course it couldn't last.

The idyll was shattered by a sickening crack as the car, and our hearts, stopped short. We hardly dared look. When we did, it couldn't have been worse as we realised that the car, like our trip, was collapsing in a welter of improbabilities. A one-in-a-million accident: there, under a sea of sand was just one tiny rock, and we had hit that tiny rock a glancing blow at just the right speed and angle to snap a front suspension bolt. That snapped bolt in turn had taken the entire mounting for the right-hand wheel arm with it, reducing the mounting clamp to a chunk of jagged, broken metal, displacing the steering-column, twisting the gearbox and contorting the engine-supports. The car lay at the drunken angle of a ship heading for the bottom, and we locked eyes in horror.

"This is it," whispered Elise. "The Big One."

For a long time we stood in appalled silence, hardly daring to utter the unutterable as we realised just how stranded we were. There was no question but that a repair was beyond the scope of my ability, my toolkit or my spare-parts reserve. Could it really be true that just one glancing bump could spell not only an end to all the dreams and hopes, but also the first time in years when our grin and bear it philosophy might be hopelessly inane? What do you do in the middle of the most nowhere version of nowhere in the world, when your vital transport becomes an immovable heap of expensive scrap? Civilisation, such as it was, lay hundreds of kilometres distant across empty sands where we would hardly last hours. And even if you could hitch a lift out with one of the infrequent travellers if you were able to attract their attention, what about all your precious possessions - those possessions you have always said you could do without if it came to the crunch, but now here's the crunch and what you have really got is a Linus-blanket attachment to several hundred kilos of baggage? Never mind all our stuff - what about Cliff's 19 pairs of socks we had promised to safeguard until his return?

We took sober stock, secure at least in the knowledge that we had food and water for days, even a week at a pinch. I crawled under the chassis and fiddled and improvised and pondered, and emerged greasy and failed, all messed up and no place to go. Then we sat down to wait, and hoped, through the first day and well into the second, and suddenly a puff of dust appeared far off and we waved and leapt to attract attention.

Through the haze appeared one of the oddest overland vehicles we have ever seen, our own included: a thirty-year-old five-ton Berliet removal truck, its cavernous interior fitted out with crude bunks, a huge stove and oven, a normal household sink and table and little else in its spartan decor. Three young French occupied this mobile barn, a truck they were wrestling to Africa's West Coast in the hope of making a little money by selling it there. Together we attacked our collapsed suspension, but it wasn't long before they were as defeated as I had been.

We suggested they take Elise to the first town some days away, Arlit over the border in Niger where she could get tools and parts while I stayed to protect the car in the desert.

"Non non non, absolument non!" they forbade. "Among the Tuareg are many bandits, it is very, very dangerous! We will pull you to the border."

Easier said than done, with the car un-towable in the normal way because of the crippled suspension. The only solution was to piggyback it, and with ropes and improvised slings we hoisted the front up against the back of their ancient truck, watched by the inevitable Tuareg who disappeared at the first sign of a camera.

The drive was a nightmare, as the Méhari smashed repeatedly into the back of the truck with every bump. First to go was the plastic grille, then the brackets holding the jerrycans, then the bumper, then even a front window, and the intolerable strain on the back wheels began to splay their suspension-arms outwards. Elise was travelling in the truck to save weight, and with each noisy crunch, her heart bled for me sitting alone in our rapidly-disintegrating car. I couldn't even hoot when things went badly wrong, for the hooter had been wrenched off kilometres ago. The truck lurched this way and that as all three French tried to drive at the same time, each convinced he had spotted the easiest route.

The game old Berliet was designed for the roads of France, not the deep sand of the Sahara, and with its rigid suspension under five tons of weight, and with only two-wheel-drive and the added drag of our car, it bogged every few minutes while a sandstorm brewed.

Like automatons we piled out each time, grabbed for the heavy sand-mats and shovelled or scraped the sand from the wheels with our bare hands. A spinning of wheels, curses in three languages and the ungainly convoy would lurch forwards, sometimes only a few metres at a time before bogging again. As the long, sweaty day dragged on the sandstorm eddyed and swirled, until it was a race against time to get to the border before being engulfed immovably; we swathed ourselves in towels against the stinging of a million bee-like attacks and hiccuped slowly onwards.

We were in bad shape when we reached In Guezzam. But the storm abated enough to drive the truck on its own back into the wilderness, to see whether we could scavenge from one of the many abandoned cars, the ones which didn't make it. The desert track is littered with dead 2CV's - not an omen nor a non-advertisement for the car, for there are only half a dozen types of vehicle which even attempt the Sahara and the 2CV is one of them. We stripped an entire suspension unit polished smooth by years of sandblasting and in perfect unrusted condition, then laboured semi-fruitlessly into the night to mount it on our car, finally defeated by our lack of specialised tools.

A pending deadline and an expiring visa took our benefactors on with profuse apologies the next day, leaving us in the one-street village to struggle on alone with the repair as the sandstorm crescendoed again. Swathed in towels with slitted eyes peering out, and working as much by feel as by sight, I drew on reserves I never knew I had, determined not to give in, struggling with recalcitrant bolts and bits of homemade metal while the sand penetrated every fold and every orifice, and hair and beard turned Christmas-card white.

I was all that moved in that beleaguered village, and every couple of hours a friendly Tuareg would struggle across to advise me to stop. Across the plain, nomads sat huddled around their hot coals, the sand piling-up against their backs. Their camels squatted, eyes tightly shut. But stubborn to a fault, on I slogged, while our food and water began to run out.

Eventually as the sandstorm abated there was a repair of sorts, and I decided to risk driving; the car crept carefully through the border, slowly over every bump on the track into no-man's-land.

We managed just 4.1 kilometres before the ludicrously-inept repair gave way with another spectacular crash and the car nose-dived into the sand once more. This time we knew it was all or nothing. Either I rebuilt the suspension painstakingly however long it took, with whatever material I could scrounge, or our car, and our dreams, would be abandoned to push up sand dunes.

The next days were the hardest we had known. Sweating and struggling, we took apart the cobbled first repair and with a hacksaw blade for which we had no holder and our semi-plastic drill (never, never would I skimp on tools again!) we spent hour after laboured hour sawing, shaping, cutting, drilling, trying to build a new bracket for the sheared suspension arm. As the sun beat down we spent a cruel seven hours just drilling one hole through the super-strong chassis, several hand-blistering hours more sawing a piece off the rear chassis to serve as a support.

This time we had the social advantage of being on the relatively well-travelled stretch between two borders, and we were alternately helped and hindered by passing traffic. Police from both Algeria and Niger came to chat with us each evening; an English tour-group truck stopped to offer tea and sympathy and paperback books to while away the stupendously-quiet desert nights; two young Germans in a VW bus offered their condolences but we already had plenty, so they rolled up their sleeves and mucked in with the repair, leaving us a few of the dozens of tins of ready-to-eat stews which were their sole sustenance for a month in the desert.

Among the most memorable of our visitors was the Oompah-blaring truck of the Munich ear, nose and throat specialists mentioned in an earlier chapter; I can only hope that they were better at fiddling in ears than with our recalcitrant axle-shaft, for they left it in a worse state than when we started, only adding to my problems. But their appearance did wonders for our spirits, helping us to see once again the absurd side of travel as they whirred and clicked their cameras at us to preserve the images of the poor travellers they had "rescued." And at the end of it all, unable to find any more mechanical challenges to bodge, they gave us a tube of sweets and a packet of chewing-gum to see us through our adversity and oompahed off through the desert once more, while their wives endured glumly and dreamed of home.

At least they stopped, which is more than can be said of most of the "Peugeot people." Making up the bulk of the Saharan traffic, these are the Europeans who cross the Sahara by the least-difficult route for a little adventure and the hope of a lot of gain. Their ultimate aim is to sell cars, usually the much-sought mechanical ships of the desert esteemed by North- and West-Africans, Peugeot 404's and 504's. Indeed, so prized is the old 404 that Western Europe is gradually becoming denuded of secondhand models as they find their way by one means or another to Africa.

It is manifestly unfair to lump all the Peugeot people together as uncaring travellers with all the compassion and sensitivity of a rhino, paying no heed to the cardinal rule of the desert: stop and offer help to anyone in trouble. But not only were we rarely offered assistance - just as often they would coat us in a cloud of dust as they roared past, desperate to cover as many kilometres as possible because time is money even in the timeless Sahara, when a few days saved might make another profitable journey possible towards the end of the season. Giving them the due they don't always deserve, another occasional reason they didn't stop was simply the fear of losing sand traction with their stock-standard two-wheel-drive cars, if they slackened the hurtling momentum which sometimes smashed their cars to scrap.

Their attitude is best summed up in what must be the most unrelentingly humourless travel book ever written, the recent German "Abenteur Sahara," in which Peugeot driver Rainer Falk manages the seemingly impossible feat of making desert travel sound less romantic than a stolid wodge of knackwurst. He tells the story of two French co-drivers, who add a new twist to the mercenary expeditions by stealing, not buying, their 404's in France. Once through to Niger or Togo or somesuch they sell the stolen car, but keep a spare set of keys so they can re-steal it the same night and make a run for the border, selling it again in the next country....

We had the last laugh on one such nice soul, a rotund Teuton who studiously looked the other way as he hurtled past in his shiny Mercedes saloon, blanketing us in grit as he ignored us in our time of trouble. Twenty kilometres and a day on, we found him stranded in the sand. Logically, a Mercedes is not designed for the rigours of the desert, and his clutch had burned out. Pointedly we made a great show of offering him water, but were dismissed with an arrogant wave.

"I do not need your water," he sneered as he scanned the empty horizon with his binoculars. "I have arranged for a lift."

Indeed he had. That evening, miles further on, we watched as a dust-cloud on the horizon turned into a heart-warming sight. There was the Mercedes being towed at the end of a long rope, behind a Tuareg truck being driven as only Tuaregs can enjoy: flat-out at about 140 kilometres an hour, bouncing and slewing across the rutted desert. The Mercedes was in spectacular flight like a puppet on its drunken string, launched repeatedly skywards with metal-rending protest and making repeated emergency landings as bits fell off and the driver clutched white-faced at the madly-bucking wheel. Couldn't be happening to a nicer guy.

As for us, the painstaking repair held, and we puttered through Niger's Agadez and out of the Sahara, greeting with almost orgasmic rapture the first stretch of tarmac we had driven in three turbulent months. Much worse was yet to come, but for the moment we were happily unaware of the gathering clouds. It was enough that even if the recently-new car looked like it had just relived War and Peace, we had come through relatively unscathed.

We had crossed this magnificent wilderness in more than 3,000 kilometres top to bottom - but there was still so much we wished to see, for the Sahara is more than just sand. It was not to be; a sheaf of non-renewable visas had expired during our protracted misadventures. We fretted, too, about the imminence of the rainy season further south which would make the jungles of Zaire, horrendous at the best of times, utterly impassable. The rest of the Sahara would have to wait, from Libya to Mali and on to West Africa. Even the mystic and exotic Timbuktu, though returning travellers mused that it was no more mystic nor exotic than a freshly-laid camel-turd. There would be other times - times which are still at the very top of our agenda, merry masochists that we may be.

Black Africa lay ahead as our diplodocus adventure continued: lots of long thin bits and the occasional central solid bit. We would continue in the well-established pattern of our travels - hitting some of our targets with demented accuracy, missing others, but being buoyed up throughout by the glorious preposterousness of it all. And this despite the recommendation by a well-intentioned Indian journalist, previewing our newspaper-serialised account so far: "This is a story you should not fail to miss."

16
THE AGONY AND THE EXIT STAMP

It was my own fault, really, for stopping at a red light in the cut and thrust of West African traffic when nobody else does. A sickening crunch, and a battered Peugeot initiated anal intercourse with our Méhari.

Within moments a crowd coagulated as the guilty party began screaming doubts about my parentage. Onlookers shouted their versions of the accident. A policeman bellowed at us all and thrust his hand through the window to take away my driving licence, possibly forever. Traffic belched to a halt and tumultuous bedlam reigned, and at that moment a Tuareg vendor tried to sell me a watch.

"Good price, good watch!" he struggled to make himself heard above the uproar in French as he shoved a nasty timepiece through our window.

"No."

"Salaud! Why you stop for the light, stupid foreigner?"

"I am police. Give me your licence."

"In my country we stop for red lights, strange as it seems."

"Is a very good watch, no jewels, very cheap. You buy."

"Remove your watch from my car, I'm having an accident, dammit!"

Gaggles of children joined the fray with the standard greeting for foreigners, all the French they knew uttered in one breath:

"Bonjour ça va cadeau!" - Hello how are you (give me a) present.

"Merde, you shall pay for my damage, idiot Anglais..."

"For you I make a special price for this priceless watch..."

"I'll shove your bloody watch down your cakehole!"

"Now now Terence, he's only trying to make an honest living. Where's your sense of humour?

"Bonjour ça va CADEAU!"

"Show me your passports."

"Sense of humour? Right now I'm entitled to the sense of humour of a pain-crazed rhinoceros. Can't even enjoy a decent accident without some walking tourist trap trying to tap you on the wallet, mutter mutter grumble..."

"Bonjour cadeau ça va!"

"Give me your insurance papers and you must wait here six weeks for the court case..."

"BONCADEAU.....!"

"My last offer only 500 francs, you buy..."
"Bonjour ça va..."
"Okay you don't buy watch, I have genuine traditional African doll good quality made in Hong Kong...."
"See what you did to my Peugeot, imbecile!"
"Bonjour..."
"QUICK, THAT MAN STOLE MY PURSE!" shrieked Elise, as the crowd parted obligingly for the fleeing thief.

The policeman, upholder of the law, had to do something. He stopped reading my licence upside-down, then pointed the direction the thief had taken. Most helpful; I pounded off in pursuit while the salesman pressed a plastic giraffe on the now-gibbering Elise, the policeman wrote in his book, the man who had shortened our Méhari ranted on about my family origins back into prehistory, and children bonjourçavacadeauxed at me as I thundered past, in the vain hope that gifts would shower down on them as I ran.

The thief got away. And so, eventually, did we.

If you think we were unfortunate, pity poor Cliff. As his long-awaited letter now revealed, he had spent days almost disappearing up his own rear, trying to get out of Algeria. In Spain he became enmeshed in a swamp of bureaucracy when he tried to buy a secondhand 2CV and equip it with the necessary trans-Africa customs guarantees, so in desperation he went to France, then to England and finally settled for an off-the-shelf new car at phenomenal expense.

Back down to Spain, then stranded for days in Morocco because an obtuse immigration official didn't like his face or the quality of his bribe or somesuch. Finally into Algeria, and halfway to Tamanrasset his shiny new 2CV fell into the daddy of all potholes and had to limp back slowly to Europe, mortally wounded. As for more of the same, said his letter, thanks but no thanks and he had run out of esteem for the whole insane idea.

That night we auctioned his 38 socks on the Niamey campsite. Central Africa beckoned, and we would do it on our own - a prospect which we greeted with mixed emotions when travellers piled on their horror stories around the campfire. Conny from Germany had been held up by bandits after they broke six of his truck's windows with catapults. New Zealand hotel-chef Lawrie, soaking six teabags into treacle-like tea and then mashing them with a spoon for good measure, was replacing the window of his Land-Rover for the fourth time. A French group had been stripped and robbed at gunpoint in Sudan.

Pshaw, it couldn't happen to us. Or could it? The very next night as we camped free near the city, we were woken in a flood of adrenalin by the massed sound of throaty, raucous African voices charging in our direction - the closest we've ever heard to the heart-stopping war-chant from the film "Zulu," and with sinking hearts we knew we were about to be the next Rorke's Drift. The "danger" turned out to be a harmless military exercise, and a soldier came across to greet us.

"Bonjour," he said. "Ça va? Cadeau?"

I'd like now to tell you a funny story about Nigeria. But there aren't any. Untypically, we had over-reacted to the scare-stories about this enormous country and sped through almost without stopping.

Mercifully, we managed to avoid Lagos, repeatedly voted the world's worst posting in surveys by whingeing expatriates, and said to make Hades seem like a weekend break. I can't vouch for that, but it is true that travellers we met often spent an entire day fighting through the chaotic traffic just to get from one side of town to the other. And to this day I treasure a cutting from a years-old Lagos newspaper, a parliamentary transcript printed when the country was debating a switch to driving on the right. It reports the words of an Honourable Member standing up in the House to offer his considered, and serious, opinion.

"To facilitate a smooth changeover on our roads," he proposed, "the switch should be gradual. Traffic will continue as normal, except that in the first week official vehicles will move to the right, goods vehicles in the second week and private vehicles in the third."

Cameroon, according to the books, had eight million inhabitants. All of the natives were friendly, and all of them lived along the road we were travelling. One long, continuous, endless village it seemed, as we bounced over the corrugated track and spent ages at the end of each day trying to find a camping spot away from the peering crowds - usually without success, and when you opened your eyes at five in the morning, there would be the massed hordes lined up outside the car, shouting "TOURIST!!" and waiting for the show to begin. We came to Africa to see, not to be seen, and I began to experience the first twitching symptoms of a debilitating Greta Garbo-ish "I want to be alone" phobia which has plagued me ever since.

It was in Cameroon that we stumbled across one of the most pathetic people we have seen in years.

Along a mountain road, we were flagged-down by a French priest, Father Pierre. After exchanging a few words he almost begged us to spend the night with him at his mission-station, tucked away miles from anywhere in the middle of the bush. As the evening wore on in a constant topping-up of wine-glasses, he blurted out the sorry story of his lonely existence so far from his beloved France.

Father Pierre had run his mission for nine years, at first with the help of two nuns who had later departed because they were "psychologically ill." His careful requests for repatriation were turned down repeatedly - he had God's work to continue in the Cameroons, and that was his lot.

The morning after we arrived, Sunday and the "highlight" of a priest's week, he dressed in his priestly robes and finery, as usual, and went out to ring the bell to summon his flock to Mass, as usual. And nobody came. As usual. Anyone who recalls that classic heart-rending scene from Charlie Chaplin's "Goldrush," when he prepares his pitiful dinner for the girl who never comes, will know how we felt about Father Pierre that sad Sunday morning - one among an endless eternity of sad Sundays, as far as we could guess though his pride would never let him admit it.

"Oh yes," he said bravely. "Sometimes they come - if I promise them a cadeau."

The Central African Empire had recently crumbled after its cannibal Emperor Bokassa's reign of terror and his obscenely-expensive coronation. The Republic which he left behind was crushingly poor, reputedly Africa's poorest country, yet it had one of the continent's most bloated bureaucracies thanks to a strange arrangement whereby civil service salaries were paid by France.

It showed. Bureaucracy ran rampant in a land where not only does one require entry and exit visas, but travellers are even stamped with a flourish through the smallest villages which will have just a handful of inhabitants - and a travellers' check-post. Visas for a country are one thing - visas for a city quite another, and the C.A.R. even required separate entry and exit visas for anyone visiting the capital, Bangui. Woe betide you, too, if you wished to whizz through Bangui without pausing to savour its dubious delights, because the rules said that once in you could not leave for 48 hours.

The formality farce left its mark on the hapless traveller. At first you would stop dutifully at each checkpoint, filling-in yet again the ledger produced by an illiterate soldier, writing your name, address and all the other useless information. Umpteen ledgers on, the previous entries began to follow a pattern which echoed your own impatience: Donald Duck, address Disneyland; The Man in the Moon; Superman from Krypton; C. U. Later, of Alligator; A. Hitler, (Cpl.), late of The Bunker, Berlin; even the memorable J. Christ Esq., of flat 26, Heaven. And others more basic.

Near one town, we were stopped at four separate roadblocks in the space of a kilometre, this time in hopes of a bribe. Police would check lights, indicators, horn, and woe betide your pocket if any didn't work. In one case two consecutive checks took place within sight of each other, but it made no difference to the routine. "Bonjour, ça va, cadeau," said the more pleasant of the operators, but we had the last laugh on one with less gall than the rest.

"Bonjour," he said. "Ça va?" And as our faces darkened in anticipation he lost his nerve in the middle of his cadeau:

"Vous n'avez pas une petite ca-, er, ca-, carnet?" ("Do you not have a little... carnet," the customs document for the car).

In Bangui itself we wandered to the post office in the hope of word from home. Like others in the queue ahead of us, we produced our passports at the Poste Restante section, and mail appeared. The African standing at the next counter was fascinated by this magic, and dug in his pocket for his own identity document. He presented it, and waited.

The postal clerk was puzzled: "Have you any letters addressed to Poste Restante?"

"No," replied the African - but was still crestfallen when no mail appeared.

From Bangui we juddered on over mountainous corrugations which threatened to rattle the car to pieces. Elise was now fighting the first stages of the malaria which, this time, she would eventually cure herself, and every bump was like a bomb to her nerves. A hundred kilometres in a day was about as much as she could stand.

Bolts began to rattle loose, the petrol-tank mounting bracket sheared, our cupboards began to judder to bits, and one shock-absorber threatened to seize solid under the strain, but on we crashed.

By now we had accepted with only occasional depression that there was usually little point in stopping to study village life, for as soon as we did village life would stop and study us, and so the Kennedy Circus rolled on. It wasn't long before we met the Belgian family who chose to live in a 44-foot freight container.

Paul was an engineer contracted to look after the road - the only road - through the C.A.R. Once his gang had levelled out the worst of the corrugations in one section he would move on after a few months to another, reaching the end before starting at the beginning again several hundred kilometres back and so on into the mists of Sisyphean time. His ingenious solution to the problem of keeping a roof over his family's head in this constant shifting was to take a standard shipping container, cut doors and windows in it, slap some insulation and partitioning on the interior and cover the whole thing with a sun canopy. The result was a surprisingly comfortable three-bedroomed mobile home which could be picked up and trucked to the next site, along with the tank which would be built on a nearby hill to provide running water.

Spending time with Paul and his Thai wife gave us a working insight into the African, one which our normal passing-throughness could never provide. And as we talked deep into the night on the concrete verandah of his container, we realised how impossible it is for Europeans to ever really grasp the African mentality.

How could we ever accept, for example, that stealing is not so much a crime, more the perceived rightful appropriation of goods from someone who has more than the "stealer" and who should therefore be forced to share his wealth? How could we ever accept the lack of motivation which means that few Africans will work unless actually forced to do so? And how could we understand how nations can starve when their people live on the most fertile soil in the world - all for the lack of any initiative to go out and prepare the fields, do a little work, and wait to reap the bounteous harvest? There is malnutrition in areas where the food drops from the trees; there is rampant theft among people who hardly have anything worth stealing; there is a total disinterest in preparing or working towards the future. Discipline is an unknown concept, and why should a man sow for the future when God or the gods might well strike his field barren, or cause some other great disaster? Thus villages exist in a time limbo, their inhabitants achieving nothing, progress nonexistent, civilisation passing them by as they simply drift through life as generations before have done, living a precarious existence, suffering an appalling mortality rate, and leaving no mark on the world when they have gone. I once envied them their peaceful, carefree and lazy lives as we drove through villages immobilised and paralysed by apathy, lethargy and drunkenness, with sex the national sport and babies the unstoppable aftermath. These days I'm not so sure.

Do not adjust your mind - there are only two more footnotes to the diatribe about this chunk of wart-emblazoned world.

The first is a tale of two morals - ours and the Africans'. A local teenage girl was caught regularly in school, enjoying a bit of your full leg-over with boys on the desks between lessons. Outraged, the (European) headmaster called in the girl's parents. They quite understood the principal's chagrin.

"You are right, this is not good," agreed the father. "In future she must do it at night."

The second is a gag an expat told which almost has the ring of reality about it. It has two old colonial buffers discussing the difficulty of introducing rugby to Africa.

"The problem with these local chappies," droned one, "is teaching them the team spirit of the game."

"Quite right," agreed the other. "Trouble is when you're out there on the field and you pass them the ball, they simply hang on to it. For weeks, sometimes..."

In the next weeks our dream-trip turned to a nightmare, leaving us as dizzy and dazed as a pilot whose helicopter turns round while the rotor stands still. A punch-drunk catalogue of disasters threatened to sap us of the very spirit which had kept us on the road for years: debilitating illness; wounds which went septic; the most atrocious roads ever with a brave Elise struggling to hold the car from toppling over - onto her - as I picked a way through 45° ruts; building our own bridges over rivers; besieged by vicious tsetse-flies and clouds of mosquitoes which could even bite through towels; a fight with a drunken Zaire official; a late-night attack with machetes and burning torches; the car's braking system on the blink; a very complete breakdown mechanically and almost mentally - and driving over that $150 chicken. For a fortnight the trip was as much fun as a funeral and we thought that's what it would be as things went from bad to worse to appalling.

Those were the main points of the news and from here on the plot sickens.

Zaire has been the nemesis of many a hapless traveller and we were prepared for the worst. It wasn't enough, and if there are any points to be awarded for sheer suicidal foolhardiness, I reckon we earned a ten. Our troubles started with that damned chicken even before we crossed the border.

It's like this: when you run over anything in Africa, you pay on a sliding scale, depending on your stature and how loudly you dare argue. Bouncing along the potholed road to the Zaire border we sent a chicken to the great coop in the sky, and recklessly decided to save the money and make a foot-on-the-floor run for it.

Shouldn't do that on roads which make the Moon look like a circular autobahn. We hit the inevitable gulley and our car did another passable impression of a manic mole. Our axle had sheared, our engine mountings no longer mounted, and we were well and truly in it again.

Hard though it is to believe, the breakdown happened just three kilometres away from the last Citroën garage on our entire route through Africa. We spent the night among the local villagers and the next morning I set off on foot into Bambari to commission the repair. After several hours of trying, the grizzled French expatriate "mécanicien" managed to get his 40-year-old towtruck going. He rattled and clanked us back to his premises, then dug in his garden for an old 2CV he thought he had buried there "some time after the war." Cannibalising the necessary parts, he put our plastic humpty-dumpty together again - and demanded an exorbitant $150. Still, we never were charged for the chicken.

We were ready for Zaire - if we could provide some diesel fuel for the ferry crossing the border-river. When we found the diesel, the ferry's battery was flat and they asked for our little power-pack - which they drained in two seconds flat and still the ferry lay lifeless. Back and forth we were poled in dugout canoes while negotiations dragged on, and finally we waited a day while their battery was sent to a garage for recharging. When it came back someone had stolen the diesel, and we were sent for more...

Sit tight, it gets worse. Much worse. We had feared the onset of the rainy season in Zaire, which turns its notorious track into a quagmire. At least we had beaten the rainy season. By twenty minutes. The skies opened and drizzled down on us, but at this stage we were still so excited about the real jungle which loomed around us that we executed a little song and dance around an imaginary maypole. Further along the bridlepath-wide track, astonished Africans gawped at our rain-dance - and fled into the bush in terror.

As the storm electricity built up, we started the long hard haul along a road which had deteriorated utterly since the Belgians were the last to work on it before pulling out two decades previously.

We slithered, crashed, bounced, crawled and pussyfooted our way over the most appalling terrain we had ever seen. Whole sections of the road had been washed away and we would disappear down, down, down into vast ruts and gulleys, often with the car leaning sideways at 45° and Elise, fighting down her understandable fear and panic, heaving for all she was worth from outside to stop the car from falling over, and falling over onto her at that. There were endless rivers and streams to cross, sometimes bridged by old rotting planks with half-metre gaps between them, and sometimes not. If you were unlucky you slithered down the bank in four-wheel-drive and forded the river in hope, or you gathered what wood you could and rebuilt your bridge, or at best you inched forward with your heart in your mouth while your partner crouched in front of the car, pointing you a little left, a little right, s-l-o-w-l-y so that the tiny 2CV wheels wouldn't slip between the bridge-plank gaps and plunge you through.

For us it was bad enough; for an English family in an old Commer van coming later it was well-nigh impossible, because the van had its rear wheels further apart than its front ones, so that if the front ones stayed on the planks the rear ones fell through and vice-versa. Frequently, if you'll forgive me for saying so, their Commer came to a full stop, and it took them weeks. We managed the first nightmare 74 kilometres in "only" three days.

Then we arrived at the immigration post, where I committed the worst crime a traveller can perpetrate with an official here: I lost my temper, something which happens as infrequently as leap year. With only one way into Zaire the consequences could have been disastrous.

I sensed he was bad news from the first waft of alcohol and the first bleary stare from his bloodshot goldfish eyes - a man with as much kindly warmth in him as an electric chair. His conversation was an arrogant bark, and with no other way into Zaire all we could do was grit our teeth and our pride, and bob yessir, nosir. His authority was total and Hitlerian in that isolated jungle outpost, and it wasn't long before he had me fuming inside and running a private taxi-service for his benefit. With ill-concealed malice I ferried him back and forth between his various women, while he revelled drunkenly in the luxury of a white chauffeur and lied that the precious rubber-stamp we needed would be found at the very next stop, always the next stop.

On the fifth village rendezvous, as he sat supping beer with wife number three while I fought off the children pulling at everything pullable on the car while they demanded bon-bons, stylos (pens) and other sundry cadeaux, my hackles performed vertical take-off in a mushroom-burst of red fury, and I roared off back to Elise at the customs post, leaving him stranded with kilometres to walk. Honour and temper satisfied, but oh god what had I done?

He was not a happy man when we saw him the next morning, though like me he was by now more steamed-down about the whole affair. Greed overcame his inclination to "lose" the rubber-stamp forever and send us back the horrendous 74 kilometres we had come, for we considered it an appropriate time to break the rules and give him a cadeau. Our gift of a book raised his village status no end, but I've often wondered since what a semi-illiterate French-speaking

African with nary a word of English made of the collected and quite frequently impenetrable poetry of Dylan Thomas...

We drove away from the eye of that storm in a teacup before he changed his mind, and straight into a night-time attack.

It had not been an easy day, and just this once we neglected to take some of the most basic precautions of travel. There was no question of getting off the road to sleep, for the "road" was a steep-banked track flanked by thick jungle, and we were in any case the only traffic for days, so we elected to camp just anywhere along the route. As dusk fell we wearily pulled to a halt in the middle of the track and began to prepare our meal. We should have been warned by the sounds from a nearby village, but after fighting bureaucracy and the route all day we hardly felt like socialising, to "establish our credentials" and make sure we didn't frighten the ever-superstitious locals. Neither did we feel much like looking for another spot less populated. But grudgingly as the sound of drumming became more insistent, we started the car and at least drove a couple of kilometres on. It was a pointless move.

As we ate, we felt the uncanny stare of eyes through the undergrowth, though we couldn't be sure. From the invisible village the drums throbbed on, and we laid ourselves to bed a little uneasily. But then all through Africa you hear drums, and feel watched, so surely it's all right?

It wasn't. The noise swelled and was joined by shrieks of drunken shouting. Then it came closer, and closer, and all sleep now banished we tried not to communicate our anxiety to each other while we grappled to unhook the mosquito-net and grabbed for our clothes. Now the racket was within a hundred metres. I peered out through a crack in the curtains and my heart stopped.

"Shee-yit!" I gasped. "Stand by to repel boarders. There's a dozen coming at us with machetes and burning torches!"

I don't believe the man who says he can confront such a situation fearlessly. Give or take a few fools and swaggerers we are all frightened, and as the aggression and alcohol came at us in wafts it was all we could do to shout to them haltingly, asking what they wanted. Fortunately one spoke a little French, and I stalled for time by telling them who we were and that we meant them no harm, while Elise frantically cleared the driving-seat in readiness for a getaway. The French-speaker said we had scared them, and as he did so one of his alcohol-fuelled colleagues held his fiery torch against our back-curtain and the mood grew steadily nastier with the first hack of a machete on the bodywork. Elise groped for a towel and water, ready to smother a burning curtain.

"It is better that you go, NOW!" said the spokesman. "Or there will be bad trouble!" We needed no urging. I leapt behind the wheel, turned the key - and the engine flooded. By this time the shouting had reached a crescendo as the drunken warriors began rocking the car, striking it with their machetes and trying to set fire to us.

"Oh god, start!" I pleaded as the engine coughed again and the shouting reached fever-pitch - and then we were off, bucketing down the track at full-tilt as Elise watched in horror while a warrior stumbled after us, his torch held to our flapping curtain which miraculously stayed unlit. Darkness and the world's worst road nothwithstanding, we didn't dare stop our inglorious flight for 10 kilometres until we were halted by the next broken bridge. The shaking took longer to stop, and for the first time we broke open our first-aid bottle of 80% Austrian rum. If this wasn't medicinal purposes, what was?

Had it happened just two days later this story would have been untold, for the car was about to be crippled totally, leaving us a sitting target for any evil-doers, drunkards, or people just plain frightened by our presence as those villagers apparently were.

By way of a preview our brakes packed up the very next day, and I eventually had to cut a panel out of the floor with our truly unmissable Swiss Army knife to make the repair.

It seemed like a big job at the time. In the light of what was to happen next, it was very small beer. Without warning as we drove through a village, the car gave a crack and a lurch, and we were grounded again. No, not yet another relapse of my ham-handed Saharan repair, for that had been fixed professionally back in Bambari. But as a probable after-effect of that strain, a spring-rod had given way. So, within the next ten minutes, did our sorely-taxed jack, and we slept that night at an impossible angle and with the drunken permission of the village headman whose domain we had so unwillingly invaded.

I dreaded the next days, not only because by this stage we were both fighting the symptoms of severe illness, possibly brought on by the fields of insect-bites blanketing our bodies. I knew only too well that any work I might do would be with the noisy, close and malodourous participation of the entire village. I fought not to be paranoid about the press of people, while Elise had her work cut out to make sure that tools and parts put down didn't disappear into the crowd forever.

On the other hand, we would never have managed without the crowd, for without a jack it was only people-power which could raise our car each time. We quickly learned that the men were useless at this job, either unable, or unwilling, or just plain uncoordinated. Six women were a better bet, and Elise soon had a team of human jacks (or perhaps more appropriately jills?) drilled and happy to show up their menfolk. The repair dragged on as people drifted in to offer fruit for money, or one lonely egg. Less cosily, people came constantly to beg and cadge, not just singly but sometimes assailing us in whole families (the assumption being, no doubt, that the family which preys together, stays together?).

As the repair progressed the village chief offered us food. Great idea - we were hungry. Then he came with the food, a grilled monkey-hand. We were not so hungry. With its pink palm upwards it was unnervingly reminiscent of those we have loved, but how to refuse the kind offer? Elise came up with the solution when she passed it back to the chief, intimating that as he was the most important among us he should have the honour of this delicacy, while we tucked instead into the proffered stew of cassava/manioc and plantain. It could have been worse - like writer Redmond O'Hanlon in the Amazon, we could have been required to suck out the eyes of the monkey and swallow them. ("I was surprised how easily they separated from their stalks," he recalls in his recent book "In Trouble Again." Only later did he find it was a practical joke played by the village chief...)

Our labours were interrupted by a delegation of women; they had screwed up the courage to ask Elise whether they might "borrow" me for some time.

"Why?" she asked, intrigued.

The women looked at her as though the answer was self-evident.

"Because we want white babies, of course." Elise was flattered to have been asked, but refused on my behalf; I had no say in the matter.

"But madame," they persisted, "only one night!"

It is true that any modest service I might have been able to render would first have had to overcome a mighty barrier - the women's very noticeable beauty-enhancement. Rancid butter mixed with goat fat and spread liberally over the liberally-spread ladies does little for the Western male libido.

While I tinkered on, Elise performed a routine tyre-change. The locals enjoyed it heartily, though men constantly wandered over to warn me not to let her do it; a mere woman could not possibly do such things properly. They were even more flabbergasted at my own evening duty: washing-up the dishes. A woman doing man's work was ridiculous enough, but a man doing women's work? Aaaii, strange indeed are the ways of the white man...

Elise was invited to join a group of women for a day in the fields. They walked for nearly two hours to get there, then dug, ploughed, harvested, gathered firewood and collected water.

"On the way back over terrible, steep tracks in the murderous heat," she told me later, slightly shamefacedly, "they were burdened with firewood over their shoulders, full water-containers in their hands and full baskets on their heads. But I wasn't carrying anything - and I held them up because I was on the verge of collapse. When we came home I was close to exhaustion, but they had to get stuck into the cooking for the men, who had been smoking, drinking, gossiping and playing games all day..."

My tinkering finally blocked the broken spring with a bar of metal, and we set off, the whole car's weight now held by just two bolts. Exactly 26 kilometres later the bolts sheared and we had to wait hours for passing humanity, trying to assemble enough wandering women to raise the car once more as I started from scratch. By now the fever was racking us both, and we also had to fight off the hordes of black flies and other biting beasts while we worked in the merciless, sapping heat as the jungle loomed oppressively around us.

Several hours later we set off once more - for just three kilometres,and "crack" it went again.

Now, finally, it was all just too much. How do you cope with a despair so black, so bleak it is a morale quicksand? Someone once said farce is tragedy speeded up, but though we could cope with farce, the tragedy it left in its wake now threatened to floor us. Bowed by this farrago of disaster heaped upon disaster, racked by fever, attacked mercilessly day and night by every manner of flying and biting thing, no sign or support of a white man in days, drenched in the sweat of our illness and the killing tropical sun, our habitual high spirits ebbed away to hopelessness as the trip lay in ruins.

The way things were going, show us a silver cloud and there was sure to be a dark lining around it, and just at that moment we might have prayed for a giant hand to break through the cloud and spirit us away out of Africa. Conscience urges you to plug on regardless; human frailty cries "Let me out!" But in the middle of that jungle-nowhere there's not even that ultimate option, of giving up, for there's only one way out of the mess and that's on. In all the years of travel we had, for the first and only time, really met our match, and with no-one looking we clasped each other tightly and indulged in the catharsis of a quiet, unashamed weep.

Then, fighting waves of sickness, back to that bloody suspension. From here on in, it could only get better. Surely?

There's a cherished line in the trail-blazing review "Beyond the Fringe," when the British greet the outbreak of World War Two with "Never mind, let's put on the kettle and have a nice cup of tea." It certainly soothed our troubled breasts, when a British tour-truck driver did just that for us.

His "Encounter Overland" group was the first sign of traffic we had seen in days, and it was all we could do not to make idiots of ourselves by kissing his feet. Tea over, he and the second mechanic hauled out a toolkit which could have rebuilt the Tay Bridge. While they fiddled on, the group's nurse did her best with the worst and most infected of our insect bites, and several hours later we were on our way again. But slowly, very, very slowly, because what we still had was non-suspension on one wheel, the whole held by three bolts and still liable to shear at the slightest bump.

We had been told of a missionary with welding equipment a couple of hundred kilometres on. They were the longest kilometres of our lives as we crept at no more than six kilometres per hour in low-range, padding gently over every real and imagined dent in the track and praying to a god we had long ago forsaken, holding our breath each time the car heeled-over in the murderous ruts to heap its unwieldy one ton onto the improvised bolts.

It was almost unbearable not only for the speed and the tension, but for the fight with the people en route. At six kilometres per hour you are totally vulnerable as you pass through the villages. People pester, they grab, kids hang on and try to ride sending your sense of impending doom haywire; people beg, they cadge. In one village where we refused to stop, a local trying for a cadeau got so angry he actually wallopped Elise on the arm, leaving a large red weal. All that and trying to nurse a crippled car to safety, too.

We limped into the town of Buta with all the vivacity of pennies falling into mud. We drove out one week later with our car, and our spirits, miraculously restored. Two young Norwegian missionaries are owed more than they can ever know - a moral debt which is all the odder considering our fairly frank rejection of any and all religion, other than the facetious "Devout Hedonism" I sometimes fill-in on forms which ask such things. We've never been too sure about the overall good which missionaries do, either - but if our souls could still be saved, Harald and Arnhild would have done it, not with any of the trappings of their creed but simply with help, companionship, penicillin, coffee and a welding-torch.

They were the most untypical missionaries you could hope to find: in their late twenties, he vital and energetic with flowing long hair, she carrying the younger of their two children African-style on her back, while the child carried its doll in the same way, at the same time. The mission-station was all that held together the fabric of local life now that the Belgians had been replaced by a black administrative void. Even the local police relied on the mission for communication with the outside world, for the Edvardsens had the only radio for miles around which worked. Zaire's government seemed unable to provide its rural folk with even the basics like education and health care, and as the situation got steadily worse it fell to the missionaries to fill the gap.

As one veteran expat put it so succinctly: "Zaire is going backwards with remarkable speed. It's currently at about 1905 and heading rapidly for the turn of the century."

Harald turned his garage into a car-assembly plant for us, rebuilding part of the suspension almost from the ground up, while I stood gormlessly by under the influence of fever and the antibiotics they had given us.

Before we left, the Edvardsens told us of the trials they had endured to set up their church.

"It took time and a lot of frustration," recalled Harald, "particularly when so many of the Africans placed in charge hadn't joined because they were especially religious, but simply because it gave them power over others. Then while getting the money to build the church was one problem, having the building materials constantly stolen was another.

"When we finally got it going, perhaps rather foolishly we decided to run it on European lines. At the very first service we passed the collection plate into the congregation. It was never seen again."

17
JOHN THOMAS TO THE RESCUE

We stood our ground on the jungle-backed river-bank, arguing gently with the ferry-captain as he puffed at his pipe stuffed with brown paper and banana leaves. Behind him the first-mate hammered and hacked with rusty wire and string made of goathair, trying to repair his standard African footwear: sandals with a tyre-tread for the sole and strips of inner-tube looped into uppers.

Who could blame them for trying to charge a fare on their officially-free ferry? We were the only customers in days, and the Zaire government hadn't paid their salaries for four months - though there were rumours that local civil servants might be lucky once the rainy season passed and the salary-truck could get through.

Stubbornly we maintained that was none of our business, and I offered only the last five litres of diesel fuel we had carried several hundred kilometres. Diesel trucks don't get through, either, and as every sensible traveller knows, no fuel, no ferry. The captain puffed away implacably - but then motioned us to drive aboard. The diesel engine belched into life, and we set off into the middle of the wide river. Then the engine died.

"Ah, my tourist friends!" beamed the captain. "The engine she just now not working."

"Not working? But we're in the middle of a fast-flowing river! Why don't you drop the anchor?"

"No anchor."

"The current will sweep us down!"

"Not if I start the engine."

"So start the engine!"

"You are my friends?"

"Yes, whatever you say, just start the engine; I think I hear rapids."

"Ah, if I start the engine for my friends, my friends must show their thanks."

"Blackmail! This is a free ferry."

"No cadeau, no go."

We gave in with good grace. You had to admire his style, and did we ever have a choice? Elise produced some brewers yeast tablets, told him they were powerful medicine to make him strong and that he shouldn't, under any circumstances, take more than one a day. The first mate, like all Africans, wanted the status of wearing a sticking-plaster, and Elise applied an Elastoplast to a scratch which had healed some time the previous year. Then the captain, popping a pill, lost his pipe overboard.

His disappointment was almost palpable, but the stern old skipper could not allow himself to show it. Neither could the crew, who had almost but not quite sighed in unison as the pipe disappeared. It would be a disgraceful thing to show pity in this hardest of worlds; only women are so weak. But we could feel sorry, so sorry at this grievous loss that we gave him more pills, and a little money to buy a new pipe. He grunted his appreciation gruffly; our friend for life, he started the engine and saved us from being swept through the rapids and out inexorably towards the Atlantic. Powerful stuff, brewers yeast, and things were looking up.

Now all we had to do was find a hundred litres of petrol in the next town, Kisangani, to see us out of the jungle and into Uganda. Many had tried, most had failed.

The gods were with us - or if they weren't, certainly two friendly local Dutch expatriates were, armed with their precious permit which entitled the holder to petrol. Heavy with our stash of cash - our hundred litres needed a wad of funny-money as thick as two London telephone directories - we watched what happens when inflation runs riot and there's less to the value of money than meets the eye.

The petrol attendants had neither cash-register nor wallets. As customers handed over hundreds of notes at a time, the money was thrown into a large suitcase perched on the pump. Every twenty minutes, the manager came to replace the suitcase with another.

In Kisangani we were as happy to see other travellers as they were to see us, and we formed an odd little convoy to take us through the rest of the jungle. Karel and Connie were two Hollanders whose trip was fuelled by coffee, or so it seemed as he swallowed up to 16 cups a day and they supplemented their liquid diet by making popcorn in the back of their cavernous truck. The unlikely nature of the convoy was completed by the exotically-named English tour group, "Economic Expeditions," a gloriously-motley bunch travelling through Africa at half the price asked by the more conventional operators. That they did it sitting sideways on the back of a tip-truck which would be sold at the end of the run partly explains the "Economic," and there was none of the passenger molly-coddling found in other groups. There, if a truck got stuck its paying passengers would often sit back and wait for the driver to sort it out. With "Economic," if they did that they'd still be stranded in Africa.

On we lurched together down the ludicrously-named Pan-African Highway; a rude, rough slash through the undergrowth, it lacked only one letter to make its name appropriate: an "i" in the middle of Pan, as we bucked, crashed, juddered and smashed along it through overhanging vegetation which reached out triffid-like to snatch at unwary Economic-ers on the back of their tip-truck.

Near a pygmy village we were surrounded by the little people offering us goods. They proffered bows and arrows, bananas, or fast-food just-heat-and-eat frogs still squirming in an imprisoning tied banana-leaf. In return they wanted valuable merchandise: empty tins and old bottles.

By the town of Beni, near the Ugandan border, we allowed ourselves a celebratory meal and several yelps of relief. We had done it! Nearly a thousand tough kilometres on through the maze-like, treacherous jungle and the hard times were over, give or take a few trigger-happy soldiers in the next war-torn country.

Wrong again. The last 50 kilometres took days as the Economical truck bogged repeatedly in the "poto-poto," the cloying mud of the Virunga mountain area.

As often as Economic or our Dutch friends bogged down (we never did, either here or in the Sahara; our car just fell apart instead), our convoy was blocked by queues of sunken trucks. In good, fatalistic, what-the-hell African style, once a truck squelched stuck in the mud, drivers would just shrug, wander off with other stranded drivers for a good time together and wait for better days and the dry season. Sometimes for weeks at a time...

Entry into Uganda was a doddle, though there was a tense moment when an armed soldier pointed his loaded AK-47 at the Economic travellers, telling them they must be escorted to the Immigration office under guard.

"Okay," said the traveller nearest the business end of the barrel. "But why should you have to walk? Jump on and we'll give you a lift."

"Aaii, thank you sir," said the soldier - and passed up the AK-47 while he climbed aboard.

In principle Uganda was no longer at war after its post-Idi Amin civil strife. In practice it was a country of countless little private armies, all armed to the teeth with leftover matériel and out to get what they could while anarchy still prevailed. By roadblock number 19 in the first afternoon our passports had been thumbed relentlessly right-way-up and upside-down, but we at least still enjoyed the relative immunity of a white skin. The locals were not so blessed, and were milked mercilessly of what few belongings they had as the price for getting through each barrier.

The capital Kampala was just as lawless, and the campsite once we had found it turned out to be a shattered, bombed and blasted mess. Half of Economic's passengers took one look and opted for a hotel instead. It was not a wise decision. As the city echoed to its usual gunfire that night, they heard the sound of shrieking, shots and assault with very grievous bodily harm along their hotel corridor. There was no need to go out to investigate - the blood trickling under their door told them more than they wanted to know.

Our sojourn on the ex-campsite was just as convivial. After forming a laager with our three vehicles, we six thought it prudent to mount an all-night rotating watch. In the middle of Economic-driver Martin's spell, we were woken by shouts as he went in hot pursuit of a thief who had stolen one of our jerrycans.

In the chase the thief dropped his booty and ran. Ten minutes later as we sat around the campfire castigating Martin for being so foolhardy in a country with as many guns as people, the thief reappeared just outside the fence and our vision.

"Give me my jerrycan," he shouted. "I am armed!"

Fortunately for us he wasn't, and "his" jerrycan continued to be ours. But it was a long night.

(A year or so later we heard how Martin came badly unstuck in Uganda while transacting the sale of another truck. The buyers passed over the money for the vehicle - then held him up at gunpoint. Martin resisted, and was shot. He managed to drag himself, bleeding profusely, to a nearby police station to beg for medical help, but the officers on duty refused to call an ambulance until they had spent an hour taking down details, during which time Martin fainted repeatedly. He eventually recovered in England, and as far as we know is still running tip-trucks to Africa).

Once into Kenya we were on familiar territory. Surely now we'd be dealt a few more of life's easy cards? We weren't to know there were still some pretty devastating jokers in the pack.

But for the moment contentment lapped around us as we basked and bounced in and out of one magnificent Kenyan game park after another. The press of people had gone, though we were still bothered by thieves and beggars. The thieves were monkeys, or an old baboon we called Boris who stole Elise's last Zaire mango when our backs were turned, and the beggars were the birds which fluttered and hovered hoping for crumbs.

Flamingoes turned Lake Nakuru pink; the plains were bursting with antelope; warthogs shuffled through the undergrowth; we threw a pebble at monkeys threatening our fruit-basket and they showed their talent for mimicry by pelting us back with rotten figs. At two in the morning a bat flapped into the car and liked it so much we couldn't separate him from the pillow, so out the whole pillow went, to be retrieved empty the next morning. At hot-springs Lake Bogoria, Elise boiled our precious, saved tin of English steam pudding on the scalding and sulphurous jets coming out of the ground.

Elephants were unpredictable, as they blundered one day into our Samburu campsite and shocked themselves and us. Floating logs we could have sworn were floating logs turned into crocodiles and floating logs we could have sworn were crocodiles turned into floating logs. All that really disturbed our mobile shangri-la was the small matter of being charged by a herd of angry buffalo...

Dusk had just started to drape as we decided to camp for the night off the main road. Gently we turned off the tarmac, picking our way through the grass, constantly alert for dips or hidden burrows which would swallow our car.

Suddenly we saw a brown movement off to one side. Then another, and the horizon was bristling with buffalo. Buffaloes are creatures than which there are few more dangerous, either because of their cunning, their tenacity, or their sheer unforgiving stupidity. Which puts them at least one character trait up on us.

"Don't worry," I told Elise glibly, "they won't take any notice of us. Relax!"

That's when they charged.

Hearts in our mouths and foot flat on the floor it was to hell with the suspension and get the fornication out of there! We hurtled over the rutted ground, our engine screaming its protest several thousand r.p.m. over its limit, ditto our heartbeats, as the thunder rumbled on in our mirror and we invoked all the saints we had renounced years ago to let bygones be bygones and give us a break.

Only just, 28 horsepower was barely faster than a dozen buffalo-power; hence this book. The moment was no less harrowing in retrospect, when we began to doubt the next morning that the attackers had indeed been buffalo, rather than the ubiquitous and playful gnu, or wildebeest. Whatever the case, being on the receiving end of Africa's wildlife certainly does wonders for any emotional anorexia you may be suffering.

Very much later, touring the Masai Mara game reserve with our Dutch colleagues, we did something similar, this time breaking the very strict rules. We almost got what we deserved.

Rather than pay the exorbitant campsite fees, we decided to chance our luck and look for a sheltered bush for the night. For the first time ever since we had driven our wonderful 4x4, I managed to bog it in the mud, and by the time we were on solid ground again it was dusk. Karel set off on foot to search for a suitable camp-spot, followed by Connie, while we stayed with the cars to clear the caked mud.

Minutes later the bush burst apart as Karel set a new world sprint record. His face like a sheet, he yelled at Connie:

"Run, in God's name, RUN!!"

They fell into their truck, pale, speechless and paralytic with fright. "Lion," gabbled Karel. "Big one. Bush. I wanted, piss. On him, almost!!!"

When the police came to arrest us, having watched the whole (illegal) charade through distant binoculars, our shaken companions were almost glad to see them. And to spend the night in a locked barracks, fine or no looming fine.

Ah, Mombasa! Kenya's fabled ocean playground and tropical host to all sorts of exotic delights: sun, sand, sea, surf, thieves, AIDS, malaria.... And all so wonderfully unmarred by discretion and good taste.

So there we were a few hours down the coast from the city, lying around on the beach under the signs warning that "The management is not responsible for any injury caused by falling coconuts." We were swept away with ennui and stirring up complacency, wallowing in the Good Life as we washed away the cares of the road's past difficulties in the warm Indian Ocean waters, pausing only to brush away the flies and the vendors selling plastic giraffes and unspeakable wooden elephants.

On the 10th of the month we were badly bitten by mosquitoes. On the 11th I had a neck so stiff I could have modelled for the maker of those plastic giraffes. On the 12th I tried to stand up, but a drunken wobble spread down my spine and the ground came up to say hello. On the 13th I was sweating like a manic sponge, and on the 14th malaria was almost visibly oozing out of every pore, body dehydrating rapidly and thermometer 40°C and rising as I threatened to strangle myself on my own contortions.

The next section is brought to you courtesy of the manufacturers of "Help," the wonder remedy, as I wasn't too handy with a notebook at the time.

Elise and our Dutch friend set off in search of a doctor and if it wasn't so tragic it would have been funny, as they and the European doctor managed to miss each other in the maze of the local hotels for three hours, after which he went back home to the faraway city. By late afternoon I was semi-comatose and it was the bush clinic or nothing, as the Dutch bundled me into their truck and went crashing through the undergrowth in search of the elusive red cross.

To anyone familiar with the more genital aspects of English slang, I'm almost embarrassed to say I owe my life to a John Thomas. The redoubtable Doctor Thomas, West Indian, very black and very competent, hooked me up to just about every bit of equipment he could muster in that rude, thatch-roofed hospital hut in the middle of nowhere. Drips, injections, pharmacy-loads of pills, and all the while Elise sat holding my hand and hoping, as the fever ebbed and flowed like the tide and John Thomas warned of the worst if cerebral malaria took hold.

The next day I was over the hill, and probably have been ever since. The fever was broken; and with John Thomas beaming at me ear-to-ear in triumph and Elise weak with relief I shook his hand limply, silently vowed never to use his name in vain again, and was carried out to recuperation, spared sight of the bill for fear of a relapse.

Uneventful and animal-filled weeks later we were in Tanzania's Serengeti Park for the second time in a decade, appalled at the deterioration. After the relative opulence and efficiency of Kenya, the very apparent collapse of Tanzania's peculiar system of socialism had turned the country's economy into a quagmire. Tourism had virtually collapsed, taking the park facilities down with it. In some of the game lodges staff couldn't even supply visitors with a glass of water, let alone the more sophisticated lubrication most tourists expect. It was all infinitely sad, but at least the animals were still there, in abundance, even if the occasional wildebeest or zebra ended up on the game lodge dinner-table for lack of normal steak. An interesting taste sensation, but after trying both of them we have to admit that Dunlop, Goodyear and Michelin probably do it better, and less chewily.

As the country crumbled almost visibly around us, with cars grinding to a halt for lack of spares, shops closing because they had nothing to sell, we suddenly found ourselves stranded near the foot of Kilimanjaro with no petrol. Rumour had it there was fuel in the town of Arusha, and we limped in on our last drops.

Readers with memories of the 1973 Arab oil-boycott may remember having to queue for petrol. But not, I'll wager, for three days solid.

The petrol station opened each day for half an hour, and each day like everyone else in the long, winding queue, we pushed our car forward, then carried on life on the pavement, sleeping in our queued car at night. At the end of the third day we reached the front of the queue.

The attendant was apologetic.

"Sorry, now all finished sir," he said.

"What, finished just today, or finished-finished?"

"Finished-finished."

"When will you get new petrol."

"Don't know sir. Maybe August. Maybe not."

Foreign passports and a bit of bluster eventually saved us, when I barged into a local bigwig's office, waving my passport and lying through my teeth about all the valuable foreign exchange we were bringing in as tourists, (true enough - but it was going straight into the black market at six times the official rate), and warning that we would only continue to bring it in if we could have petrol. We were allocated enough to get us to the next town - where we had to go through it all again.

Still, at least eggs were in good supply, so we wouldn't starve.

"How much are they?" I asked the girl in the egg-shop.

"One shilling each."

"Okay, I'll take ten."

She reached proudly for her calculator.

"Um," she pondered as she jabbed at the keys. "Ten eggs at one shilling each, that's, um, um... No, no good; ten eggs, times one shilling, um..."

I waited patiently for the answer, then gave her a 50. But I hadn't the heart to walk out with the 45 I got back in change.

The Malawian manager of the lakeside rest-house wrote down our details with pedestrian slowness.

"Your family-name?"

I told him. It went down as "Candy."

"Address?"

"London, England."

"L-u-n-d-n," he wrote at snail speed. Elise decided to be friendly with some small talk.

"It's a long way, huh?" she said of our address.

"L-o-n-g-w-e-h-u-h..." he wrote.

But such nice people, despite the fact that Customs confiscated our all-Africa guidebook because it was "subversive." With its geographical background information, addresses of hotels and the rest of the travel trivia it was no more subversive than a royal wedding or a furniture catalogue, but unfortunately it just happened to mention in passing that Malawi might not be as entirely democratic as the Westminster system envisaged. Dynamite stuff in the wrong hands, so off with its head.

The smothering over-niceness of the Malawian people eventually drove us along a dry deserted river bed in search of a little privacy for a while. It lasted only until the very first sleep-encrusted hint of dawn the next morning. There was a knock on the car window. I peered out blearily - and I was staring into one of those wonderfully-African all-teeth smiles which makes every other smile you ever saw a leer.

"Good morning," it beamed. "I have come to greet you!"

"What? Greet....? Good grief man, it's ten past five in the morning. I'm still sleeping."

"That's quite alright sir," said the smile. "I will wait."

So he did, and finally there was nothing for it but to arise and be greeted. Darius turned out to be a student desperately anxious to practise his English, and to convince us that Malawi was indeed, as the tourist brochures had it, "The Warm Heart of Africa." The rest of the day he dragged us from one set of mud huts to the next, while we revelled in the opportunity to wallow in the richness, the dusty panorama of everyday village life.

We were introduced to his first mother, his second mother, ("My father has only two wives at the moment,"), and then the village elders, for whom young Darius went into the most uncomfortable, and to us almost demeaning, walk on his haunches as a required token of respect for one's elders, almost pressing himself to the ground as he shuffled lest he give offence. The inevitable "mealie-meal," the staple diet of ground, boiled maize flour, appeared and was served as we swallowed and smiled our thanks, burning our fingers as we rolled balls of it African-style without the use of any implements. "A wonderful food," enthused Darius. "I can eat it all day." As do some of the children to the exclusion of anything else, their distended bellies and listless looks a sure symptom of the first signs of the "kwashiorkor," a beri-beri deficiency disease brought on by this endless, inadequate diet.

It was a day damaged only by our silly mistake on leaving. We bowed and hand-shook our profuse thanks to one and all, genuinely grateful for this insight into Africa, then turned to go. As we did, a village elder growled something at Darius, who acknowledged by going into another simian crouch before scuttling off to do his grandfather's bidding. He returned with a live, squawking upside-down chicken.

"For you to eat," he thrust it out. "My third grandfather wants you to take it."

It flapped, and bit Elise's hand, and there was a quick bit of mind-boggling as we contemplated the feather-filled chaos it would bring to our Méhari. Elise was quickest off the mark with a polite excuse.

"Thank you," she said. "It is very nice, but, but - - er, we only eat vegetables."

Translated, our refusal of their gift was greeted with disbelief, then with hurt. But the mistake was made and there was no going back.

We should have accepted, and set the bird free a few villages further. But I knew full well what would happen once it fluttered into our car. Quicker than you could say "Kentucky Fried" Elise would be stroking the damn thing, then feeding it, then harnessing it on a leash for walkies, and before we knew it we'd be off to the vet for a poultry-passport to see us through the frontiers. Hell, after she read how Noël Coward once took a lobster on a leash for a walk in Paris, anything was possible.

Crime is endemic in Africa, but in Zambia we found a thief so hardened that if he had been the Titanic, the iceberg would have sunk.

Rule One in Zambia is never to leave your car unattended; it tends to shrink in your absence. A traveller we met lost two hubcaps from his VW bus in Lusaka, the capital, while filling-up at the petrol station. A tidy-minded man, he decided to replace them immediately and parked outside a hole-in-the-wall shop selling secondhand hubcaps.

"VW Kombi, hm?" said the friendly owner. "No, I don't have any hubcaps in stock - but my other branch does. Let me give you a coffee and I'll send for them."

Our friend supped gratefully, pleasantly surprised at the hospitality and helpfulness, and when the two hubcaps came they were pronounced suitable and he paid the asked price.

Yes, you probably know what's coming. He had just bought his own two remaining hubcaps, removed from his bus while he waited. The police merely shrugged.

Even knowing all that, I still found it hard to believe as I sat in the front of our car waiting for Elise to shop, that a thief could have the gall to try breaking-in at the back. I shouted; he ran; I moved into the back of the car to forestall another attempt; and he tried to break in at the front... And a policeman stood and watched it all with utter disinterest.

At the Livingstone/Victoria Falls campsite, two young Dutch backpackers asked if we minded whether they slept close to our car for safety. Sure, no problem - but we didn't quite realise they were so paranoid about the risks that they actually slept right underneath our car, squeezed between the chassis and the ground. Had they warned us in advance, we would have been spared the embarrassment of having to apologise for using our improvised funnel-toilet in the night, its contents emptying through a plastic tube in the floor...

Their shoes were stolen notwithstanding.

Crime must flourish in a society which has so little - though in Zambia that's an odd factor: that there's so little to steal.

So many of the basics are missing, as the country's repeated food riots showed. Batteries, razor-blades, toilet-paper, sugar - everything is in short supply at one time or another.

Even the duty-free shelves of Zambia's international airport carried a full supply of shortages. Where they could have been creaming precious foreign-exchange from the thousands of international transit passengers each week, all that was on display was a counterfull of locally-made cigarettes whose tobacco fell out if you held them upright, one mottled bar of Cadbury's, a bottle of suspiciously-pale Black Label Whisky, and a dog-eared copy of an old Cosmopolitan.

But never mind, at least we could order a beer. One. When we asked for another the waiter said we'd just had it. And when we rejected the unspeakable sandwich he brought, he simply shrugged, turned on his heel and ate it himself.

The situation was far better in neighbouring Zimbabwe. Or was it? The five-page menu in a local restaurant there opened-out as interestingly as an ostrich-feather fan and offered several score dishes. Only on reading the small print did you realise that everything was a permutation of five ingredients:

"One egg; one egg and chips; two eggs; two eggs and chips; three eggs.....one egg, one tomato and chips; two eggs, one tomato and chips; one egg, two tomatoes and chips; one sausage without chips; one sausage, one egg.....three eggs, three tomatoes, three sausages, three slices of bacon, and chips....."

Botswana must have the world's noisiest sunsets. The sun doesn't so much sink over its dusty, scrub horizon, as crash cacophonously.

Elephants trumpet, lions roar, hyenas howl. The evening becomes redolent with whole exchange-fulls of warbling-telephone crickets. Beetles belt out a barrage of dripping-tap plops amid the plaintive cries of the night ape, the swishing and squeaking of bats, the night-splitting stentorian echo of grazing hippos in search of their nightly 200 kilos of fodder, the barking of baboons and the chatter of monkeys. Come dawn, the day shift takes over.

Away from its boring towns and cities, Botswana is the Africa of everyone's imagination: wild and distinctly dangerous, a country bigger than France but with one-sixtieth of the population, and where man is vastly outnumbered by animals.

Around 84 per cent of the country is desert, 17 per cent is set aside for wildlife and less than 2 per cent bears the imprint of human habitation. Some 1,000 kilometres from top to bottom or from side to side, it has just two main asphalt roads. For the rest you're on your own - and just how much on your own was made clear when I found myself locked into a staring match with a two-metre green mamba, one of the most deadly of Africa's snakes.

There we were in the heart of the continent's biggest swamp, the Okavango, just us and our hired canoe poler/guide, with the nearest town and help a minimum three days away. Mamba venom is fatal and we carried no serum, I remembered in curiously slow motion as I stared into those unblinking black eyes one metre away.

The handbooks say - with all the clinical logic which comes so easily to authors at their desks - that you should remain dead still. Eminently sensible, but even as my brain was rationalising this advice, my legs had made their own decision and I was scrambling away at a speed to do credit to a cheetah. Startled, the snake moved too - fortunately in the opposite direction.

After that reprieve, even finding a blood-sucking leech attached to one of your extremities is a distinct anticlimax, and for the leech the Surgeon-General's warning about smoking being hazardous to health rang true as we struggled to release its grip with the prescribed burning cigarette.

In 1989 Botswana announced a swingeing new policy aimed at attracting only the most up-market of tourists, pricing its attractions out of the pocket of more modest movers. Infinitely sad, for though East Africa has its fabled game reserves, Botswana has the advantage of being more unspoiled and relatively untouched by development, the press of population growth and mass tourism. For three days we were the only human beings in the Moremi reserve, an area the size of Holland. In a week on the Makgadikgadi Salt Pans, which would comfortably contain Belgium, it was just as deserted, with tens of thousands of flamingoes and marabou storks and a few straggling herds of buck. We shared the core of the Okavango Swamps with hippos, crocodiles, a few hardy local fishermen - and at least one green mamba.

In the sprawling Chobe reserve along the Zambian border, a week's travelling brought us into contact with half a dozen rangers, about the same number of tourists, three lions, dozens of giraffe and zebra, warthogs scuttling around every bend, antelope too numerous to even begin classifying, and more than a hundred elephants - one of which took it into his head that the park was suddenly overpopulated by two tourists too many.

He charged, and we did the most logical thing possible under the circumstances - we panicked. As three tons of trumpeting adolescent thundered our way, I threw the car into reverse and tried to put my accelerator foot through the floor. Hopeless, of course, when reverse gear is good for just 25 kilometres per hour and a well-tuned elephant can cruise at 50.

The good news was that the elephant changed his mind. The bad news was that we had reversed straight into a mudpool and after we brought our rampaging adrenalin under control it took an hour of digging, winching and sweating to get our shaken expedition back on the road again. We were at least less scathed than the tourists whose VW bus had been overturned by an angry elephant, though they suffered only scratches. Ditto the park visitors in a little VW-beetle who had the distinct bad luck to trundle round a corner and straight into the back legs of an adult elephant facing away from them. V-e-r-y slowly his legs buckled, and he sank his several tons gently onto their car, which spread itself over the track. They got out in time.

It's only a century or so since Botswana was "discovered" by the white pioneers. The true discoverers of the country - the bushmen - are now all but wiped out. Indeed, if one expatriate taxidermist in the dusty safari town of Maun is to be believed, until 1950 the Great White Hunters could get licences not just to kill elephant, big cats, antelope, rhino and the rest, but to shoot bushmen too.

We opted for something completely different in our travels, and for just this once parked our car under a thorn tree and set off in a hired dugout canoe with a black Botswanan guide. For the eight days we took a tent, umbrellas, sun cream, first aid, maps, a camera, binoculars, books and a small supermarket of tinned food. Our guide took five kilos of maize meal and a fishing net.

Day in and out we drifted through the maze of clear water which belies the murky images conjured up by the word "swamp." Along the banks, overgrown with reeds, waterbuck whuffed and bolted, fish eagles stared down at us impassively, otters splashed and dived, hippos drifted along running a taxi service for white egret birds cadging a lift on their broad backs. Occasionally there was the vicarious thrill of seeing a crocodile slither into the swamp, and with the heat at a searing 40°C the many swims we needed were fraught with an enervating sense of danger as we took it in turns to scan the clear water while the others cooled off.

Each afternoon we chose an uninhabited island on which to camp, hoping fervently that we had not set up our tent on one of the countless hippo paths. We had once been fortunate when a nocturnal hippo decided to scratch his bum on our car and almost turned us over, but out here, two tons of night-grazing hippo has no compunction about striding straight through a flimsy piece of canvas.

Now and then we would go walking, quietly grateful to the inventors of toilet roll as we followed time-hallowed advice, marking the route we had taken with bits of tissue on branches every hundred metres for fear of blundering off forever into the bush and oblivion. In eight enervating days we sampled everything - and everything sampled us, from mosquitos and spiders to that infamous leech and the heavy-duty tsetse flies. The piper would eventually be paid when I wrestled first with hepatitis, then with the debilitating water-borne disease bilharzia which sneaked up to lay me flat whenever I least expected it over the next two years.

Back in the car again, we wangled some permits and pointed ourselves westwards along the notorious Caprivi Strip, so long a no-go zone for tourists in the war of attrition between South Africa and Namibia's fighters for freedom, Swapo. Scanning every bump lest a landmine be lurking, we rattled on to Rundu on the Angolan border - a fortress town where every home had its own sandbagged bunker. Residents lived in fear of Swapo attacks, though experience showed there was not always too much to fear.

The IRA could have learned a lot from Swapo. Consider the attack which took place on a northern Namibian town just before we arrived. Two Swapo guerrillas from Angola (and I swear this is true, though only the battle-hardened locals could believe such a farce), decided to invade Namibia on a couple of rusty bicycles. Not only did they pedal hundreds of kilometres inland on their rickety machines, but they did it carrying a massive mortar which they then pointed at the town. It wiped out an unoccupied cowshed. They were captured because one of the getaway bikes had a puncture, and with two people on the other one they were not exactly a match for the six Land-Rovers, three armoured cars, two troop carriers and a helicopter sent to intercept them. Yep, a dirty business, war.

It was in awesome Namibia that we scavenged our first meals from a litter-bin.

No, we weren't that hard-up. Not quite. But as we stood gazing in wonder at the "Mukorob" or Finger-of-God landmark, a 34-metre tower of stone which has perched for tens of thousands of years on the spectacular eroded pinnacle of a hill, we were filled with wonder - both for the rock, and the behaviour of the German package-tourists in the bus next to us.

Obviously replete with a recent breakfast, they were throwing out their entire, provided "luxury packed lunches." Unopened. Well, I mean, in our position, wouldn't you, you know...? No? Well, if the idea bothers you, rest assured that it couldn't happen today. No indeed, because after standing for tens of thousands of years the Finger of God blew down in a storm soon after we had left.

On through some of the finest sights in Africa we trundled - the magnificent Etosha Game Reserve; the picturesque German coastal town displaced halfway across the world, Swakopmund; Africa's answer to the Grand Canyon - the inspiring, and lonely, Fish River Canyon; one-horse desert towns where even the horse had died... And then came news which curtailed our gentle Trundle Trundle Little Car, as we learned that a ship's timetable was about to close the chapter on this epic phase of our travelling lives, nearly 50,000 kilometres and more than a year on.

We had to speed through South Africa, aiming for the port of Durban and an ancient cargo vessel. Our Dutch shipping sources said it was the last one still to defy both sanctions and economics, by plying the route between Southern Africa and our goal once more, the Persian Gulf, from where we could drive the "easy" 10,000 kilometres back to Western Europe. It was either that, or drive all the way back up Africa. Given our average couple of calamities per country we would never survive.

The 16-day voyage stretched to 36 because of threatened cyclones, port strikes and mechanical trouble and we saw a lot of sea. Driven to distraction as the only passengers on this floating Robinson Crusoe island, I read the entire ship's library of 60 books, with no end of fascinating titles to choose from: "The Mariners Mirror," and "The Beginners Guide to Waterway Craft" (in Norwegian...), to "Edwardian Canals" and the most mind-numbingly, conversation-stoppingly sedative of all, "Dredging Today." Elise lay locked in mortal combat with her seasickness, not helped by the combined wafts of bilge and a cargo of six million eggs. That and the mention of yet another five-course meal at the captain's table - nay, the only table - enlivened by the skipper's interminable and lively-as-stewed-lead stories of raging seas and wartime exploits.

Certainly a trip with a difference, though, port-hopping back up Africa. That's theoretically not possible from boycotted South Africa, but lots of the shipping company's folding greenery changed hands in Mozambique, where the authorities issued a complete new set of paperwork obliterating any mention of naughty South Africa. By paying $50 a day we had been accepted as "nominal" members of the crew and issued with seamen's cards, so there we went on a memorable little sail marred only occasionally by excruciating boredom, next to which even watching grass grow would have been exciting.

Our car was buried under several tons of oranges bound for Oman ("Product of Botswana," they were stamped, and when Botswana produces oranges we should head for the spaceships because the Greenhouse Effect will be utterly out of control). Thirty-six days, with just the captain, and us, and his Chinese crew who spoke little English but did wonders for our morale in the teeth of the storms. As the ship shuddered alarmingly each time its screws were lifted high out of the foaming, lurching waves, they smiled as they showed us how they always keep their valuables permanently sewn inside their lifejackets. Just in case.

Today that rustbucket is pushing up seaweeds, but this time it got us there, just - though there were anxious moments when the ship veered away in totally the wrong direction and plunged off to Pakistan in search of a cargo, before finally turning back for the Gulf despite fears that we might become Iranian target-practice in the then-tense Straits of Hormuz.

Still, at least it was better than a conventional ocean-liner cruise, among the typically geriatric passengers sailing towards that final horizon. A cruise-liner crewman who popped across for a chat in Mombasa confirmed our worst fears.

"Anyone who doesn't think cruising is a dying trade should take a look in our kitchens at the end of a voyage," he mused.

"We carry so many retired people, we had seven in our fridges at the end of one long trip. And there are so many blue-rinses aboard, if you flew over by helicopter you'd have difficulty spotting the pool."

The ship docked in Bahrain, and police promptly arrested Elise once more as an illegal immigrant. We were home.

18
A LONG WAY FOR NOTHING?

So far, so peculiar. The equivalent of seven times around the globe we had looked at half the world, and somewhat less happily half the world had looked at us. But like the girl who said sex was a pain in the arse, were we doing it right?

Reduced to its core, overland travel entails sitting in a car while the world pans past. Someone once said and it might have been me, that it narrows the mind and broadens the buttock. More than 300,000 kilometres, 74 countries and hundreds of frontier-crossings on, we began to have our doubts. Could we have come a long way for nothing?

Might there actually be something to that Paul Theroux contention that travel, so broadening at first, eventually contracts the mind? At the very least our broadened minds were displaying cultural stretch-marks. And as for getting as much out of it as we used to? Inevitably as everyone past the intense emotional awakening of teenagehood knows, it gets progressively harder to savour every new experience with that depth and freshness you had in youth, no matter how hard you fight not to go gently into that good night.

True, the battering on the last African slog had taken its toll. We had never expected it to be a Dairy Box trip filled with soft centres, where every scene would be wrapped in foil, with fillings smoothly coated and offering a succession of pleasurable surprises. But neither had we been fully prepared for the sheer scale of that ragbag of adversity which caused our first physical and emotional grey hairs.

And whither the wide-open spaces? In many parts of Africa, the population actually doubled in the years between our first and last journey, with wildlife in retreat, and it showed. The continent is getting poorer, too, and hungrier year by year. A recent fictional character warns of a proposed African trip: "It's too late now. Africa isn't too friendly these days."

The simple truth is that all Third World travel is becoming steadily more difficult as populations and bureaucracy, like Topsy, just grow and grow. And if people are more numerous, it's also sadly true that for the traveller they are becoming less different. One-world culture is on the march in its T-shirts and jeans, drinking from Coke-cans and bearing ghetto-blasters which swop the jungle beat for disco. What's the point of venturing to far-off lands, when they do things exactly the same way there? The inexorable tide of development not only makes the world a steadily less-beautiful place - it makes the open spaces ever harder to find, and it hems them in a welter of restrictions. And how much is being ruined, too, by the cultural rape and rapine of mass tourism?

And yet...

Settling into "Dunroamin" suburban life, keeping down with the Joneses and measuring our lives against our neighbours' like socks in the wash has little appeal. Anyway, once you've had enough kids to make your mortgage seem worthwhile, it's too late to send them back or stuff them into a shoebox if you change your mind. No, we were born to wander and wander towards our non-pensions we certainly will, but how?

We have dabbled at a few ideas, trying walking, cycling, canal-boating, clopping along with a horse-and-cart and even crewing on a veteran sailing ship. They were all, well, different - but as full-stop alternatives to our usual life on the road these experiments offered more false endings than a Beethoven symphony. In the final analysis we soon realised that we are good at one thing only; asking us to do something else is like trying to persuade a train to drive off its tracks and break out across open country.

Then there's the love-affair with that silly plastic car; in comfortable discomfort it takes us where we want to go without entirely scrambling our ideals, and that's that. A children's pantomime character once said he didn't like adventures because they leave you late for dinner. As long as we've got our car, we can have our adventures and our dinner too.

Besides which, having been made honorary members of several of the 100-plus 2CV clubs around the world, we wouldn't dare change. At the colourful biennial international gatherings of upwards of a thousand 2CV's at a time, we have revelled in the camaraderie and have accepted the odd prize for our long-distance lunacy. We even attended the car's official 40th birthday party near Clermont-Ferrand in France in 1988. There amid fanfares which were extremely good for business, a local mayor named a new, empty street after the car's instigator - though I confess the odd doubt about sincerity when, staying late after the ceremony, we saw the municipal workmen remove the new road name...

Others may travel in more style than we do. But then as Cocteau noted, style is for some people a complex way of doing simple things; for others (like us) it is a simple way of doing complex things. The limit of our ambition is simplicity itself: to keep driving into every corner of the circular globe at more or less the same pace, for as long as we can. You could put our aspirations on a postcard.

Armchair psychologists may make something of it - of all the literary bric-a-brac of an earnest adolescence, the only piece I've never thought of discarding is this trenchant little poem:

There's a race of men that don't fit in, A race that can't stay still;
So they break the hearts of kith and kin; And they roam the world at will.
They range the field and they rove the flood, And they climb the mountain's crest;
Theirs is the curse of the gypsy blood, And they don't know how to rest.
If they just went straight they might go far; They are strong and brave and true;
But they're always tired of the things that are, And they want the strange and new.

We have to continue travelling for the same reason that when there is an itch, one tends to scratch it. Seventeen years since we started, I still can't really tell you why, because one journey I've never been too good at is the voyage into one's head, the meander into paperback psychology. I leave that to the likes of "Manwatching" zoologist Desmond Morris, who maintains that in our pursuit of the simple outdoor life we are reliving our animal past. Where others opt for accountancy or quantity-surveying, as the years sailed by we simply found, without quite willing it thus, that we had ticked the box marked "Other" on life's long career list. Some are born bums, others have bum-ness thrust upon them and like the man said, "once a bum, always a bum."

We simply have to keep going. The alternative is too ghastly to contemplate: settling down to an endless mental retravelling of our trips so far, rehashing our dog-eared stories as we head gracelessly towards old-bufferdom, battering listeners towards eye-glazing boredom with endless reminiscences of "When we were in India...," ending up as isolated as a loony with a sore throat in Hyde Park Speakers' Corner, and perceived as having to carry a government health warning like a pack of cigarettes.

George Bernard Shaw once listed the seven deadly millstones afflicting mankind as food, clothing, firing, rent, taxes, children and respectability. We have avoided all but the first three - but there is a price to pay.

We have a roof over our head, but it measures just one square metre. All we have in the world is what we can carry. We chose to have no children, without whom it all becomes possible. We don't have the security safety-net of any state's welfare system - not unreasonably, considering that for most of the 17 years, we have avoided the taxman through the simple and legal expedient of not having lived anywhere, or at least anywhere taxable.

We can neither endure nor enjoy the normal social round. We become closer companions to each other with each new challenge we crest; but our few really good friends are astonishingly scattered and only see us when they do, and sometimes when they least expect it halfway across the world. When we make new friends, we leave them. It gets quite frequently lonely, though Steinbeck said there is no cure for loneliness except being alone, and we've certainly got plenty of that; he struck another familiar chord when he said he was born lost and took no pleasure in being found.

Yet for all the rootlessness, the always-itchy feet, even the loneliness of the long-distance trundler, we wouldn't have life any other way - because it's incomparably free, fresh and constantly renewing. Upmarket gypsies, or in the trendy jargon of today's economists, "non-productive units," we reach the parts that others want to reach, and it's the only way we know to be as happy as hogs in slop. 'Tis a far, far better thing that we do, we tell ourselves as we sift the morse-code jumble of our unfulfilled dreams to consider where to next: Central and South America, Australasia, Eastern Europe, another bash at Timbuktu? Indeed, in the short time since this book was begun we have been part of an international convoy of 2CV's bouncing across Russia to snarl-up traffic in Red Square. And we have had to abort another African jaunt mid-Sahara, when the first bombs fell in the Gulf War and outraged Algerians took to using Europeans - any Europeans - as stone-throwing target-practice to vent their displeasure. But that, as they say, is another story. What is certain is that by the time this book rises with or without trace, we'll be well on our way again. "Not just anywhere; everywhere."

With our feet planted firmly in the clouds it is, if you like, a happily eccentric lifestyle. Actually, being called "a couple of ridiculous eccentrics" was probably the nicest compliment a despairing family-member could have paid us, though she meant it as an insult. Bernard Levin - not exactly the most uneccentric of men himself, witness his recent trans-Europe trudge in search of Hannibal's elephant footsteps - wrote: "We shall know that civilisation has ended when the last eccentric dies." It was Levin who also said that the British take their pleasures sadly, if not masochistically. For two Brits at least, one real and one adopted, I'd like to think he's wrong as that "urge to be someplace else" takes us once more. Judge for yourself.

And so this book is not the valediction, the swan-song of two "wandervogeln" hinted at the start of this word-salad. We will continue going where we haven't really decided to go, wherever that is. And in doing so, we will achieve something. Whatever that is. Never mind the length, feel the quality.

Of course it depends on our health. Seventeen years of collecting international germs the way others collect stamps, has left its indelible mark. Malaria, dysentery, bilharzia, hepatitis, poverty...

Yet of every illness in the book, there's only, really, one disease which absolutely, utterly, has the final say in what we do. In both of us the virus is chronic. In both it recurs with quartz-crystal regularity.

It's called wanderlust.

ABOUT THE WRITER:

Terence Kennedy was born in Northern Ireland in 1949 and grew up in Africa. He has worked variously as a newspaper reporter and columnist, a "spectacularly inept" railway clerk, a rock and jazz drummer, a radio and television scriptwriter and announcer, and a magazine editor. Most recently responsible for two Middle East guidebooks, he has contributed to publications as far removed geographically and ideologically as Britain's august Financial Times, and an oddball magazine for displaced foreigners written in Bahrain, edited in Singapore, published in London, printed in Hong Kong and distributed from Cyprus...

Other than the obsessive travelling which spawned this book, his interests include Beethoven, contemporary jazz, the Titanic, and the international gaggles of Citroën 2CV enthusiasts found in over a hundred clubs.

His travel companion and wife Elise is Dutch, and after meeting in the early 1970's the two decided to go away together - "not just anywhere; everywhere." The tally so far: 74 countries. Thanks to their eccentric lifestyle and with no job, no family of their own and no fixed abode they have "managed to avoid all but the first three of Shaw's seven deadly millstones afflicting mankind: food, clothing, firing, rent, taxes, children and respectability."